THE GOVERNING PRINCIPLES OF ANCIENT CHINA

Based on 360 passages excerpted from the original compilation of Qunshu Zhiyao

群书治要 360

第二册 〈汉英对照〉

2019年9月修订版

[唐]魏　征　褚遂良　虞世南等编
马来西亚汉学院　译著

世界知识出版社

图书在版编目（CIP）数据

群书治要 360. 第二册 ： 汉英对照 / （唐） 魏征，（唐） 褚遂良，（唐） 虞世南编 ； 马来西亚汉学院译著. -- 北京 ： 世界知识出版社，2019.10
ISBN 978-7-5012-6082-9

Ⅰ. ①群… Ⅱ. ①魏… ②褚… ③虞… ④马… Ⅲ. ①政书—中国—唐代—汉、英 Ⅳ. ① D691.5

中国版本图书馆 CIP 数据核字（2019）第 179234 号

群书治要 360. 第二册：汉英对照
Qunshu Zhiyao 360. Dierce: Hanying Duizhao

⊙策　　划——上海正道影视发展有限公司
⊙编　　者——（唐）魏征 褚遂良 虞世南等
⊙译　　者——马来西亚汉学院
⊙责任编辑——薛　乾
⊙责任出版——王勇刚
⊙装帧设计——义　慧
⊙出版发行——世界知识出版社
⊙地　　址——北京市东城区干面胡同 51 号（100010）
⊙经　　销——新华书店
⊙网　　址——www.ishizhi.cn
⊙印　　刷——艺堂印刷（天津）有限公司
⊙开本印张——880×1230 毫米　1/32　16.75 印张
⊙字　　数——180 千字
⊙版次印次——2019 年 12 月第一版　2019 年 12 月第一次印刷
⊙标准书号——ISBN 978-7-5012-6082-9
⊙定　　价——60.00 元

Table of Contents
目录

Chapter One
君道 THE WAY OF A LEADER

Chapter Two
臣术 THE ART OF A MINISTER

Chapter Three
贵德 ESTEEMING VIRTUES

Chapter Four
为政 ON THE SUBJECT OF ADMINISTRATION

Chapter Five
敬慎 RESPECTFULLY CAUTIOUS

Chapter Six
明辨 DISCERNING

前言

Preface

At the beginning of the Zhenguan Era, Emperor Taizong (599–649) of the Tang dynasty decreed that *Qunshu Zhiyao* (*The Compilation of Books and Writings on the Important Governing Principles*) be compiled. At the tender age of sixteen, Taizong enlisted himself in the army, and joined his father's forces to try to stop the turmoil that was going on in the society. For more than ten years, he dwelt himself in military matters. After he ascended to the throne at the age of twenty-seven, he laid down his armor and began to promote culture and education, paying particular attention to the principles of governing and bringing peace to the country. He sought to rejuvenate the nation from the aftermath of civil strife by restoring order to life, lessening the burdens of ordinary people, and increasing prosperity.

Although Taizong was an intelligent, brave, and eloquent man, he regretted that his earlier military expeditions had prevented him from obtaining much formal education. He also learned from the mistakes made by the fallen Sui dynasty and realized that to start a new dynasty was no easy task, and to sustain it would be even harder. Hence during his reign, he encouraged his ministers to point out his mistakes and to candidly criticize his imperial policies. To make up for lost time, Taizong ordered two advisors, the honorable Wei Zheng and Yu Shinan, to comb through all the historical records on imperial governing principles from the *Six Classics*, the *Four Collections of History* and the *Hundreds of Schools*[1], and to extract the most important lessons related to the cultivation of oneself, management of family, good government, and ways to bring about peace in the world. The result was a collection, titled Qunshu Zhiyao, carefully excerpted from 14,000 books and 89,000 scrolls of ancient writings—500,000 words in all, and covering sixty-five book categories—dating from the era of the Five Legendary Emperors[2] to the Jin dynasty[3].

This truly is a treasured compilation on governing principles that can bring about peace and order, which "when used in the present, allows us to examine and learn from our ancient history; when passed down to our descendants, will help them learn valuable lessons in life." Those were the words written by Advisor Wei Zheng in the preface of the completed

---

[1] The *Six Classics* are: *Shijing* 诗经 (*Book of Odes*), *Shangshu* 尚书 (*History of Antiquities*), *Yili* 仪礼 (*Etiquettes and Ceremonies*), *Yuejing* 乐经 (*Book of Music*), *YiJing* 易经 (*Book of Changes*), and *Chunqiu* 春秋 (*Spring and Autumn Annals*). *Sishi* 四史 (*The Four Collections of History*) are: *Shiji* 史记 (*The Records of History*), *Hanshu* 汉书 (*The Book of Han*), *Houhanshu* 后汉书 (*The Book of Later Han*), and *Sanguozhi* 三国志 (*Records of the Three Kingdoms*). *Zhuzi-Baijia* 诸子百家 (*The Hundreds of Schools*) are schools of philosophies that sprang up during the Spring and Autumn, and Warring States periods, circa 770 -221 BC.

[2] The Five Emperors of antiquity (circa 2600 BC) are: Emperor Huang 黄帝, Emperor Zhuanxu 颛顼 , Emperor Diku 帝喾 , Emperor Yao 尧 , and Emperor Shun 舜 .

[3] Jin dynasty (265-420)

compilation. Emperor Taizong was extremely pleased with the broad yet concise compilation and would not let the books out of his sight. He said: "The collection has helped me learn from the ancients. When confronted with issues, I am very certain of what to do. This is all due to your efforts, my advisors." From here we can see that the subsequent peace and prosperity of the Zhenguan Era was attributed greatly to this compilation! This treasure is truly a must-read for all politicians.

However, by the beginning of the Song dynasty, *Qunshu Zhiyao* disappeared from circulation. This is due to the fact that Chinese woodblock printing was not well developed at that time. The *History of Song* also did not show any record of this compilation. Fortunately, the Japanese Kanazawa Bunko museum collection had a complete manuscript hand-copied by Japanese monks during the Kamakura period (1192–1330). The Japanese returned the books to China in the 60th year of the reign of Emperor Qianlong, and they became the master copy for the *Four Series Books* published by the Commercial Press (Shanghai) as well as publications used by Chinese Taiwan.

At the end of 2010, I was fortunate to obtain a copy of *Qunshu Zhiyao*. I read the work repeatedly, and I was filled with immense joy that eternal stability and peace to the entire world can be brought about by the cultural teachings of our ancient saints and sages. I deeply feel this is so. The most important thing is that the Chinese people themselves must truly comprehend and embrace this traditional culture, to stop doubting and start believing. The teachings of the saints and sages constitute an embodiment of the true self-nature of all beings that transcends time and space. Even now, they still hold true. The key learning point hinges on two words: "sincerity and respect." The article "Summary of the Rules of Propriety" says: "Always and in everything let there be reverence." Emperor Kangxi of the Qing dynasty said: "When a ruler interacts with his people, the element of respect is fundamental." He also said: "All the teachings that have been passed down through thousands of years are no more than sincerity and respect." The prominent Song scholar Chengzi said: "Respect triumphs over all evils." These sayings illuminate the fact that in order to cultivate ourselves, advance our virtues, help people, and benefit the world, only sincerity and respect can enable us to perfectly achieve these. If we lack respect and sincerity toward the teachings of ancient sages and virtuous emperors, little benefit will be gained even if we have read the ancient texts extensively. Confucius stressed that he only cited the teachings of others and created nothing of his own. He believed in and loved the teachings of the ancients.

The honorable Dr. Sun Yat Sen, in his speech on the Three Principles of the People (Principle of Nationalism, Fourth Lecture), said: "The advancement in science and material civilization in Europe only happened mostly in the last 200 years. But when it comes to the essence of political philosophy, Europeans still need to look to China for answers. Gentlemen, you all know that our world's best scholars come from Germany. But today's German scholars are studying Chinese philosophies as well as Buddhism from India to correct the bias in science."

British historian Professor Arnold Toynbee asserted: "In order to resolve the social problems of the twenty-first century, we must rely on the teachings of Confucius and Mencius, and on Mahayana Buddhism." Look at the chaos and uncertainties that we face today. If we truly want to save the world and save China, only traditional Chinese cultural education will provide the answers we seek. The wisdom, the ideas, the methods, the experience, and the results of governing, which are all in

Qunshu Zhiyao, are crystallized from thousands of years of trials and tribulations. They are indeed precious! If we can fully comprehend and apply these principles, world peace and individual bliss can be achieved naturally. If we do not follow these principles of governance, we will be inviting endless catastrophes and tragedies.

I realized that the reappearance of *Qunshu Zhiyao* indicates the sacred mission of this compilation. I am happy to print 10,000 copies, to be published by the World Book Company, to be given away to political parties and various leaders in China,and around the world, for them to learn about the essence of governing. This way, a harmonious society and a peaceful world will not be far away. I am pleased to know that *Qunshu Zhiyao* will soon be circulated again in the near future. At the invitation of Ms. Yan Chu I wrote these few words to express my heartfelt praise for the realization of this project.

Chin Kung
December 28, 2010
Hong Kong,China

编译组序

Qunshu Zhiyao 360 Editorial Notes

Qunshu Zhiyao, The Compilation of Books and Writings on the Important Governing Principles is a compilation containing advice, methods, and historical notes on the successes and failures of the imperial government of China. This compilation takes us through thousands of years of Chinese political thinking, and offers us some valuable leadership principles which not only helped the great Tang Emperor Taizong to establish the glorious Reign of Zhenguan, but will also prove valid as points of reference for contemporary leaders. As for the general public, this compilation is a great source of inspiration for self-improvement, family management and human relations.

Our Centre's advisor, Venerable Prof. Chin Kung, is mindful of the importance of passing on traditional Chinese culture. When he received a copy of the *Qunshu Zhiyao* at the end of 2010, he immediately commissioned the World Book Company to print the compilation for distribution, as he deeply believed that this compilation contains remedies that can cure today's problems. In 2011, when Prof. Chin Kung came to

Malaysia and visited the Prime Minister, the honorable Dato' Sri Mohd Najib Razak, and the former Prime Minister, Tun Dr. Mahathir Mohamad, he briefly introduced the contents of the book to them. Both leaders expressed their wish to see the English translation as soon as possible. Hence, Prof. Chin Kung came up with the idea of extracting 360 quotes from *Qunshu Zhiyao* and translating them into modern Chinese and other languages to facilitate easy daily reading. He entrusted the Chung Hua Cultural Education Centre with the task, and this marked the beginning of the *Qunshu Zhiyao* 360 project. Prof. Chin Kung hopes that over the course of the next ten years, 360 quotes will be selected each year from the compilation to be translated into different languages and distributed internationally. He believes that this is the biggest contribution toward peace that China can offer to the world.

Qunshu Zhiyao is made up of extracts from various classics, histories, and the works of the saints and sages. It consists of a total of sixty-six books compiled in fifty scrolls/volumes. This version of *Qunshu Zhiyao 360* groups the contents of *Qunshu* into six chapters, namely: The Way of a Leader, The Art of a Minister, Esteeming Virtues, On the Subject of Administration, Respectfully Cautious, and Discerning. Each chapter is given sub-headings that substantiate the related key points. It is hoped that this series will enable readers to grasp the essence of *Qunshu Zhiyao*.

When the task of translating *Qunshu Zhiyao 360* into English began, many kind individuals from Australia, Canada, China, Singapore, United Kingdom, United States and Malaysia took time out of their busy schedules to help us complete this project. Without their generous contribution, this translation would not have been possible. Here, we would like to express our sincerest gratitude to all of them.

We continue to look forward to receiving your input as to how this abstract may be improved, especially in places where meanings might have been wrongly conveyed during the course of translation.

Last but not least, may all of you enjoy a blissful family life and career, and let us join our hands to bring PEACE to this world.

Sincerely,
English Translation Group of *Qunshu Zhiyao 360*
August 2014

About *Qunshu Zhiyao 360*, Vol. 2

Like its predecessor, this translation was done based on the Chinese annotations of *Qunshu Zhiyao* 360, Vol. 2, compiled by our associates at the Chung Hua Cultural Education Centre, in March 2013. Our learned colleagues have brought to our attention that there are in fact excerpts from sixty-six books instead of sixty-five as originally mentioned in Vol. 1 of this book series. Unlike Vol. 1, where Chinese annotations were omitted, we have included the Chinese annotations for bilingual readers who may want to know more about the source of our translation.

The original compilation of *Qunshu Zhiyao* was not meant only to collect excerpts from the original books, but more so on extracting important points that the editors Wei Zheng and his members thought were important for Emperor Taizong to observe. So some sentences from the original works could have been omitted from the compilation purposely by Wei Zheng. For readers who wish to understand further about the quotes, it is advisable to read the original texts from where the quotes were extracted.

Conventions Used in this Edition

Junzi and "a man of noble character" are used simultaneously in this translation to indicate the special connotation of *Junzi* in the Chinese world, which cannot simply be described by a single English term. *Junzi* embodies an ideally ethical and capable person, sometimes meaning a power holder, which is its original sense. The term is a compound word composed of two written characters, which separately means "ruler's son." Under the changing social conditions of the Warring States period, the concept of birthright was replaced by the notion of an "aristocracy of merit," and in the Confucian school, the term *Junzi* came to denote an "ethical aristocrat," or, "a man of noble character," rather than a future king. The hallmark of the *Junzi* was his complete internalization of the virtue of *ren* (benevolence) and associated qualities such as *yi* (righteousness), *li* (propriety), *zhi* (wisdom) and *xin* (trustworthiness).

The term for "ruler" in the original Chinese is gender neutral. This book has chosen to use masculine pronouns and possessive pronouns, partly to enable the sentences to flow more smoothly, and partly to reflect the norms of ancient China where government was run mostly by men. No gender bias is intended here, particularly in view of the fact that today's women have increasingly taken up important positions in government.

Italics: Indicates non-English word, book title, and transliterated Chinese terms.

Romanization system: This book uses the Hanyu Pinyin romanization system for transliterated names and terms. Exceptions for figures whose customary transliteration is more common than pinyin, like Sun Yat Sen, the founding father of the Republic China, or, whose English name is more familiar to Western readers, such as Confucius.

Names of emperors:

i. According to *Shi Ji* 史记 (*The Records of History*), the Five Emperors 五帝 (denoting much more reverential status than the modern term "Emperor") are Emperor Huang 黄帝 , Emperor Zhuanxu 颛顼 , Emperor Diku 帝喾 , Emperor Yao 尧 , and Emperor Shun 舜 .

ii. From the Xia dynasty to the Qin dynasty (2100– 221BC), rulers usually held the title *Wang* 王 , "King". Example: King Cheng 成王 , King Kang 康王 , King Wen 文王 and King Wu 武王 . With the division of China into separate Warring States, this title had become so common that the unifier of China, Qin Shi Huang 秦始皇 (the "First Emperor of Qin dynasty"), created a new title of *Huangdi* 皇帝 "Emperor", thus claiming legendary status for himself. The title of Emperor of China continued to be used for the remainder of China's imperial history, right down to the fall of the Qing dynasty in 1912.

iii.Before the Tang dynasty: Use posthumous names, such as Emperor Wu of Han dynasty 汉武帝 .

iv. Emperors of the Tang, Song, Liao and Jin (1115–1234) dynasties: Use temple names, such as Tang Taizong 唐太宗 ("Emperor Taizong of Tang dynasty.")

v. Emperors of the Ming dynasty and Qing dynasty: Use era names (same as reign names), such as Emperor Kangxi 康熙 .

Order of names:

i. Personal names in Chinese present the family/clan name first. For example, Lin Xiangru 蔺相如 , with "Lin" being the family name.

ii. In ancient China, the word *zi* 子 is given to one's respected teacher after the teacher's last name. In this case, *zi* will join the last name like, Zengzi 曾子 , Mozi 墨子 .

iii. Book titles named after the author: Last name and given name will be separated. For example, the book *Mo Zi* 墨子 , was written by Mozi, founder of the Mohist School.

iv. Where a respectable title consists of two words, such as Tai Gong 太公 , Qing Zi 卿子 , the title will not be joined to the last name. Example: Jiang Tai Gong 姜太公 (The Grand Duke Jiang), Sun Qing Zi 孙卿子 (The Respectable Master Sun).

君道 Chapter One

THE WAY OF A LEADER

修身
Character Building

甲、戒贪
Guard against greed

1. 圣人守其所以有，不求其所未得。求其所未得，则所有者亡矣；修其所有，则所欲者至矣。

（卷四十一　淮南子）

【白话】圣人安守自己本具的性德，而不贪求自己未获得的。贪求自己未获得的，反而已拥有的会丧失掉（因为贪求则无福，更有甚者会贪赃枉法，将福报折尽）；如果修养自己本具的性德，想得到的就会自然得到（因为性德具有无量的智慧德能福报）。

1. A sage abides in his innate virtues and does not crave for anything beyond that. If he craves for more, he will end up losing all his accumulated blessings. But if he continues with his cultivation of morality, he will naturally attain what he hopes to achieve.

Scroll 41: *Huai Nan Zi*

2. 绝无益之欲，以奉德义之涂[1]；弃不急之务，以修功业之基。其于名行，岂不善哉？

（卷二十八　吴志下）

【注释】①涂：同“途”，引申指途径，门路。

【白话】断绝无益的欲望，来遵循道德仁义之路；放弃无关紧要的事情，来修习建功立业的根基。这对自己的名声与品行，难道不是很有益的吗？

2. Eliminate detrimental desires so that one can pursue the path of righteousness; give up unimportant endeavors so that one can be better prepared for future undertakings. Is this not a useful way of carving out a reputation and moral character for ourselves?

Scroll 28: *Wu Zhi,* Vol. 2

3. 福生于无为，而患生于多欲。故知足，然后富从之；德宜君人，然后贵从之。故贵爵而贱德者，虽为天子不贵矣；贪物而不知止者，虽有天下不富矣。

（卷八　韩诗外传）

【白话】幸福产生于内心知足而无所外求，而忧患产生于人的欲望过多。所以一个人知道满足，然后富裕会随着到来；德行适合领导民众，然后尊贵就会随之而来。所以看重爵位而轻视德行的人，虽然做了天子也并不高贵；贪求财物而不知休止的人，虽然拥有天下也并不富足。

3. Contentment breeds happiness, but excessive cravings breed misery. While a contented person may enjoy wealth eventually, a virtuous leadership brings forth nobility. Hence, a person who craves for titles of nobility but disregards moral integrity cannot be deemed a man of honor despite becoming a ruler; and a person with endless cravings for wealth will never be contented despite owning the whole world.

Scroll 8: *Han Shi Wai Zhuan*

4. 有以欲多亡者，未有以无欲危者也；有以欲治而乱者，未有以守常[1]失者也。

（卷四十一　淮南子）

【注释】①常：常规，常道。

【白话】有因为欲望太多而灭亡的，没有因为无欲而陷入危险的；有因为想要治理却混乱的，没有因为遵循常道却失败的。

4. While some have ruined themselves due to endless desires, no one has ever courted danger because they do not have cravings. While some have tried to run a good government but ended up in chaos, no one has ever failed to be a good ruler because he followed the righteous path.

Scroll 41: *Huai Nan Zi*

5. 三代[1]之兴，无不抑损情欲；三季[2]之衰，无不肆其侈靡。

(卷二十九　晋书上)

【注释】①三代：指夏、商、周。②三季：指夏、商、周三代的末期。

【白话】夏、商、周三代之所以兴盛，无不是因为领导者对自己的七情五欲加以节制；三代末期的衰败，无不因肆意奢侈浪费。

5. The Xia, Shang and Zhou dynasties enjoyed reigns of prosperity because the rulers exercised a strict restraint over their cravings and desires. The consequential downfall of the three dynasties was due to unrestrained spending and excessive luxuriating.

Scroll 29: *Jin Shu*, Vol. 1

6. 日月欲明，浮云盖之；河水欲清，沙石秽[①]之；人性欲平，嗜欲害之。夫纵欲而失性，动未尝正也，以治身则失，以治国则败。

（卷四十一　淮南子）

【注释】①秽：污染，玷污。

【白话】日月本欲明亮，却有浮云遮蔽它；河水本欲清澈，却有沙石污染它；人性本欲宁静，却有嗜欲妨害它。如果放纵欲望而丧失了本性，那么行动就没有正确的时候，以这种心态修身则自身会陷入危殆，以这种心态治国则会使国家衰败。

6. The sun and the moon would always shine brightly, but the clouds enveloped them; the water in the river would always be as clear as crystal, but the sand and stones polluted them. Humans by nature would always want to have inner calmness, but desires and cravings tainted their minds. If one is in pursuit of endless cravings, he might lose his conscience and commit acts of misdeeds. This would cause him serious consequences, and if he is the ruler of a country the whole nation would be at stake.

Scroll 41: *Huai Nan Zi*

7. 天下之愚，莫过于斯，知贪前之利，不睹其后之患也。

（卷十二　吴越春秋）

【白话】天下没有比这更愚蠢的了，只贪图眼前的利益，而看不到身后的祸患。

7. Of all the foolishness in the world none can be worse than an inability to see the dire consequences trailing behind immediate gains.

Scroll 12: *Wu Yue Chun Qiu*

8. 今人之所以犯囹圄[1]之罪，而陷于刑戮[2]之患者，由嗜欲无厌[3]，不修度量[4]之故也。

（卷四十一　淮南子）

【注释】①囹圄：音 líng yǔ / ㄌㄧㄥˊ ㄩˇ。监狱。②刑戮：受刑罚或被处死。③厌：满足。④度量：法度。

【白话】人们之所以犯监禁之罪，而遭刑罚、杀戮之祸，是因为其嗜欲没有止境，（心灵堕落）而不以法度自我要求的缘故。

8. People become criminals and face imprisonment or execution because they could not restrain their endless desires and exercise self-discipline.

Scroll 41: *Huai Nan Zi*

9. 夫物暴长[①]者必夭折，功卒[②]成者必亟坏。

（卷二十二　后汉书二）

【注释】①暴长：急遽生长。②卒：突然。后多作“猝”。

【白话】任何东西迅猛生长必然会夭折，功业仓促而成必然会很快衰败。

9. Anything that grows rapidly will come to a premature end. Any achievement that is hastily gained over a short period of time will soon wane away.

Scroll 22: *Hou Han Shu*, Vol. 2

乙、勤俭
Be frugal and diligent

10. 俭，德之恭[①]也；侈，恶之大也。

（卷二十九　晋书上）

【注释】①恭：通“洪”。大。

【白话】节俭是伟大的美德，奢侈是严重的恶行（因为节俭可培养爱敬之心，奢侈则产生很大后患）。

10. Frugality is a great virtue; extravagance is a great misdeed.

Scroll 29: *Jin Shu*, Vol. 1

11. 古言非典义，学士不以经心；事非田桑，农夫不以乱业；器非时用，工人不以措手；物非世资，商贾不以适市。士思其训，农思其务，工思其用，贾思其常。是以上用足而下不匮。

（卷四十九　傅子）

【白话】古时，言谈不符合经典义理的，学士不会留心；不是耕田养蚕之事，农夫不因之而扰乱本业；器具不适宜当时使用的，工人就不动手去做它；物品不是社会需要的，商人不把它运到市场。士人想着圣贤的训诲，农民想着务农，工人想着器物的实用，商人想着经营常用的物品。因此，在上者用度充足，百姓的需要也不缺乏。

11. In ancient times, scholars would ignore talks that were irrelevant to classical learning; farmers would not disrupt their chores for matters that were unrelated to farming; craftsmen would not produce utensils that were irrelevant for the seasons; and merchants would not supply things that had no demand in the market. Scholars

were mindful of the teachings of the sages; farmers were mindful of farming; craftsmen were mindful of the practicality of the utensils; and merchants were mindful of the supply and demand of daily necessities. Hence, the supply of goods for men in high positions remained sufficient and the daily needs of the general public were met.

Scroll 49: *Fu Zi*

丙、惩忿
Refrain from anger

12. 损。君子以惩忿窒欲。可损之善，莫善损忿欲。

（卷一　周易）

【白话】君子看到损卦，就知道应当善于掌控自己的愤怒，克制自己的欲望。

12. The oracle of *Sun* 损 [1] implies “decrease”. When a man of noble character (*Junzi*) notices the *Sun* oracle, he understands that he should control his anger and restrain his desires.

Scroll 1: *Zhou Yi*

---

[1] The hexagram *Sun* 损 ䷨

13. 秦始皇之无道，岂不甚哉？视杀人如杀狗彘①。狗彘，仁人用之犹有节。始皇之杀人，触情②而已，其不以道如是。而李斯又深刑③峻法，随其指而妄杀人。秦不二世而灭，李斯无遗类④。

（卷四十九　傅子）

【注释】①彘：音 zhì / 业`。猪。②触情：触发情绪。③深刑：严刑。④遗类：指残存者。

【白话】秦始皇残暴无道，岂不是太严重了吗？看待杀人如同杀猪狗。猪狗，仁人使用它们尚且有节制。始皇杀人，只是因触怒了自己而已，他不按道义行事达到了如此程度。李斯又进一步施行严刑峻法，按自己意图胡乱杀人。结果秦朝不满两代就亡国，李斯也全族绝灭。

13. Had not the inhuman brutality of Emperor Qin Shi Huang gone to the extremes? To him, killing human beings was like slaughtering domestic animals. Any person with a conscience would only slaughter domestic

animals sparingly. Emperor Qin put people to death simply because he was agitated by them and had no regrets about his acts of cruelty. To make matters worse, his Prime Minister, Li Si, imposed laws with harsh punishments and killed anyone who opposed him. Consequently, the Qin dynasty reigned for less than two generations and Li Si was executed together with his whole clan.

Scroll 49: *Fu Zi*

丁、迁善
Emulate good deeds

14. 子曰:“见贤思齐焉,见不贤而内自省也。”

（卷九　论语）

【白话】孔子说:“看见贤人,便应当想着向他看齐;看见不贤的人,便应当自我反省(是否有和他类似的情形)。”

14. Confucius said: “When we see men of worth, we should try to emulate them; when we see people lacking in morality, we should reflect and ask ourselves whether we have anything in common with them.”

Scroll 9: *Lun Yu*

15. 太上乐善，其次安之，其下亦能自强也。

（卷三十五　曾子）

【白话】人最高的境界是乐于为善，其次是习惯为善，其下是能够勉励自己努力为善。

15. It is considered the highest form of virtues when one enjoys doing kind deeds; less so if kind deeds are done habitually; lesser still when one encourages oneself to do kind deeds.

Scroll 35: *Zeng Zi*

戊、改过
Correcting our own mistakes

16. 益。君子以见善则迁，有过则改矣。从善改过，益莫大焉。

（卷一　周易）

【白话】君子看到益卦，就知道见到别人的善言善行就应该努力效仿，有过错就要立即改正。

16. The oracle of *Yi* 益 [2] implies “increase”. When a man of noble character (*Junzi*) notices the *Yi* oracle, he understands that if he discovers the good points in others he should strive to emulate them. If he makes a mistake, he should rectify it instantly.

Scroll 1: *Zhou Yi*

---

[2] The hexagram *Yi* 益 ䷩

17. 人谁无过？过而能改，善莫大焉。

（卷五　春秋左氏传中）

【白话】哪个人没有犯过错误？犯了过错能改正，没有比这更大的善行了。

17. To err is human. There is nothing greater than the initiative to mend one's fault after committing it.

Scroll 5: *Chun Qiu Zuo Shi Zhuan*, Vol. 2

18. 太上不生恶，其次生而能夙绝之，其下复而能改。

（卷三十五　曾子）

【白话】人最高的境界是没有恶念，其次是有了过错能早早地断绝，其下是错误复犯后终能改过。

18. The highest state of mind is to have no evil thoughts; less so is when a mistake is corrected soon after it is made; lesser still is when a frequently committed mistake could be eventually corrected.

Scroll 35: *Zeng Zi*

19. 子曰："君子不重则不威，学则不固。主忠信，无友不如己者。过则勿惮改。"主，亲也。惮，难也。

（卷九　论语）

【白话】孔子说："君子内心和外表不庄重，便没有威仪，学问都不坚固。亲近忠信之人（以他们为师），不和与自己志不同道不合的人交朋友。有了过失，不要怕改正。"

19. Confucius said: "If a man of noble character (*Junzi*) does not discipline his mind and dignify his demeanor, he will not only lose the respect of others but will also lack a firm footing in his studies. So he should befriend trustworthy people and avoid the company of those who are incompatible with his ideals. When he makes a mistake, he should have the courage to rectify it."

Scroll 9: *Lun Yu*

敦亲
Be Respectful of Relatives

20. 刑①于寡妻②，至于兄弟，以御③于家邦。刑，法也。寡妻，寡有之妻，言贤也。御，治也。文王以礼法接待其妻，至于其宗族，以此又能为政，治于家邦。

（卷三　毛诗）

【注释】①刑：法。指以礼法相待（依郑玄笺注）。②寡妻：嫡妻。③御：治理。

【白话】修养德行首先给自己的妻子做个好榜样，处处以礼法相待，由此扩展到作为兄弟们的表率，进而就可以用来治理一家一国了。

20. In cultivating virtues, a man should first set a good example in his relationship with his wife, treating her courteously at all times. He then extends this manner further to become a role model to his brothers and sisters, and applies the same principles further to govern a country.

Scroll 3: *Mao Shi*

21. 君之于世子也，亲则父也，尊则君也。有父之亲，有君之尊，然后兼天下而有之。

（卷七　礼记）

【白话】君王对于世子，从亲疏关系而言是父亲，从尊卑关系而言则为君王。君王对于全国民众既具有父亲的亲爱，又具有君王的尊严，然后才能君临天下、拥有百姓。

21. A king is related to a crown prince as father-and-son, but according to the royal hierarchy relationship, they should be classified as a king and his subject. A king should care for his people as dearly as a father to his children, and uphold his sovereignty before he could run his administration well and gain the full support of his people.

Scroll 7: *Li Ji*

22.《传》曰:“周之同盟[①],异姓为后。”诚骨肉之恩,爽[②]而不离。亲亲[③]之义,寔[④]在敦固。未有义而后其君,仁而遗其亲者也。

(卷二十六　魏志下)

【注释】①同盟:《左传·隐公十一年》及《三国志·陈思王植传》通行本均作“宗盟”。宗盟,指天子与诸侯的盟会。②爽:差失;不合。③亲亲:亲爱亲属。④寔:同“实”。确实,实在。

【白话】《左传》上说:“周朝天子与诸侯盟会,异姓诸侯排列在后。”实在是因为骨肉之间恩情深厚,即使有过失也不会离弃。亲爱亲属的道理,确实应当敦厚坚贞。未曾有忠义的臣子会怠慢君主,也未曾有仁德之人会遗弃自己的亲人。

22. The book of *Zuo Zhuan* says: “When the Zhou emperors held counsels to form alliances with the patrimonial lords, members outside the Zhou clans were seated at the back.” Indeed the deep-rooted affections among relatives

would always be prioritized and this close relationship would still be maintained despite disputes. Family ties should be genuine and faithful. Never had faithful and honorable subordinates neglected their leaders, nor benevolent individuals abandoned their relatives.

Scroll 26: *Wei Zhi*, Vol. 2

23. 君子笃于亲，则民兴于仁；故旧不遗，则民不偷①。

兴，起也。能厚于亲属，不遗忘其故旧，行之美者也，则皆化之，起为仁厚之行，不偷薄。

（卷九　论语）

【注释】①偷：浇薄；不厚道。

【白话】在位的君子，若能厚待他的父母兄弟，民众就会兴起仁爱之风；不遗弃他的旧友故交，民众就不会对人冷淡无情。

23. When people holding high positions could show filial piety to their parents and care for their siblings, this examplary role model would evoke compassion in others. So, by not deserting old friends, everyone would become caring toward each other.

Scroll 9: *Lun Yu*

反身
Self-Reflection

24. 孔子曰："人能弘道，非道弘人也。"故治乱废兴在于己，非天降命不可得反也。

（卷十七　汉书五）

【白话】孔子说："人能光大道义，不是道义去光大人。"所以国家的安定与动乱、兴盛与衰亡，都决定于君主自己，而并非天命不可挽回。

24. Confucius said: "While a man could enhance the Great Way, the Great Way could not enhance him." Hence, a ruler is the decisive factor that will determine whether peace or disorder can prevail in a country, and it is not a fate that cannot be changed.

Scroll 17: *Han Shu*, Vol. 5

25. 子路问君子。子曰："修己以敬。"敬其身也。曰："如斯而已乎？"曰："修己以安百姓。修己以安百姓，尧、舜其犹病①诸②！"病，犹难也。

（卷九　论语）

【注释】①病：难，不易。②诸："之乎"二字的合音字。

【白话】子路问怎样才算君子。孔子说："以敬来修治自己，使身心言语统归于敬，处处合礼，这就可以算是君子了。"子路又问："这样就够了吗？"孔子说："修治自己来让百姓得到安乐。修治自己进而令百姓得以安乐，这件事就是连尧、舜那样的圣君，恐怕也难做得周到呀！"

25. Zilu asked Confucius what constituted a man of noble character (*Junzi*). Confucius said: "By cultivating respectfulness in all our speech and actions, we can be deemed a man of noble character."

"And is that all?" asked Zilu.

Confucius replied: "He cultivates himself so he could bring peace and happiness to the people. Cultivating oneself to bring peace and happiness to the people is something that even emperors Yao and Shun found difficult to accomplish."

Scroll 9: *Lun Yu*

26. 主者国之心也，心治[1]则百节[2]皆安，心扰则百节皆乱。治犹理也。节犹事也。以体喻也。

（卷四十一　淮南子）

【注释】①治：指心绪安宁平静。②节：骨节。人身骨骼联接的部分。

【白话】君主好比是国家的心脏，心安则全身都会安定，心乱则全身都会紊乱。

26. A ruler is like the heart of a nation. Thus, when the heart is at ease the whole body will function properly, but when the heart is uneasy, all the bodily functions will be disrupted.

Scroll 41: *Huai Nan Zi*

27. 故天下不正,修之国家;国家不正,修之朝廷;朝廷不正,修之左右;左右不正,修之身;身不正,修之心。所修弥①近,而所济弥远。禹②、汤③罪④己,其兴也勃焉,正心之谓也。

（卷四十九　傅子）

【注释】①弥:更加,愈发。②禹:姒姓,名文命,鲧之子。又称大禹、夏禹、戎禹。后被选为舜的继承人,舜死后即位,建立夏代。③汤:契的后代,子姓,名履,又称天乙。商开国之君。④罪:归罪于。

【白话】所以,天下不正就要整治国家,国家不正就要整治朝廷,朝廷不正就要整治身边的臣子,臣子不正就要加强自身的智慧德能,自身不正就首先要调整自己的思想。所整治的愈切近,所成就的愈远大。夏禹、商汤常常检讨自己的错误,国家的兴盛就很快,这是调整自己思想的结果。

27. When unhealthy social trends are rampant, a ruler should work on transforming the nation. When the country is declining, a ruler should work on transforming the ruling administration. When the ruling administration is inefficient, a ruler should reshuffle his administration and substitute incompetent ministers with capable ones. If the ministers are corrupted, a ruler should rely on his wisdom and morality. To be an efficient administrator, the ruler should first regulate his mindset and mentality. So, the closer he arrives at the core of the problems, the better accomplishments he would attain. King Yu of the Xia dynasty and King Tang of the Shang dynasty used to reflect and correct their inadequacies, and thus the two dynasties flourished swiftly and enjoyed reigns of prosperity as a result of the regulation of the right mindset.

Scroll 49: *Fu Zi*

28. 唯不推心①以况②人，故视用人如用草芥。使用人如用己，恶③有不得其性者乎？古之达④治者，知心为万事主，动而无节则乱，故先正其心。其心正于内，而后动静不妄，以率先天下，而后天下履正⑤，而咸保其性也。斯远乎哉？求之心而已矣！

（卷四十九　傅子）

【注释】①推心：以诚相待。②况：比，引申为推及；推测。③恶：音 wū / ㄨ。相当于“何”、“怎么”。④达：通晓；明白。⑤履正：躬行正道。

【白话】正是没有推己及人去体谅他人，所以看待用人如用草芥。如果任用别人就像任用自己，（如此感同身受）怎么会不了解人民的性情（顺应民心而治）呢？古代能通达治国之道者，明白心是万事的主宰，行为无节制，就会使国家动乱，所以首先端正自己的思想心态。假如思想心态端正，无论动还是静，都不会胡作非为，自己做天下人的表率，天下人就会践行正道，从而皆能保有其良善的本性。这些要求遥远吗？不过是求之于自心而已呀！

28. If a person shows no sense of empathy, he would treat others like dirt. If he treats others the way he treats himself, there is no reason why he would not make the populace feel at ease. Ancient wise rulers were well aware that the mindset plays a key role in all matters, and that unrestrained behaviors would bring instability to the country. Therefore every ruler should first regulate his mindset and adopt the right mentality in everything he does. By exemplifying an ideal role model, the people would emulate his virtues and thus revert to their innate kindness. Are these requirements unapproachable, as they are all about regulating the mindset?

Scroll 49: *Fu Zi*

29. 故上老老[①]而民兴孝，上长长而民兴悌，上恤孤而民不背。所恶于上，无以使下；所恶于下，毋以事上。

（卷七　礼记）

【注释】①老老：以敬老之道侍奉老人。

【白话】所以在上位的人能尊敬老年人，那么百姓的孝敬之风就能兴起；在上位的人能敬事长者，那么百姓的爱敬之风就能兴起；在上位的人能体恤孤苦无依的人，那么百姓之间就不会相互背弃。不喜欢上司对自己的一些做法，就不要这样去对待下属；不喜欢下属的一些行为表现，自己就不要以同样的方式来对待上级。

29. If a ruler could show respect to the elderly, the people will emulate his virtues by observing and promoting filial piety. If a ruler could show respect to his seniors, the people will emulate his virtues and learn to be caring. If he helps the weak and needy with compassion, the people will not forsake each other. If we dislike

the manner our seniors treat us, we should not do the same to our subordinates. If we dislike the manner our subordinates treat us, we should not do the same to our seniors.

Scroll 7: *Li Ji*

30. 尧舜率天下以仁，而民从之；桀纣率天下以暴，而民从之。

（卷七　礼记）

【白话】尧王、舜王以“仁”领导天下，百姓就跟着他行仁；夏桀、商纣以暴戾横行天下，百姓就跟着他做坏事。

30. Through the benevolent reigns of emperors Yao and Shun, the people emulated their virtues and grew compassionate. When kings Jie and Zhou ruled with brutality, the people emulated their corrupted ways and grew violent and immoral.

Scroll 7: *Li Ji*

31. 夫上之所为，民之归[1]也。上所不为，而民或为之，是以加刑罚焉，而莫敢不惩。若上之所为，而民亦为之，乃其所也，又可禁乎？

（卷五　春秋左氏传中）

【注释】①归：趋向，归附。

【白话】上位者的所作所为，百姓会趋向效法。上位者所不做的事，而百姓有人做了，因此加以惩罚处分，就没有谁还敢不加以警戒。若上位者所做的，百姓也有人做了，这乃是势所必然的，又怎能禁止得了呢？

31. The people would naturally observe and emulate the conduct of those in higher authority. If the people do things that the authorities forbid, they will be penalized and everyone will heed this as a warning. But if members of the public are found guilty of violating the same law that the authorities used to defy, are the offenders punishable by law, as they are only trying to do what their authorities are doing?

Scroll 5: *Chun Qiu Zuo Shi Zhuan*, Vol. 2

32. 孔子曰："人而不仁，疾之以甚，乱也。"故民乱反之政，政乱反之身。身正而天下定。是以君子嘉善[1]而矜不能，恩及刑人，德润穷夫[2]。施惠悦尔，行刑不乐也。

（卷四十二　盐铁论）

【注释】①嘉善：赞美善人。②穷夫：鄙贱之人。

【白话】孔子说："对待不仁的人，憎恶得太过分，那就必然立即作乱了。"因此，下民乱了，要从朝政上反省原因；朝政乱了，要从执政者自身反省原因。自身思想观念、行动举措都正确了，天下自然安定。所以，君子能够赞美善良的人，又能够同情那些不能为善的人，对受刑的人给予恩惠，对鄙贱之人也施与恩德。在施与恩惠时内心满怀喜悦，而在不得已需要执行刑罚时就会感到难过。

32. Confucius said: "To carry your dislike of an immoral man to the extreme will push him to rebel instantly." Thus when there is a civilian rebellion, the government should reflect upon its administrative policies, and the head of government should reflect on his shortcomings that led to the failing of the administration. When the conduct and policies of a leader are properly regulated, there will be peace and stability in the country. Therefore, a man of noble character (*Junzi*) would compliment kind people while empathizing with those who refrain from doing kind deeds, besides giving counseling to prisoners and helping the needy. He is overjoyed when given an opportunity to serve, but would be deeply saddened if he has no alternative but to carry out punishments.

Scroll 42: *Yan Tie Lun*

33. 是以天万物之覆[①]，君万物之焘[②]也。怀生[③]之类，有不浸润于泽者，天以为负；员首[④]之民，有不沾濡[⑤]于惠者，君以为耻。

（卷四十七　政要论）

【注释】①覆：保护；庇护。②焘：音 dào／ㄉㄠˋ。覆盖，引申为庇荫。③怀生：指有生命之物。④员首：指百姓。⑤沾濡：浸湿。指蒙受恩泽。

【白话】因此，上天是万物的庇护者，君主是万物的保护者。凡是生灵，只要有一个没有得到滋润，上天就会觉得有所亏欠；百姓之中，只要有一人没有得到君王的恩惠，君主就会觉得这是耻辱。

33. Heaven is the guardian of all things while the ruler is the protector of all things. If a sentient being is deprived of heaven's bounties, heaven would deem this as an inadequacy. If a civilian is deprived of the ruler's bounties, this is deemed a disgrace in the eyes of the ruler.

Scroll 47: *Zheng Yao Lun*

34.《象》曰：山上有水，蹇[1]。君子以反身[2]修德。除难莫若反身修德也。《彖》曰：蹇，难也，险在前也。见险而能止，智矣哉！

（卷一　周易）

【注释】①蹇：音 jiǎn / ㄐㄧㄢˇ。跛行艰难。②反身：反求自身。

【白话】《象传》说：山上流水跌宕曲折而下，行动艰难，这是蹇卦的象征。君子看到此卦，就想到在困难之时应该反省自身，修养自身德行。《彖传》说：蹇卦，象征着艰难，就是前面有危险的意思。看到险情能够停止，这是明智之举啊！

34. According to the book of *Xiang Zhuan*, the oracle of Jian 蹇 symbolized water on the mountain flows in sweeping meanders down steep, inaccessible mountains, making our journey extremely difficult. When a man of noble character (*Junzi*) reads this he should turn his attention to himself and cultivate his character. The book

of *Tuan Zhuan* says: "The oracle of *Jian* 蹇 [3], implies obstructions, dangers ahead. In such a situation it is wise to take a break in view of the danger."

Scroll 1: *Zhou Yi*

---

[3] The hexagram *Jian* 蹇 ䷦

35. 修己而不责人，则免于难。

（卷四　春秋左氏传上）

【白话】修养自己的德行，而不去责难别人，就会免于遭受祸难。

35. We should cultivate our own character instead of putting the blame on others. In this way we can keep misfortunes at bay.

Scroll 4: *Chun Qiu Zuo Shi Zhuan*, Vol. 1

尊贤
Be Respectful of Wise and Able Ministers

36. 仁人也者，国之宝也；智士也者，国之器也；博通①之士也者，国之尊也。故国有仁人，则群臣不争；国有智士，则无四邻诸侯之患；国有博通之士，则人主尊。

（卷四十二　新序）

【注释】①博通：广泛地通晓；了解各种事理与知识。

【白话】有仁德的人是国家的珍宝；有才智的人是国家的重器；博通的人是国家所尊贵的。因此，国中有仁者，那么群臣就不会争权夺利；国家有智士，那么国家就没有四邻诸侯侵扰的担忧；国家有博通的人，那么国君就会受到尊崇。

36. A benevolent person is esteemed as a national treasure; a wise person is esteemed as a national asset; a learned scholar is esteemed as a national nobility. Thus, the presence of benevolent people will prevent power struggles among ministers; the presence of wise people will solve problems relating to possible invasions by neighboring countries; and the presence of learned

scholars will educate the public about showing the highest respect to the ruler.

Scroll 42: *Xin Xu*

37. 尊圣者王；贵贤者霸；敬贤者存；嫚[1]贤者亡。古今一也。

（卷三十八　孙卿子）

【注释】①嫚：亵渎，轻侮。

【白话】尊重圣人的君主会称王于天下；重视贤人的君主会称霸于诸侯；恭敬贤人的君主，国家会存在；怠慢贤人的君主，国家就会灭亡。从古到今都是一样。

37. A ruler who revered men of virtues would reign over the world; a ruler who attached great importance to men of virtues would be the leader of the lords; a ruler who honored men of virtues would preserve his country, while a ruler who neglected men of virtues would drive his country to destruction. This has been true since the ancient era.

Scroll 38: *Sun Qing Zi*

38. 夫善人在上，则国无幸民。谚曰：“民之多幸，国之不幸。”是无善人之谓也！

（卷五　春秋左氏传中）

【白话】有德行的人处于上位，国中就没有心存侥幸的人。俗话说：“如果百姓多存侥幸心理，那将是国家之不幸。”说的就是没有有德之人在上位执政啊！

38. With virtuous people holding high positions in the government, no one would leave things to chance. An idiom says: “When the people leave things to chance, misfortune would befall the nation,” indicating a situation where no able and virtuous people are serving in the top administration.

Scroll 5: *Chun Qiu Zuo Shi Zhuan*, Vol. 2

39. 无善人则国从之。从亡也。《诗》曰："人之云①亡，邦国殄瘁②。"无善人之谓也。故《夏书》曰："与其杀不辜，宁失不经③。"惧失善也。逸书也。不经，不用常法。

（卷五　春秋左氏传中）

【注释】①云：句中助词，无义。②殄瘁：同义词连用，指困穷，困苦。③经：常法。

【白话】没有贤人，国家就会随之衰败。《诗经》说："贤人不在了，国家就遭祸殃。"这是由于失去贤人的缘故。所以《夏书》说："与其错杀无辜，宁可失之于不用常法。"就是害怕失去贤人。

39. Without the service of able and virtuous people, a country will soon decline. The book of *Shi Jing* says: "In the absence of the able and virtuous, the country will soon be overcome by misfortunes." Hence, the book of *Xia Shu* says: "Being blamed for not following normal procedures is far better than to execute innocent people by mistake." This indicates that ancient rulers were extremely concerned about losing people of virtues.

Scroll 5: *Chun Qiu Zuo Shi Zhuan*, Vol. 2

40. 故王者劳于求贤，逸于得人。舜举众贤在位，垂衣裳，恭己无为，而天下治。

（卷四十二　新序）

【白话】当君主的人寻求贤才是辛劳的，得到了贤才就轻松了。大舜举用了很多贤能的人，使他们各得其位，自己垂衣正身，恭谨律己，凡事不用亲为，就使得天下太平。

40. A ruler labors to find good people, but once they are found he can relax and enjoy a reign of prosperity. Emperor Shun assigned many wise and able men to the right tasks, and so all he did was to uphold his sovereignty and there was a reign of peace.

Scroll 42: *Xin Xu*

41. 古者明王之求贤也，不避远近，不论贵贱，卑爵以下贤①，轻身②以先士。

（卷三十六　尸子）

【注释】①下贤：屈己以尊贤。②轻身：谦卑降低身分，不自恃。

【白话】古代明智的君王为国家寻求贤良人才，不论关系亲疏，不管地位尊卑，都会放下自己的爵位来迎接贤良人才，降低自己的身分来善待有德士人。

41. The wise rulers of the past would seek virtuous people to serve the country. Irrespective of whether his relations with them were close or distant, or whether their social status was low or noble, he would humble himself and regard them as distinguished people who would lead the country toward success.

Scroll 36: *Shi Zi*

42. 今君之位尊矣，待天下之贤士，勿臣而友之，则君以得天下矣。

（卷三十一　六韬）

【白话】如今君主的地位尊崇，若对待天下的贤士，不把他们当作臣下，而以朋友相待，那么君主就可以得到天下了。

42. "Today, Your Lordship has attained supreme status, and if you can treat worthy individuals as close friends rather than subordinates, you will eventually rule over the world."

Scroll 31: *Liu Tao*

43. 周公摄[①]天子位七年，布衣[②]之士，执贽[③]而所师见者十人，所友见者十二人，穷巷白屋[④]所先见者四十九人，进善者百人，教士者千人，官[⑤]朝[⑥]者万人。当此之时，诚使[⑦]周公骄而且吝，则天下贤士至者寡矣。

（卷四十三　说苑）

【注释】①摄：代理。②布衣：借指平民。古代平民不能衣锦绣，故称。③贽：初次见人时所执的礼物。古代礼制，谒见人时携礼物相赠。④穷巷白屋：穷巷，冷僻简陋的小巷。白屋，指平民或寒士的住所。⑤官：授给某人官职；使为官。⑥朝：拜访。⑦诚使：假使。

【白话】周公代理天子执政七年（非常礼贤下士，同时不吝分享智慧经验及培养人才），未做官的读书人中，他带着礼物以尊师之礼拜见的有十人，以朋友之礼会见的有十二人，优先接见的穷巷陋屋中的贫寒之士有四十九人，随时向自己提供善言的有上百人，受到他教导的读书人有上千人，被选拔在官府朝廷服务的有上万人。在那时，假使周公对人骄傲而且吝啬，那么天下的贤士来见他的就很少了。

43. For seven years the Duke of Zhou acted as the regent. During that time, he brought gifts as a token of first visit to ten civilian scholars in the capacity of a student paying respect to his teachers; met twelve people as friends, and gave priority to meetings with forty-nine humble scholars in their meager dwellings. About a hundred people were ready to offer him advice anytime; more than a thousand students came under his tutorship; and tens of thousands of officials were personally selected by him to serve in the government. Worthy men from all over the kingdom would not have served under him if he was arrogant and mean.

Scroll 43: *Shuo Yuan*

纳谏
Be Receptive to Counsels from Ministers

44. 为人君之务，在于决壅①；决壅之务，在于进下；进下之道，在于博听；博听之义，无贵贱同异，隶竖牧圉②，皆得达焉。

（卷四十七　政要论）

【注释】①决壅：消除壅蔽。②隶竖牧圉：指奴役、童仆、放牧、养马的人。圉，音 yǔ／ㄩˇ。

【白话】做君主的关键，在于能够去除蒙蔽；去除蒙蔽的关键，在于能够让下属进谏；让下属进谏的方法，在于广泛地听取各种意见；广泛地听取意见，就是要能够做到无视下属的高低贵贱，即使是奴役、童仆、放牧、养马的人，也要能够让他们的意见传达进来。

44. The key to success of a leader lies in the fact that the bare truth should never be concealed from him. Thus, he must allow his subordinates to remonstrate with him and be keen to accept a wide variety of counsels and suggestions, irrespective of whether they came from the nobles or the lowly. Be they servants, houseboys, herdsmen or stablemen, everyone must be allowed to express their views.

Scroll 47: *Zheng Yao Lun*

45. 欲知平直，则必准绳[①]；欲知方圆，则必规矩[②]；人主欲自知，则必直士。唯直士能正言。

（卷三十九　吕氏春秋）

【注释】①准绳：测定物体平直的器具。准，测平面的水准器；绳，量直度的墨线。②规矩：规和矩。校正圆形和方形的两种工具。

【白话】想要知道物体是否平直，就一定要依靠水准器和墨绳；想知道是否方圆，就一定要依靠圆规和矩尺；君主想知道自己的过失，就一定要依靠直言之士。

45. If you need to determine perpendicularity, you should use a plumb rule with a plumb line. If you need to determine whether it is a circle, you use compasses; to determine a square, use an angle rule. If a ruler wishes to know where he has gone wrong, he should seek the help of someone who dares to point out his shortcomings.

Scroll 39: *Lü Shi Chun Qiu*

46. 古之贤君，乐闻其过，故直言得至，以补其阙[1]。

（卷四十九　傅子）

【注释】①阙：疏漏。

【白话】古代的贤明君主，乐于听人指出自己的过失，所以能听到正直的话，藉以补救缺点。

46. The ancient sage-rulers were keen to know where they went wrong and thus were able to hear honest and upright remonstrations to remedy their shortcomings.

Scroll 49: *Fu Zi*

47. 明君莅众[1]，务下之言，以昭外也；敬纳卑贱，以诱贤也。其无拒言，未必言者之尽用也，乃惧拒无用而让[2]有用也。

（卷四十四　潜夫论）

【注释】①莅众：治理百姓。②让：通“攘”，排斥。

【白话】贤明的君主治理百姓，务求臣下之言，来昭示于朝廷外；恭敬地接纳卑贱之人，来吸引贤士。君主不拒绝进言，未必所有的进言都采用，只是担心拒绝无用的意见而会使有用的意见受到排斥。

47. In running his administration, a wise ruler expected the words of his ministers to be made public, while encouraging remonstrations even from men of inferior status to attract worthy people to serve in his government. He would not decline remonstrations, not because he expected to adopt all counsels given, but rather, to ensure that invaluable advice was never rejected in the process.

Scroll 44: *Qian Fu Lun*

48. 仁君广山薮[1]之大，纳切直[2]之谋。

（卷二十二　后汉书二）

【注释】①山薮：山林与湖泽。薮，音 sǒu／ㄙㄡˇ。②切直：恳切率直。

【白话】仁德的君主有着像高山、湖泽那样大的胸怀，可以接纳恳切率直的谋略。

48. The magnanimity of a benevolent ruler—being as mighty as a mountain and as vast as a lake—would enable him to be ever ready to accept straightforward and earnest strategic plans.

Scroll 22: *Hou Han Shu*, Vol. 2

49. 今群臣皆以邕为戒，上畏不测之难，下惧剑客之害，臣知朝廷不复得闻忠言矣。夫立言无显过之咎[①]，明镜无见玼[②]之尤[③]。如恶[④]立言以记过，则不当学也。不欲明镜之见玼，则不当照也。愿陛下详思臣言，不以记过见玼为责。

（卷二十四　后汉书四）

【注释】①咎：罪过，过失。②见玼：显露瑕疵。见，同“现”，显现、显露。玼，玉的斑点，引申为缺点、毛病。③尤：过失，罪愆。④恶：音 wù/ㄨˋ。讨厌，憎恨。

【白话】今天群臣都以蔡邕的下场为鉴戒，上怕受到难以预料的灾难，下怕有刺客来行刺，臣知道朝廷不会再听到忠言了。发表言论不该因指出过错而被责处，明镜不该因照出污点而被怨尤。如果讨厌设立史官秉笔直书记录过失，那就不该学习古人（设立史官）。如果不想被镜子照出污点，就不该去照了。希望陛下仔细考虑臣说的话，不因为指出过错和反映污点而责备大臣。

49. As everyone in the imperial court regarded the fate of Cai Yong as a painful lesson, ministers are now exercising extra care not to offend those of senior rankings for fear of courting trouble or being assassinated. I know that truth will no longer be heard in the imperial court. But should a person who disclosed the plain truth deserve punishment? Should we lay the blame on a mirror because it reflects our blemishes? If a ruler worries that open remonstrations of his shortcomings will be recorded in history he should not have encouraged remonstrations to be given. If one does not want his blemishes to be reflected in a mirror he should not have looked himself in the mirror. May Your Highness consider my words carefully and pardon the ministers who have revealed your shortcomings and inadequacies.

Scroll 24: *Hou Han Shu*, Vol. 4

50. 能容直臣，则上之失不害于下，而民之所患上闻矣。

（卷四十九　傅子）

【白话】能容纳正直的臣子，则君主有失误也不会贻害百姓，而百姓的忧患君主也能听到。

50. If a ruler can tolerate and heed the advice of upright ministers, the impact of his mistakes will not bring disaster to his people, and the hardship suffered by his people can also be brought to his attention.

Scroll 49: *Fu Zi*

51. 君明则臣直。古之圣王,恐不闻其过,故有敢谏之鼓[①]。

(卷二十六　魏志下)

【注释】①敢谏之鼓:设于朝廷供进谏者敲击以闻的鼓。

【白话】君主圣明臣下就正直。古代圣明的君王唯恐听不到自己的过错,因此设立了让进谏者敲击以便领导者知晓的鼓。

51. An honorable ruler would naturally have upright ministers. As ancient sage-rulers were worried that they might not be able to realize and rectify their shortcomings, they implemented the “remonstrating drum” to allow remonstrators to beat the drum in order for them to express their views.

Scroll 26: *Wei Zhi*, Vol. 2

52. 尧舜之世，谏鼓谤木[①]，立之于朝，殷周哲王，小人[②]怨詈[③]，则洗目改听，所以达聪明[④]，开不讳[⑤]，博采负薪[⑥]，尽极下情也。

（卷二十三　后汉书三）

【注释】①谤木：相传尧舜时于交通要道竖立木柱，让人在上面写谏言，称“谤木”。②小人：平民百姓。③怨詈：怨恨咒骂。詈，音 lì / ㄌㄧˋ。咒骂。④聪明：指明察事理。⑤不讳：不隐讳。⑥负薪：指地位低微的人。

【白话】尧舜的时候，在朝堂设敢谏之鼓，立诽谤之木，殷周二朝的圣王，对待百姓的怨骂，总是洗耳恭听，真诚接受，所以才能够明察事理，让别人直言不讳，广泛听取普通百姓的意见、全面细致地了解民情。

52. During the reigns of emperors Yao and Shun, the remonstrating drum was set up in the court, and wooden pillars were erected in major hallways to allow civilians to inscribe their complaints. The sage-rulers of the Yin and Zhou dynasties would listen attentively to people's complaints and deliberate on the truth of what was spoken, and allow people to speak their minds without prohibition. After listening to their suggestions, the ruler would be in a better position to judge the situation of his people.

Scroll 23: *Hou Han Shu*, Vol. 3

53. 禹之治天下也，以五声听。门悬钟鼓铎[1]磬[2]，而置鼗[3]，以待四海之士，为铭[4]于笋簴[5]曰："教寡人以道者击鼓；教寡人以义者击钟；教寡人以事者振[6]铎；告寡人以忧者击磬；语寡人以讼狱者挥鼗。"此之谓五声。是以禹尝据一馈而七起，日中而不暇饱食。曰："吾不恐四海之士留于道路，吾恐其留吾门廷[7]也！"是以四海之士皆至，是以禹朝廷间，可以罗雀[8]者。

（卷三十一　鬻子）

【注释】①铎：音 duó／ㄉㄨㄛˊ。古代乐器，大铃的一种。古代宣布政教法令或遇战事时用之。青铜制品，形如钲而有舌。其舌有木制和金属制两种，故又有木铎和金铎之分。②磬：古代打击乐器，状如曲尺。用玉、石或金属制成。③鼗：音 táo／ㄊㄠˊ。有柄的小鼓。④铭：刻写在器物上的文辞。⑤笋簴：即"笋虡"，音 sǔn jù／ㄙㄨㄣˇ ㄐㄩˋ。古代悬挂钟磬的架子。横架为笋，直架为虡。⑥振：挥动，摇动。⑦门廷：宫门、朝门外的地方。⑧罗雀：形容门庭寂静或冷落。

【白话】禹王通过聆听五种声音来治理天下。朝堂门上悬挂着钟、鼓、铎和磬，旁边摆放着鞉，以此接待天下士人，并在悬挂钟磬的木架上刻着铭文，说："以道教导我的请击鼓；以义教导我的请敲钟；教导我如何处理国家大事的请摇铎；告知我国家忧患的请击磬；告诉我诉讼之事的请摇鞉。"这就是所谓的五声。因此，禹王曾经在吃一顿饭的期间七次起身处理政务，一直忙到正午都没有时间吃饱饭。禹王说："我不怕天下的贤者停留在路上，我担心没有及时听取宝贵建议并加以处理，而让他们滞留在我的门庭啊！"因此天下士人纷纷到来，也因此，禹的朝廷很清静。

53. King Yu governed his kingdom through the application of "five sounds" generated by musical instruments. On the door of the imperial court hung a bell, a drum, a proclamation or war bell, and a chime stone; another small revolving drum with a handle was placed beside them. Visiting scholars were greeted by the following words, engraved on the wooden rack: "Please hit the drum if you want to teach me the Great Way; strike

the bell if you want to teach me about honor; shake the proclamation or war bell if you want to teach me about administrative affairs; hit the chime stone if you want to brief me about national issues, and if you want to discuss lawsuits please swing the revolving drum." These were the functions of the "five sounds". It was said that on one occasion, King Yu was interrupted seven times during a meal to attend to official matters and could only finish his meal by noon. King Yu said: "I do not worry about sages idling along the road, but am worried that I might not be prompt in receiving invaluable advice from these people and neglected them at my courtyard." Thus, learned men came from all over the kingdom to offer valuable ideas to Yu and so there was lasting peace and order during his reign.

Scroll 31: *Yu Zi*

54. 昔高祖[1]纳善若不及,从谏若转圜[2]。

（卷十九　汉书七）

【注释】①高祖:指西汉高祖刘邦。②圜:音 yuán／ㄩㄢˊ。同“圆”。

【白话】当年汉高祖采纳善言唯恐来不及,听从谏言就好似转动圆形之物那样顺畅迅速。

54. Emperor Gaozu of the Han dynasty was always ready to accept good advice and would never hesitate to listen to remonstrations as surely as spinning a round object.

Scroll 19: *Han Shu*, Vol. 7

55. 通直言之涂，引而致之，非为名也，以为直言不闻，则己之耳目塞。耳目塞于内，谀者顺之于外，此三季[①]所以至亡，而不自知也。

（卷四十九　傅子）

【注释】①三季：指夏、商、周三代的末期。

【白话】敞开直言之路，招引获得谏言，不是为取得好名声，而是认为听不到正直的言论，自己就会耳目闭塞。自己耳目闭塞，阿谀的人又凡事顺从自己，这就是夏、商、周三代末年的君主灭亡的原因，而他们自己却不知道。

55. Allowing open remonstrations against the government was never meant to leave a good impression, but rather, due to the fact that if upright opinions were not heard, the ruler might be veiled from the plain truth. Being concealed from the plain truth and surrounded by irresponsible subordinates who were flatterers-these were the crucial factors leading to the downfall of the Xia, Shang and Zhou dynasties, even without their knowledge.

Scroll 49: *Fu Zi*

56. 扁鹊不能治不受针药①之疾，贤圣不能正不食（食疑受）善言（善言作谏诤）之君。故桀有关龙逢②而夏亡；纣有三仁③而商灭。故不患无夷吾④由余⑤之论（论作伦），患无桓、穆之听耳。

（卷四十二　盐铁论）

【注释】①针药：针灸、药物。②关龙逢：桀的臣子。桀作酒池塘丘，为长夜饮。龙逢力谏被杀。逢，音 páng／ㄆㄤˊ。③三仁：指微子、箕子、比干三人。④夷吾：即管仲。⑤由余：一作繇余，春秋时天水人。为秦穆公出谋划策，使秦位列春秋五霸。

【白话】扁鹊不能医治不接受针灸和药物的疾病，贤人和圣人也不能纠正不接受劝谏的国君。因此，夏桀虽有关龙逢，夏朝还是灭亡了；殷纣虽有微子、箕子、比干三个仁人，但商朝还是灭亡了。可见不用担心臣子没有像管仲、由余那样好的见解，就怕国君不能像齐桓公、秦穆公那样愿意听取谏言。

56. Even the great doctor, Bian Que, could not cure illnesses that were not receptive to acupuncture and medicine; and even the saints and sages could not help rulers who were not open to sensible advice. Despite having faithful ministers such as Guan Longpang[4], the Xia dynasty came to an end under King Jie's tyrannical rule. Another despot, King Zhou of the Shang dynasty, had able ministers like Wei Zi, Ji Zi and Bi Gan[5], but his despotic rule quickly brought the downfall of the Shang dynasty. Hence rulers should never worry that their ministers might not be as competent as Guan Zhong or You Yu[6], but should worry that they might not be able to accept remonstrations as willingly as Duke Huan of Qi and Duke Mu of Qin did.

Scroll 42: *Yan Tie Lun*

---

[4] Guan Longpang 关龙逢 was killed after he tried to admonish King Jie 夏桀 not to build the "wine pool".

[5]King Zhou 殷纣 killed Bi Gan 比干 , imprisoned Ji Zi 箕子 , and forced Wei Zi 微子 , his brother, to flee to another country.

[6]You Yu 由余 also called Yao Yu 繇余 was a high minister in the state of Qin 秦国 during the late Spring and Autumn period between 659–621 BC. He succeeded in getting the eight tribes of the west to submit to the authority of Duke Mu of Qin 秦穆公 and established Qin as one of the five hegemonic states of the Spring and Autumn period.

杜谗邪
Be Averse to Slanderous and Malevolent Advice

57. 是故为人君者，所与游①必择正人，所观览必察正象，放郑声②而弗听，远佞人③而弗近，然后邪心不生，而正道可弘也。

（卷二十五　魏志上）

【注释】①游：交游；结交。②郑声：原指春秋战国时郑国的音乐。郑国的音乐多为靡靡之音。故称放荡不雅正的音乐为“郑声”。③佞人：善于花言巧语，阿谀奉承的人。

【白话】所以说，做君主者，他所交往的一定要挑选正直的人，所观看的一定要选择正大光明的景象，抛开庸俗的音乐而不听，疏远谄媚的人而不接近，这样才能使邪恶之心不生，而正道也可以得到弘扬了。

57. A ruler must choose upright people to be his friends, appreciate scenery that is inspiring, and distance himself from decadent music and flatterers. In this way he can regulate his mind and promote the virtuous way.

Scroll 25: *Wei Zhi*, Vol. 1

58. 或问："天子守在四夷①，有诸？"曰："此外守也，天子之内守在身。"曰："何谓也？"曰："至尊者，其攻之者众焉，故便僻②御侍③，攻人主而夺其财；近幸妻妾，攻人主而夺其宠；逸游伎艺，攻人主而夺其志；左右小臣，攻人主而夺其行；不令之臣，攻人主而夺其事。是谓内寇。"

（卷四十六 申鉴）

【注释】①四夷：古代华夏族对四方少数民族的统称，指东夷、西戎、南蛮、北狄。②便僻：音 pián pì / ㄆㄧㄢˊ ㄆㄧˋ。指君主左右受宠幸的小臣。③御侍：帝王侍从。

【白话】有人问："天子的守卫在于防御四方夷狄的入侵，是吗？"答："这只是对外的防御，天子对内的防御在于自身。"问："此话怎讲？"答："处于至高无上地位的人，'进攻'他的人很多。逢迎谄媚的侍从攻人主之心，而竞相取得其财利；人主亲近的妻妾嫔妃攻人主之心，而争夺其宠爱；放纵游乐的歌妓艺人攻人主之心，使其玩物丧志；人主左右的小臣攻人主之心，使其品行不端；心怀不善之臣攻人主之心，使其贻误大事。这些可说是内部的盗寇。"

58. Someone might ask: "Is the ruler's defense strategy targeting at the *Si Yi*[7] tribes surrounding the land of Huaxia[8]?"

Answer[9]: "This is only the foreign defense strategy of a ruler. His true defense lies in the cultivation of himself."

"Why is this so?" asked another.

Answer: "The person in the highest authority has many 'assailants'. The flatterers by his side will assail his feelings and compete for monetary favors. His wives and consorts will assail his feelings and compete for favoritism. The hedonist performers will assail his feelings and lure him to forget his missions. The junior officials by his side will assail his feelings and make him behave indecently. Unscrupulous ministers will assail his feelings and make him ignore critical issues. These are the thieves who assail and hasten the rotting of the ruling administration to its core.

Scroll 46: *Shen Jian*

[7] *Si Yi* 四夷, eponyms given to the "four barbarians" in ancient Chinese literature : the western *Rong* 戎 (western tribes), the eastern *Yi* 夷 (eastern tribes), the northern *Hu* 胡, or *Di* 狄 (northern tribes), and the southern *Man* 蛮 (southern tribes).

[8] *Huaxia* 华夏 represents China and the Chinese civilization in historical Chinese literature.

[9] In the book *Shen Jian* 申鉴, the author posed questions and answers to elaborate on his own political thinking.

59. 奸臣因以似象之言而为之容说①，人主不能别也，是而悦之，惑乱其心，举动日缪②，而常自以为得道，此有国之常患也。夫佞邪之言，柔顺而有文；忠正之言，简直而多逆。

（卷五十　袁子正书）

【注释】①容说：曲意逢迎，以取悦于上。说，同“悦”。②缪：音 miù／ㄇㄧㄡˋ。错误；乖误。

【白话】奸臣用乍听起来像是正道的话来谄媚君主，君主没有能力辨别，以为是对的而心生欢喜，混乱了自己的心思，行为日益乖离正道，却还总认为自己做得合乎道义，这是君主们的通病。那些奸佞们的言语，柔和顺心而有文采；忠正臣子的话，简朴直接而多半听来逆耳。

59. Treacherous officials often used persuasions that seemed righteous to convince the ruler. If a ruler could not discern right from wrong, he would be confused and would gradually move away from the right path,

assuming that he was still steering toward the right direction. That was a common fatal error made by most rulers. The words uttered by the treacherous are usually gentle and pleasing, flowery and full of flattery; but the words from loyal and upright officials are simple, direct, and often displeasing to the ears of the ruler.

Scroll 50: *Yuan Zi Zheng Shu*

60. 谄媚小人，欢笑以赞善；面从①之徒，拊节②以称功。益③使惑者不觉其非，自谓有端晏④之捷、过人之辨⑤而不寤⑥，斯乃招患之旌。

（卷五十　抱朴子）

【注释】①面从：谓当面顺从。②拊节：即击节，形容十分赞赏。拊，音 fǔ / ㄈㄨˇ。拍；击。节，古乐器中摈制节拍的器具，用竹编成，击之成声。③益：更加。④端晏：指子贡和晏子。⑤辨：通“辩”。指辩论的才能。⑥寤：通“悟”，觉悟，认识到。

【白话】谄媚的小人，总是笑着称赞叫好；当面奉承的人，总是击节称赞功德。更使迷惑的人觉察不出自己的错误，自认有着和子贡、晏子一样的敏捷，以及超越常人的辩才，而不能醒悟，这些正是招致祸患的旗帜。

60. A scoundrel would always laugh and throw compliments wherever he went. A stooge would always hit the bamboo drum box while lauding one's contributions. But a deluded person might be led into believing that he could be as talented and eloquent as Zigong and Yanzi. This is, unfortunately, a foolish banner that could easily court trouble.

Scroll 50: *Bao Pu Zi*

61. 昔李斯教秦二世曰："为人主而不恣睢[1]，命之曰天下桎梏[2]。"二世用之，秦国以覆，斯亦灭族。

（卷二十六　魏志下）

【注释】①恣睢：放纵暴戾。②桎梏：音 zhìgù／ㄓˋ ㄍㄨˋ。古代用来拘系犯人手脚的刑具，在手上戴的为梏，在脚上戴的为桎，类似于近世的脚镣手铐。

【白话】从前李斯告诉秦二世说："当了君主若不能放任自己、无拘无束，这就叫做把天下变成束缚自己的脚镣手铐。"秦二世采用了他的话，秦国因此而灭亡，李斯也被灭族。

61. Prime Minister Li Si advised Emperor Er Shi (the second emperor) of the Qin dynasty by saying that if a person could not act freely after becoming a ruler, it might be likened to a man being handcuffed and restricted from moving around. Er Shi heeded this and ruled ruthlessly, thus bringing the Qin dynasty to an end in just three years, and Li Si and his whole clan were executed by this tyrannical ruler.

Scroll 26: *Wei Zhi*, Vol. 2

62. 用贤人而行善政，如或谮[①]之，则贤人退而善政还[②]。

（卷十五　汉书三）

【注释】①谮：音 zèn／ㄗㄣˋ。谗毁；诬陷。②还：罢歇；止息。

【白话】任用贤德的人施行清明的政治，如果有人进谗言毁谤他，那贤人就会离去，而善政也就废止了。

62. A man of virtues appointed to run a competent administration would resign if false charges were brought against him, thus ending the efficient management of the country.

Scroll 15: *Han Shu*, Vol. 3

审断
Be Perceptive and Astute

63. 天下之国，莫不皆有忠臣谋士也，或丧师败军，危身亡国者，诚在人主之听，不精不审。

（卷四十八　时务论）

【白话】天下所有的国家都是有忠臣和谋士的，其中有折损军队、吃了败仗，危及自身乃至亡国的，实在是因为君主听了各种建议之后的决断，不严密、不详究。

63. Although there are faithful ministers and wise strategists in every country, some countries would still suffer heavy losses in battles, thereby putting their lives and the fate of their countries at stake. This is because the rulers listened to various advice but could not come up with wise decisions based on careful observation and highly critical analysis.

Scroll 48: *Shi Wu Lun*

64. 夫谗人似实，巧言如簧①，使听之者惑，视之者昏。夫吉凶之效，在乎识善；成败之机，在于察言。

（卷二十四　后汉书四）

【注释】①巧言如簧：形容人言辞巧妙动听，犹如笙中之簧。簧，笙、竽、管等乐器中振动发声的薄片，用竹、金属或其它材料制成。

【白话】谗奸之人看似诚实，花言巧语好像笙簧，让听到的人迷惑，让看到的人昏聩。吉和凶的效验，在于有能力认识何者是善；成或败的关键，在于能够详审何者论述正确。

64. People with treacherous characters may look sincere and their sweet talks are forever melodious like the music played on wind instruments, which could enthrall the audience and dazzle their eyes. It takes one who can discern right from wrong to verify the effects of good or ill doings, and the key to success or failure would hinge on one's ability to determine who is speaking the truth.

Scroll 24: *Hou Han Shu*, Vol. 4

65. 凡有血气①，苟不相顺，皆有争心。隐而难分，微而害深者，莫甚于言矣。君人②者将和众③定民，而殊其善恶，以通天下之志者也，闻言不可不审也。

（卷四十九　傅子）

【注释】①血气：血液和气息。②君人：为人君主；治理人民。③和众：使百姓和顺。

【白话】大凡有血气的万物，如果彼此不和顺，就会有竞争之心。人们交往中隐晦而难以分辨、细小却有大害的，莫过于言语。做君主的要协调众人、安定百姓、分别善恶以通达天下人的心志，对听到的话就不能不加以详察。

65. Conflicts among all beings with flesh and blood are inevitable unless they learn to live amicably with one another. Nothing is more destructive than a misleading speech. A ruler should be in good terms with the people, bring stability to the society, and be able to discern right from wrong so that he could understand fully the

aspirations of his people. For this, he will have to think and examine carefully what he hears.

Scroll 49: *Fu Zi*

66. 不用之法，圣主不行；不验[1]之言，明主不听也。

（卷四十一　淮南子）

【注释】①不验：不切实际；没有效验。

【白话】不合时宜的法度，圣明的君王不会施行；不切实际的言论，贤明的君王不会听信。

66. A sage-ruler will not implement rules that have become obsolete. A wise ruler will reject ideas that are unfeasible.

Scroll 41: *Huai Nan Zi*

67. 主察异言，乃睹其萌；主聘儒贤，奸雄乃遁[①]；主任旧齿[②]，万事乃理；主聘岩穴，士乃得实。故傅说陟而殷道兴，四皓至而汉祚长，得治之实也。

（卷四十　三略）

【注释】①遁：逃亡；逃跑。②旧齿：年高望重者；老臣，旧臣。

【白话】君主能明察反常的言论，才能看到祸乱的萌芽。君主能聘任贤能的儒士，奸雄就会逃亡；君主信任久经考验的老臣，万事才能治理得好；君主访求不求名利的隐士，这些士人的实德才得以宣扬，进而发挥教化的作用。

67. A ruler could anticipate the fermenting of an uprising if he could analyze and detect something unusual in a speech. If he engaged worthy scholars to work in his administration, ministers with treacherous characters would flee into hiding. When he entrusted administrative duties to his old and experienced ministers, everything

would be done well. Recruiting selfless wise people who come out of their reclusive cultivation will enable them to put their invaluable wisdom to good use.

Scroll 40: *San Lüe*

68. 齐侯问于晏子曰："为政何患？"对曰："患善恶之不分。"公曰："何以察之？"对曰："审择左右，左右善，则百僚[1]各获其所宜，而善恶分矣。"孔子闻之曰："此言信矣。善进则不善无由入矣，不善进则善亦无由入矣。"

（卷四十三　说苑）

【注释】①百僚：百官。

【白话】齐侯向晏子问道："执政最要担心的是什么？"晏子回答说："担心好人、坏人分不清。"齐侯说："怎么样来考察他们呢？"晏子回答说："审慎地选择左右亲信，如果左右亲信好，那么百官就会各自得到其所适合的位置，这样好人、坏人也就能辨别清楚了。"孔子听后说："这话确实如此。贤善之人得到进用，那么不善之人就没有办法进来；如果不善之人得到进用，那么贤善之人也就没有办法进来了。"

68. The Marquis of Qi asked Prime Minister Yanzi: "What are the main concerns in running an administration?"

Yanzi replied: "A ruling administration should worry about being unable to differentiate between the righteous and the evil."

"So how does one make a distinction between the two?" The Marquis asked again.

To this Yanzi said: "Observe the people who work closely with you carefully. If they are competent, they would assign tasks fit for their subordinates; in this way, the righteous and evil ones will soon be identified."

On hearing this Confucius added: "This is quite a credible statement. If people of virtues are hired, the immoral ones would not have a firm footing in the government. But if the immoral ones gain power, there will be no opportunities for people of virtues to serve in the government."

Scroll 43: *Shuo Yuan*

69. 众人之唯唯，不若直士之愕愕[1]。

（卷八　韩诗外传）

【注释】①愕愕：直言无讳的样子。

【白话】众士的唯唯诺诺，不如一位正直士人的直言谏诤。

69. A straightforward remonstration from an upright person is better than submissive responses from the majority.

Scroll 8: *Han Shi Wai Zhuan*

70. 人主莫不欲得贤而用之，而所用者不免于不肖；莫不欲得奸而除之，而所除者不免于罚贤。若是者，赏罚之不当，任使之所由也。人主之所赏，非谓其不可赏也，必以为当矣；人主之所罪，非以为不可罚也，必以为信[1]矣。智不能见是非之理，明不能察浸润[2]之言，所任者不必智，所用者不必忠，故有赏贤罚暴之名，而有戮能养奸之实，此天下之大患也。

（卷五十　袁子正书）

【注释】①信：果真；确实。②浸润：逐渐渗透。引申为积久而发生作用。

【白话】君主无不想得到贤才并任用他们，但所任用的人中总是难免有不贤的人；君主无不想抓住奸人而铲除他们，但被铲除的人中总是难免有贤能的人。像这种情况出现，是因为赏罚失当、委任官员不妥造成的。君主所奖赏的，并不是明知道这个人不应该奖赏而偏要奖赏他，一定自以为奖赏得十分恰当；君主所惩罚的，并不是明知道这个人不该惩罚却偏要惩罚他，一定是认为惩罚得恰到好处。问题在于君主的智慧不能分辨是非曲直，其贤明的程度还不能够识别渐渐渗透的谗言，所委任的人未必真有智慧，所用的人未必忠诚，所以虽然名义上是赏赐贤能而惩罚暴徒，实际上却往往惩罚了贤者而姑息了奸人，这是天下的大患啊！

70. Every ruler would dream of recruiting worthy officials to serve under him but among the people he hired, some turned against him. Despite intending only to weed out treacherous officials, it was somehow inevitable to involve a few worthy people. This happened as a result of rewards or punishments being wrongfully given and some officials being inappropriately appointed. A ruler would not have rewarded an undeserving individual if he had not believed that this award was justifiable. Likewise, he would not have wrongly punished a person if he had not believed this punishment was justifiable. The plain truth revealed that if a ruler could not discern right from wrong, while lacking the wisdom and vigilance in analyzing escalating rumors,

he might erroneously hire unwise and disloyal people to serve him. Hence it may seem as if he has rewarded the worthy and punished the villains but in actual fact he has done the opposite. This would indeed be a most tragic scourge!

Scroll 50: *Yuan Zi Zheng Shu*

臣术 Chapter Two

THE ART OF A MINISTER

立节
Uphold Integrity

71. 良将不怯死以苟免[①]，烈士[②]不毁节以求生。

（卷二十五　魏志上）

【注释】①苟免：苟且免于损害。②烈士：有节气有壮志的人。

【白话】良将不会因畏惧死亡而苟且偷生，有气节壮志的人不会毁弃节操以求活命。

71. A great general would rather sacrifice his life for the country than to lead a cowardly life. A martyr will not forsake his integrity in return for his safety.

Scroll 25: *Wei Zhi*, Vol. 1

72. 子罕[1]曰:“我以‘不贪’为宝,尔以玉为宝。若以与我,皆丧宝也,不若人有其宝。”

（卷五　春秋左氏传中）

【注释】①子罕:乐喜,子姓,乐氏,字子罕,是春秋时期宋国的卿,于宋平公时任司城,故又称司城子罕。

【白话】子罕说:“我把‘不贪’看作宝物,你把玉石看作宝物。如果你把玉石送给我,我们两人就都丧失了宝物,倒不如各人保有自己的宝物。”

72. Zihan said: “I take pride in being not greedy. You take pride in owning emeralds. If you give the emeralds to me, we will both lose what is precious to us. Would it not be better for each of us to keep the item that we treasure the most?”

Scroll 5: *Chun Qiu Zuo Shi Zhuan*, Vol. 2

73. 故旧[①]长者[②]，或欲令为开产业。震曰："使后世称为清白吏子孙，以此遗之，不亦厚乎？"

（卷二十三　后汉书三）

【注释】①故旧：旧交、旧友。②长者：年纪大或辈分高的人。

【白话】旧友和长辈中有人劝杨震为子孙置办一些私人财产。杨震说："让后世人称他们为清白官吏的子孙，把这个留给他们，不是很丰厚吗？"

73. Some old friends and family elders advised Yang Zhen to bequeath some private properties to his sons and grandchildren. Yang Zhen said to them: "If in the future my sons and grandchildren are known for being the 'descendants of an official with a clean record,' is this not a rich inheritance indeed?"

Scroll 23: *Hou Han Shu*, Vol. 3

74. 亮自表[1]后主曰:“成都有桑八百株,薄田[2]十五顷,子弟衣食自有余饶。至于臣在外任,无别调度[3],随身衣食,悉仰于官。若死之日,不使内有余帛、外有赢财[4],以负陛下。”及卒,如其所言。

（卷二十七　蜀志）

【注释】①自表:自上奏章。②薄田:贫瘠的田。有时也用以谦称自己的田地。③调度:征调赋税。④赢财:余财。

【白话】诸葛亮曾向后主上表说:“臣在成都有桑树八百株,薄田十五顷,家中子弟的衣食,已有余裕。至于臣在外任职,没有征调其它财物、赋税作为收入,随身衣食都依赖朝廷供给。如果臣有一天死去,不让家中有多余的布帛、家外有多余的财产,以致辜负陛下的信任。”到诸葛亮去世的时候,正像他所说的那样。

74. In a memorial presented to Emperor Liu Shan, Prime Minister Zhuge Liang said: "I own 800 mulberry trees and fifteen hectares of paddy fields at Cheng Du, which are more than adequate for my children. During my tenure as a government minister, I have never misappropriated any funds, including the taxes collected, and the government would always provide food and clothing for me. One day when I pass away, I will not have any surplus brocade for my family to keep, or own any surplus money and properties outside my family—this is a sign of honoring your trust in me." When Zhuge Liang passed away, everything was done exactly the way he had promised.

Scroll 27: *Shu Zhi*

75. 州之北界有水，名曰“贪泉”。父老云：“饮此水者，使廉士变节。”隐之始践境，先至水所，酌而饮之，因赋诗曰：“古人云此水，一歃①怀千金。试使夷齐②饮，终当不易心！”

（卷三十　晋书下）

【注释】①歃：音 shà/ㄕㄚˋ。饮。②夷齐：伯夷和叔齐的并称，两人曾互相礼让王位。武王伐纣时，伯夷与叔齐曾叩马而谏，认为这样做是以暴易暴，不可取。后天下归周，二人以为耻，义不食周粟，于首阳山采薇而食，直至饿死。

【白话】广州的北部有一处泉水，名叫“贪泉”。当地父老传说：“饮了这个泉的水，清廉的官员就会改变节操而贪污。”吴隐之刚踏入广州地界，便先到贪泉去，舀水来喝，并赋诗一首说：“古人说这里的泉水，喝一口就会变成贪婪的小人。假如让伯夷、叔齐这样的廉洁之士喝下，他们绝不会改变自己的初心！”

75. In the north of Guangzhou Province there is a fountain known as the "Covetous Fountain." Legend has it that even a righteous official would be transformed into a corrupted person after drinking a mouthful of water from this fountain. When a man named Wu Yinzhi arrived at Guangzhou, the first thing he did was to locate this fountain and fetch some water to drink, after which he wrote this poetic prose: "The ancients say that a mouthful of this fountain water will turn a man into a scoundrel. But I doubt honorable men like Bo Yi and Shu Qi will change their noble character even if they had drunk this water!"

Scroll 30: *Jin Shu*, Vol. 2

尽忠
Serve with Utmost Loyalty

76. 忠臣不私，私臣不忠，履正奉公，臣子之节。

（卷二十四　后汉书四）

【白话】忠臣没有私心，有私心的臣子则不忠，履行正道、奉公行事，是做臣子的节操。

76. Loyal ministers are selfless, and selfish ministers are not loyal. Integrity is about upholding justice in carrying out one's official duties.

Scroll 24: *Hou Han Shu*, Vol. 4

77. 君语及之，则危言[1]；语不及，则危行[2]。国有道，则顺命；无道，则衡命[3]。

（卷十二　史记下）

【注释】①危言：犹慎言。②危行：小心地行动，慎行。③衡命：违逆命令。

【白话】如果国君问到自己，就谨慎地发表自己的言论；若是国君没询问自己，就谨慎地做事，修养自己的德行。国君政令合乎正道时，就服从命令去做；国君政令不合乎正道时，就不受其命而隐居起来。

77. When His Highness requests for an opinion, I would speak cautiously. If he has no questions for me, I would carry out my work cautiously and focus on cultivating my moral character. When the country conforms with the *Dao* (the moral way) I will obey the orders. If the country has deviated from its moral way, I will decline to obey and revert to the simple life of a recluse.

Scroll 12: *Shi Ji*, Vol. 2

78. 夫杀生赏罚，治乱所由兴也。人主所谓宜生，或不可生，则人臣当陈所以宜杀；人主所谓宜赏，或不应赏，则人臣当陈所以宜罚。然后治道（治道上下必有脱文）耳。

（卷二十九　晋书上）

【白话】死、生、赏、罚这些处置的正确与否，和国家的安定与动乱有着密切的关系。君主说某人应该活命，倘若不可以活命，那么做人臣的就应陈述所以该杀的原因；君主认为某人该奖赏，倘若不该奖赏而该罚，那么做人臣的就应陈述其所以该罚的道理。然后才谈得上治国有道。

78. The social stability or unrest of a country is closely related to the ruler's final decisions in determining the life and death, reward and punishment of his subordinates or people. If a ruler wished to spare the life of a man who deserved the death sentence, his officials should clarify in detail why the execution should be carried out. If a ruler wished to reward a man who deserved punishment,

his officials should explain to him why the punishment should be carried out. A good government is said to be established when the above conditions are met.

Scroll 29: *Jin Shu*, Vol. 1

79. 忠臣之事君也，言切直则不用，其身危；不切直则不可以明道。故切直①之言，明主所欲急闻，忠臣之所以蒙②死而竭智也。

（卷十七　汉书五）

【注释】①切直：恳切率直。②蒙：蒙受。引申为冒着、顶着。

【白话】忠臣事奉君主，言语恳切率直则不被信用，还会危及自己的生命；如果言语不切直，又不能够阐明道理。所以切直的话，是英明的君主所急切希望听到的，也是忠臣之所以冒着死罪而竭忠尽智要表达的。

79. Faithful ministers who serve their ruler truly would risk their lives with honest remonstrations. However, their advice might not be heeded. Since implicit remonstrations might not be able to reveal the truth, a wise ruler should therefore be keen to listen to straightforward remonstrations that might put the life of the remonstrating minister at stake.

Scroll 17: *Han Shu*, Vol. 5

劝谏
Presenting Counsels

80. 臣，治烦去惑者也。是以伏死①而争②。

（卷五　春秋左氏传中）

【注释】①伏死：甘愿舍弃生命。②争：通“诤”。诤谏。

【白话】臣下，是为国君整治繁乱和解除迷惑的人。因此要冒死去谏诤规劝。

80. Ministers are individuals who help a ruler to govern well, apart from overcoming his doubts. Thus, they would remonstrate even if it means risking their lives.

Scroll 5: *Chun Qiu Zuo Shi Zhuan*, Vol. 2

81. 夫不能谏则君危，固谏则身殆。贤人君子，不忍观上之危，而不爱①身之殆。

（卷四十七 政要论）

【注释】①爱：吝惜、舍不得。

【白话】臣子不能谏诤，君主就会有危险；坚持进谏，臣子自己就会有危险。真正的贤人君子，不忍心看到自己的君主处于危险之中，因而不顾自身的危亡。

81. If ministers fail to convince their ruler with justified remonstrations, this will put him in a dangerous situation. But if they keep on remonstrating, their lives might be at stake for offending their ruler. Ministers who are men of noble character (*Junzi*) will not bear to see their ruler being caught in a dangerous situation, and will therefore risk their lives for the sake of the country.

Scroll 47: *Zheng Yao Lun*

82. 故曰："危而不持，颠而不扶，则将焉用彼相？扶之之道，莫过于谏矣。故子从命者，不得为孝；臣苟顺者，不得为忠。是以国之将兴，贵在谏臣；家之将盛，贵在谏子。"

（卷四十七　政要论）

【白话】因此（孔子）说："君主遇到危险而不去护持，君主就要跌倒而不去搀扶，那君主还要这样的臣子干什么呢？而扶持的方法，没有比谏诤更好的了。因此，做儿子的如果只是一味听从父亲的话，算不得是真正的孝；做臣子的只是一味顺从君主的意思，算不上是真正的忠。因此国家将要兴旺，贵在有能够直言谏诤的大臣；家庭将要兴旺，贵在有能够劝谏父母的孩子。"

82. Confucius said: "If a minister does not protect a ruler from danger, or help him when he is about to fall, then why should a ruler employ his service? The best way to protect a ruler is none other than through sincere remonstrations. A son who obeys a father blindly is not fulfilling true filial piety. A minister who obeys his ruler sheepishly is not being truly faithful. The prosperity of a nation relies very much on government officials who are able to remonstrate with the ruler frankly, while the prosperity of a family relies on children who are able to remonstrate with their parents."

Scroll 47: *Zheng Yao Lun*

83. 若托物以风喻，微生（生疑言）而不切，不切则不改。唯正谏直谏可以补缺也。

（卷四十七　政要论）

【白话】如果假借一些事物来进行委婉的劝谏，言辞隐微不显而不能够切中要害，不能切中要害，就很难改正错误。只有不畏强凌弱、直言地劝谏，才能补救君主的过失。

83. If one were to express a remonstration through metaphorical implications but was so ambiguous that it failed to convey the intended message, then it could never help a ruler to rectify his mistakes. So, the only way to make a ruler correct his faults is through direct and sincere remonstrations.

Scroll 47: *Zheng Yao Lun*

举贤
Nominating the Right Administrators

84. 国之所以不治者三：不知用贤，此其一也；虽知用贤，求不能得，此其二也；虽得贤不能尽，此其三也。

（卷三十六　尸子）

【白话】国家不能得到治理有三方面的原因：不知道推举任用贤德之人，这是其一；虽然知道任用贤人却求不到贤人，这是其二；虽然得到贤人却不能人尽其才，这是其三。

84. There are three factors which contribute to an unstable government. First, the right persons are not appointed to do the right jobs. Second, the right persons are identified but they decline to join the government. Third, the right persons are appointed but their talents are never put to good use.

Scroll 36: *Shi Zi*

85. 子墨子曰:"今者王公大人为政于国家者,皆欲国家之富、人民之众、刑政之治。然而不得,是其故何也?是在王公大人为政于国家者,不能以尚贤事能为政也。是故国有贤良之士众,则国家之治厚。故大人之务①,将在于众贤而已。"

(卷三十四　墨子)

【注释】①务:紧要的事情。

【白话】墨子说:"现在朝廷中从政的王公大臣,都希望国家富强、人口众多、刑律政教都井井有条。然而却不能如此,这是什么缘故呢?究其原因,在于现在朝廷中从政的王公大臣,不能把尊重贤才、重用有德能的人作为执政方略。国家拥有的贤良之士愈多,那么国家的治化就愈深厚。所以大臣们的要务,就在于使贤才愈来愈多而已。"

85. Mozi said: "Today the government wishes to make the country prosperous and populous, with law and order, and everyone receiving education. But what was the reason that stopped this from happening? It was because the government did not consider honoring virtuous and able men and appointing them to assume important positions as part of the administrative strategy. In fact, a country would enjoy political stability when run by men of virtues. Therefore the most urgent task for senior ministers now is to ensure that more worthy people are working for the government."

Scroll 34: *Mo Zi*

86. 古者取士，诸侯岁贡①。孝武之世，郡举孝廉，又有贤良文学之选。于是名臣辈出，文武并兴。汉之得人，数路②而已。

（卷二十三　后汉书三）

【注释】①岁贡：古代诸侯郡国定期向朝廷推荐人才的制度。②路：途径，门路。

【白话】古代选取士人，要求诸侯定期向朝廷举荐人才。汉武帝时，除各郡推举孝廉外，另有贤良文学之士的选拔。于是名臣辈出，文治武功同时兴盛。汉王朝获得人才，主要就是通过这几个方面。

86. The ancient government required the patrimonial lords to nominate virtuous and able people at regular intervals to serve in the imperial government. During the reign of Emperor Xiao Wu of the Han dynasty[10], besides nominating filial and honest men from prefectures to

[10] Emperor Xiao Wu 孝武 is the posthumous title of the 7th emperor of the Han dynasty, who reigned between 141–87 BC.

assume government positions, accomplished scholars were also selected to serve in official posts. As a result, many well-known and accomplished ministers and officials were created in both the civil and military wings of the government. The Han dynasty was able to recruit the service of many worthy individuals using these methods.

Scroll 23: *Hou Han Shu*, Vol. 3

87. 古之官人，君责之于上，臣举之于下。得其人有赏，失其人有罚。安得不求贤乎？

（卷三十　晋书下）

【白话】古时候任用官员，君主在上面提出（选拔的）要求，臣子在下面保举推荐。所举荐的人得当，就奖赏举荐者；所举荐的人失当，就处罚举荐者。这样臣子们能不去访求贤人吗？

87. In the past, if a ruler made a request to select officials, his ministers would submit their nominations. If the right candidate was recommended, the nominator would be rewarded. But if the wrong candidate was recommended, the nominator would be punished. In this way the ministers had no choice but to seek and nominate the best candidates for their government.

Scroll 30: *Jin Shu*, Vol. 2

88. 官者无关梁，邪门启矣；朝廷不责贤，正路塞矣。所谓责贤，使之相举也；所谓关梁，使之相保也。贤不举则有咎，保不信亦有罚。有罚则有司莫不悚也，以求其才焉。

（卷三十　晋书下）

【白话】选任官员不严格把关，不正之门就会开启；朝廷不求取贤人，入仕的正道就会阻塞。所谓求取贤人，就是让官员递相举荐；所谓从严把关，就是让保举人和被荐人互相担保。贤人得不到推荐，官员就有罪过；举荐不实，官员也要受罚。有了处罚就会让负责的官员有恐惧之心，因而能够尽力求贤。

88. If the selection of officials is not carried out under stringent measures, it will only create opportunities for malpractices in the government; and if the recruiting of virtuous officials is not encouraged, the process of searching for these candidates will be hindered. In selecting potential candidates, it means that ministers have to take turns to make nominations. To act under

stringent measures means that the nominators and the nominees are accountable for each other. If the right candidate is not recommended, the nominating ministers will be penalized; and if there are nomination frauds, the officials will also be punished. As such, officials will be deterred from malpractices and will thus strive to look for worthy talents to serve the country.

Scroll 30: *Jin Shu*, Vol. 2

贵德 Chapter Three

ESTEEMING VIRTUES

尚道
Be Respectful of the Dao

89.《彖》曰：观乎天文，以察时变；观乎人文，以化成天下。

（卷一　周易）

【白话】《彖传》说：观察天象，可以知晓四季的变化规律；观察社会的人文现象，可以推行教化而实现天下大治。

89. The book of *Tuan Zhuan* says: "In studying astronomy, we are able to understand the law of changes of the seasons. In studying human civilizations, we are able to understand the process of transformation in the human society and thus implement education and efficient administration to rule the country."

Scroll 1: *Zhou Yi*

90. 天地以顺动①，故日月不过，而四时不忒。圣人以顺动，则刑罚清而民服。豫之时义大矣哉！

（卷一　周易）

【注释】①顺动：顺应事物固有的规律而运动。豫卦坤下震上，坤为顺，震为动。

【白话】天地顺应自然规律而动，所以日月运行不会失度，四季轮转没有误差。圣人能够顺应人的天性而动，则刑罚清楚简单，万民服从。豫卦所蕴含的"顺天而动"的义理是多么的深远广大啊！

90. Heaven and earth move according to the law of nature; hence, the orbits of the sun and the moon will not cross paths and there is no irregularity in the cycle of the four seasons. The sages conformed their actions to the innate nature of humans; therefore the punishments that they imposed were simple and just, and the people faithfully obeyed them. "Complying with the law of heaven", as implied in the oracle of *Yu* 豫 [11], has such a profound and far-reaching meaning!

Scroll 1: *Zhou Yi*

---

[11] The hexagram *Yu* 豫 ䷏

91. 坤，至柔而动也刚，至静而德方，含万物而化光①。坤道其顺乎，承天而时行。

（卷一　周易）

【注释】①化光：德化广大的意思。

【白话】坤卦六爻皆阴，至柔，但一有所动便显示出刚健的特性；它的形态是至静的，但具有方正的德性，含养万物而德化广大。坤道是如此的柔顺，它总是顺承着天道而行，随着时节运转不息。

91. In the oracle of *Kun* 坤 [12], all the six lines are *yin* lines, symbolizing utmost gentleness, but when put in motion, it exudes strength and dynamism. It is always in a state of utmost stillness but owns virtues that are upright, able to nourish all things and extensively assert its moral influence. The way of *Kun* is so gentle and docile; it obeys the way of heaven and revolves perpetually in step with the seasons.

Scroll 1: *Zhou Yi*

---

[12] The hexagram *Kun* 坤 ䷁

92. 夫大人者，与天地合①其德，与日月合其明，与四时合其序，与鬼神合其吉凶。先天而天弗违，后天而奉天时。

（卷一　周易）

【注释】①合：符合、相同。

【白话】圣明之人，他的道德像天地一样覆载万物，他的圣明如同日月一样普照万物，他施理政事像四时一样井然有序，他示人的吉凶祸福如同鬼神一样奥妙无穷。他若在天时之前行事，天不违背他；若在天时之后行事，也能奉顺天道运行的规律。

92. A sage is one whose virtue encompasses everything, like heaven and earth do, and whose wisdom is as illuminating as the sun and the moon. He handles matters in an orderly way, like the regularity in the cycle of the four seasons; he can foretell good and bad fortunes, calamities and blessings as remarkably as the supernatural beings. He may precede heaven, and heaven

will not act in opposition to him; he may follow heaven, but will act only as heaven at the time would do.

Scroll 1: *Zhou Yi*

93. 子曰："天之所助者顺也，人之所助者信也。履信思乎顺，是以自天佑之，吉无不利。"

（卷一　周易）

【白话】孔子说："上天所辅助的是能够顺从正道的人，人们所扶助的是笃守诚信的人。按照诚信的要求去做事，而时刻不忘记顺从天地之道的人，能够从上天得到保佑，吉祥而无不利。"

93. Confucius said: "Heaven helps those who follow the righteous path, and people help those who are trustworthy. The trustworthy who abides by the law of nature will be blessed by heaven; thus all things will turn out to be auspicious and favorable for him."

Scroll 1: *Zhou Yi*

94. 夫道以人之难为易也。是故曾子曰:“父母爱之,喜而不忘;父母恶之,惧而无咎[1]。”然则爱与恶,其于成孝无择[2]也。史鰌[3]曰:“君亲而近之,至敬以逊[4];貌[5]而疏之,敬无怨。”然则亲与疏,其于成忠无择也。孔子曰:“自娱于檃括[6]之中,直己而不直人,以善废而不邑邑[7],蘧伯玉[8]之行也。”然则兴与废,其于成善无择也。屈侯附[9]曰:“贤者易知也,观其富之所分,达之所进,穷之所不取。”然则穷与达,其于成贤无择也。是故爱恶亲疏,废兴穷达,皆可以成义。

（卷三十六　尸子）

【注释】①咎:责怪,责备。②无择:不用挑选;没有区别。③史鰌:字子鱼,春秋卫国大夫。一生为国荐贤斥奸,死后犹陈尸以谏,以其至诚感动卫灵公。④逊:谦虚,恭顺。⑤貌:通“藐”。轻视。⑥檃括:泛指矫正。本为矫正竹木邪曲的工具。揉曲叫檃,音 yǐn/ㄧㄣˇ,正方称括。⑦邑邑:忧郁不乐貌。⑧蘧伯玉:春秋时卫国人,是一位求进甚切并善于改过的贤大夫。蘧,音 qú/ㄑㄩˊ。⑨屈侯附:战国人,其生平不详。

【白话】若循着道义来做事，就能使那些别人觉得困难的事情变得容易。曾子说："父母疼爱自己，心里高兴而不忘父母恩德；父母讨厌自己，则戒慎恐惧不惹父母生气。"既然如此，那么不论父母喜欢还是讨厌自己，对于自己成就孝心来说，没有什么区别。史鰌说："君王亲近自己，就礼敬而恭顺；君王疏远自己，就恭敬而无怨。"既然如此，那么不论君王亲近还是疏远自己，对于自己成就忠诚来说，没有什么区别。孔夫子说："在自我矫正中感到快乐，严格要求自己而不苛求别人，有才德而被废置不用，却能不郁郁寡欢，这就是贤人蘧伯玉的德行。"既然如此，那么不论被举用还是被弃置，对于自己养德行善来说，没有什么区别。屈侯附说："是否贤德很容易辨别，只要观察他富裕时如何分配财富，发达时举荐什么样的人，穷困时如何拒绝外面的诱惑。"既然如此，那么不论穷困与发达，对于自己成就贤德来说，没有什么区别。所以，无论别人对我们喜爱还是厌恶、亲近或是疏远，还是自己人生衰败、兴旺，或是穷困、发达，都可以成就自己的大义。

94. If one abides by the principles of righteousness, what seems difficult to others will be easy for him. Thus, Zengzi said: "When parents love us, we should be happy and never forget their kindness; but when they dislike us, we should have no resentment and try not to make them unhappy." Therefore, whether our parents love or dislike us, this should never affect our filial piety toward them. Shi Qiu[13] said: "If a ruler is close to us, we should respect him and listen to his orders obediently. If a ruler distances himself from us, we should also respect him without resentment." Therefore, whether a ruler is close to us or distances himself from us, it should never affect our loyalty toward him. Confucius said: "We should feel happy to be able to rectify our faults and exercise strict self-discipline over ourselves but never insist the same

---

[13] Shi Qiu 史鳅 was a senior minister who had served in the state of Wei 卫国. He was persistent in nominating able and virtuous men to serve in the administration and warned Duke Ling 灵公 to distance himself from men who would corrupt the government. Just before Qiu died, he asked his family to place his dead body in a room in the northern quarter of the house, to show to the public how he had failed to convince Duke Ling to appoint Qu Boyu 蘧伯玉 to be the premier, and therefore shamefully could not have his remains placed in the centre hall according to the custom at that time. His faithfulness did not go in vain. Duke Ling took this last advice and dismissed Mi Zixia 弥子瑕, the courtier, and promoted Qu Boyu to become the premier.

on others. A man of virtues such as Qu Boyu[14] will not feel upset when being neglected." Therefore, whether we are appointed in office or being neglected will not affect our morality and acts of virtues. Quhou Fu[15] said: "It is not difficult to differentiate a person of virtues from the rest: Observe the way he distributes his wealth when he is rich; see which type of people he nominates when he is holding a high position, and notice how he resists temptations when he is impoverished." In short, true virtues will not be affected in times of hardship or prosperity. Being loved, disliked, in good terms or being distanced, failure or success, rich or poor, all these will help strengthen our success in treading the righteous path.

Scroll 36: Shi Zi

---

[14] Qu Boyu 蘧伯玉 had served in the administrations of Duke Ling 灵公 and before that with Duke Xian 献公 and Duke Shang 殇公 who were respectively the grandfather and father of Duke Ling. Bo Yu's proposition on urging administrators to exemplify virtues to educate the people and interfere as little as possible in people's livelihood was an important factor that enabled the small state of Wei to remain neutral and survive among its more powerful neighbors. When Confucius entered Wei he was astonished at the peaceful and stable conditions of the state and attributed this to the presence of able and virtuous officials like Bo Yu.

[15] Quhou Fu 屈侯附 was the premier serving under Marquis Wen of the state of Wei 魏文侯 around 5th century BC. Not much was known about him.

95. 君子不与人之谋①则已矣,若与人谋之,则非道无由也。故君子之谋,能必用道,而不能必见受②也;能必忠,而不能必入③也;能必信,而不能必见信也。君子非仁④者,不出之于辞,而施之于行。故非非者行是,而恶恶者行善,而道谕矣。

(卷三十一　鬻子)

【注释】①之谋:《鬻子》通行本作"谋之"。②见受:被接纳,被接受。③入:接受,采纳。④仁:《鬻子》通行本作"人"。

【白话】君子不为人出谋划策则已,如果为人谋划,就一定会依循道义。所以君子的谋划,一定能做到遵从道义,但不一定会被人接受;一定能做到尽忠无私,但不一定会被人采纳;一定能做到诚实不欺,但不一定会被人相信。君子指正他人,不表露于言辞,而是体现于行动。所以要指出事情错误,就自己去把正确的做出来;厌恶恶行,就自己努力行善来予以补救和感化。这样一来,道理自然就彰显了。

95. If a man of noble character (*Junzi*) agrees to devise strategies for others, his plans will always be drawn on the basis of righteousness. Hence the strategies devised by him would hold elements of righteousness, but they might not necessarily be accepted by some people. His strategies would display great loyalty, but they might not necessarily be used. His strategies would also be trustworthy, but they might not necessarily be trusted by others. When a Junzi corrects the faults of others, he will demonstrate it in his actions. Hence, doing things in a correct manner is an effective way to remind others of their mistakes. To rectify the unbecoming conducts of others, we should carry out acts of virtues frequently so as to evoke the kindness in them. In this way, the principles of righteousness can be clearly understood.

Scroll 31: *Yu Zi*

96.《象》曰：地中生木，升。君子以慎①德，积小以成高大。

（卷一　周易）

【注释】①慎：遵循；依顺。

【白话】《象传》说：树木生于地中，是成长上升的象征。君子因此遵循道德，从积累小善做起，以至成就高尚的德行。

96. The book of *Xiang Zhuan* interpreted the oracle of *Sheng* 升 [16]— "Ascend" as follows: "Plants (wood) grow from the earth, indicating that this is a form of progressive development. A man of noble character (*Junzi*) is thus vigilant in his conduct and cultivates the act of doing kindness until he has accumulated his virtues to become a man of high morality."

Scroll 1: *Zhou Yi*

---

[16] The hexagram *Sheng* 升 ䷭

97. 帝者贵其德也，王者尚其义也，霸者迫（迫作通）于理也。道狭然后任智，德薄然后任刑，明浅然后任察。

（卷三十五　文子）

【白话】称君主为帝是重视其美德，称君主为王是崇尚其正义，称君主为霸则是因为他通晓事理。道德偏狭了才凭借智谋，恩德不厚了才凭借刑罚，圣明不足了才凭借苛察。（凭借智谋、刑罚、苛察，会产生不同的弊端。）

97. A ruler is hailed as an emperor because he is a man of high virtues. He is hailed as a king because his righteousness is revered. He is hailed as a dominator because he understands very well how things work. Only when virtues have been compromised should one rely on strategy. Only when kindness is on the wane should one rely on punishment. Only when wisdom is inadequate should one rely on stringent policing.

Scroll 35: *Wen Zi*

98. 天有时、地有财，能与人共之者，仁也。仁之所在，天下归之。免人之死、解人之难、救人之患、济人之急者，德也。德之所在，天下归之。与人同忧同乐、同好同恶者，义也。义之所在，天下归之。凡人恶死而乐生，好得而归利。能生利者，道也。道之所在，天下归之。

（卷三十一　六韬）

【白话】天有四时、地有财富，能和人民共同享用，就是仁爱。实施仁爱者，天下人就归附他。使人民免遭死亡、解除人民的困难、救助人民的灾患、接济人民的急需，这些就是恩德。广施恩德者，天下人就归顺他。和人民同忧同乐、同好同恶，就是义。践行道义者，天下人就归附他。所有的人都害怕死亡而乐于生存，喜欢得到好处和利益。能使天下人都获得利益的，就是道。有道者，天下人就归附他。

98. Heaven has its seasons and the earth is rich in its resources. Sharing these assets of nature with everyone is benevolence. Where there is benevolence, people will

pledge their allegiance readily. Sparing people from death, eliminating their hardships, rescuing them from disasters and helping those in need are acts of virtue. Where there is loving-kindness, the people will pledge their full support. Sharing hardships, pleasures, likes, and dislikes with the people are acts of righteousness. Where there is righteousness, people will pledge their allegiance. In fact, humans fear death and enjoy pleasure in life. They like to obtain benefits and advantages. To obtain benefits for all the people, that is *Dao* (the Great Way). Where there is *Dao*, people will pledge their allegiance.

Scroll 31: *Liu Tao*

99. 文王问太公曰："先圣之道可得闻乎？"太公曰："义胜欲则昌，欲胜义则亡，敬胜怠则吉，怠胜敬则灭。故义胜怠[1]者王，怠胜敬者亡。"

（卷三十一　六韬）

【注释】①怠：据前文之意，此"怠"字疑当作"欲"，译文按欲字翻译。

【白话】文王问太公："先世的圣人之道可以讲给我听听吗？"太公答："道义胜过私欲，国家就会昌盛；私欲胜过道义，国家就会衰亡；敬慎胜过怠慢，则诸事吉祥；怠慢胜过敬慎，则功业毁灭。所以道义胜过私欲者可以统治国家，怠慢胜过敬慎者就会灭亡。"

99. King Wen of the Zhou dynasty asked Tai Gong: "May I know more about the *Dao* of the ancient sages?"

Tai Gong answered: "When righteousness overcomes desire, a country will flourish. When desire overcomes righteousness, a country will perish. When respectfulness overcomes arrogance, everything will be auspicious;

when arrogance overcomes respectfulness, all achievements will be destroyed. Therefore, a government that lets righteousness prevail over selfish desires will rule effectively, and a government that lets arrogance prevail over respectfulness will be destroyed."

Scroll 31: *Liu Tao*

100. 道德仁义定，而天下正。

（卷四十三　说苑）

【白话】道德仁义落实之后，天下便自然归于正道。

100. When morality, code of ethics, benevolence and righteousness are observed, the world will naturally revert to its right path.

Scroll 43: *Shuo Yuan*

101. 有道以理[①]之，法虽少足以治矣；无道以临[②]之，命[③]虽众足以乱矣。

（卷三十五　文子）

【注释】①理：治理。②临：监视，监临。引申为统治、治理。③命：政令。

【白话】遵循道来治理天下，法规虽少，却足以使天下太平安定；不遵循道来统治天下，命令虽然众多，却只能使天下混乱。

101. When *Dao* (the Great Way) is implemented in governing, there is peace and stability in the country despite having few rules. Against the *Dao*, rules might be plenty but they will only create confusion and chaos to the country.

Scroll 35: *Wen Zi*

102. 天反时为灾，寒暑易节。地反物为妖，群物失性。民反德为乱，乱则妖灾生。

（卷五　春秋左氏传中）

【白话】上天不按四时运行就会发生灾害，大地违反万物常性就会发生妖异，人民违反德义就生出祸乱，有了祸乱就会发生灾害和怪异。

102. "If the order of the four seasons is interrupted, disasters will follow. If the earth reverses the order of nature, strange phenomena will appear." This means that if the people reject virtues and righteousness, chaos will arise; and when chaos arises, disasters and strange phenomena will prevail.

Scroll 5: *Chun Qiu Zuo Shi Zhuan*, Vol. 2

孝悌
Filial Piety and Kinship

103. 夫孝敬仁义，百行之首，而立身之本也。孝敬则宗族安之，仁义则乡党[1]重之。此行成于内，名著于外者矣。

（卷二十六　魏志下）

【注释】①乡党：同乡；乡亲。

【白话】孝敬、仁义，是各种品行当中最重要的，也是为人处世的根本。能孝敬，则家族内部就会安定；有仁义，则会受到乡亲们的尊重。这就是德行养成于自身，好的名声就会显扬在外了。

103. Both filial piety and respectfulness, as well as benevolence and righteousness are the pinnacles of moral conduct and the basic guidelines in our daily life. Filial piety and respectfulness bring stability to the family and the entire clan. With benevolence and righteousness, we gain respect from people in the neighbourhood. As we cultivate virtues, our good reputation will be attained as time goes by.

Scroll 26: *Wei Zhi*, Vol. 2

104. 夫人为子之道，莫大于宝身[1]全行[2]，以显父母。

（卷二十六　魏志下）

【注释】①宝身：珍惜身躯。②全行：品行完美无缺。

【白话】为人子之道，没有比爱惜自己的身体，保持良好的品行，从而让父母因子女贤德而得到荣耀更重要的了。

104. In our role as sons and daughters, nothing is more important than taking good care of our physical well-being and maintaining a moral conduct that will glorify our parents.

Scroll 26: *Wei Zhi*, Vol. 2

105. 曾子曰："孝子之养老，乐其耳目，安其寝处，以其饮食忠养[1]之。父母之所爱亦爱之，父母之所敬亦敬之。"

（卷七　礼记）

【注释】①忠养：指尽心诚敬奉养父母，不仅仅是照顾父母的身体而已。

【白话】曾子说："孝子奉养父母，敬备礼乐以使父母的耳目愉悦，要使父母的寝处起居安适，对于饮食各方面，都要尽心仔细地照料和侍奉。父母所钟爱的自己也应钟爱，父母所恭敬的自己也恭敬。"

105. Zengzi said: "When a filial son serves his parents, he would let them enjoy listening to melodious music, provide them with comfortable living facilities and serve them well with appropriate food and drinks. In addition, he would love what his parents love and revere what they revere."

Scroll 7: *Li Ji*

106. 人之事亲也，不去乎父母之侧，不倦乎劳辱[1]之事，唯父母之所言也，唯父母之所欲也。于其体之不安，则不能寝；于其飡[2]之不饱，则不能食。孜孜[3]为此，以没其身。

（卷四十五　昌言）

【注释】①劳辱：犹劳苦。亦指劳苦之事。②飡：同“餐”。③孜孜：勤勉，不懈怠。

【白话】人子侍奉双亲，不离开父母的身旁，不厌烦劳苦之事，恭恭敬敬听从父母的话不违背，体恤父母的需要尽力侍奉。父母身体不安，自己就无法安睡；父母没吃饱，自己就无法进食。勤勉不懈于此，终身不改。

106. As children we should serve our parents and never leave them alone. Do not get bored with laborious chores. Respectfully listen to our parents' advice and do not dishonor them. Understand their needs and try our best to fulfill them. When our parents are ill, we should

not sleep soundly, and when they have not finished taking their meal, we should not enjoy our meal before them. Observe these duties diligently and put them into practice for the rest of our lives.

Scroll 45: *Chang Yan*

107. 礼以将其力,敬以入其忠。《诗》言:“夙兴[①]夜寐,毋忝[②]尔所生。”不耻其亲,君子之孝也。

(卷三十五　曾子)

【注释】①兴:起身。②忝:音 tiǎn/ㄊㄧㄢˇ。羞辱。

【白话】遵照礼仪来尽力侍奉父母,要把恭敬融入尽孝的真诚心里。《诗经・小雅・小宛》说:“早起晚睡勤奋不懈,无愧于生养你的父母。”说的是孝子一刻也不放松自己,不让父母蒙受羞耻,这是君子的孝。

107. When attending to our parents, we should be respectful and sincere in performing our filial duties. *Shi Jing* says: “Rising early and retiring late for you have worked hard, so as not to disgrace your parents who gave you life and nourishment.” This denotes that a filial child is well-disciplined, hardworking, and will never bring disgrace to his parents. This is the filial piety shown by *Junzi*, a man of noble character.

Scroll 35: *Zeng Zi*

108. 曾子曰:“若夫慈爱、恭敬、安亲①、扬名,则闻命矣,敢问子从父之命,可谓孝乎?”子曰:“是何言与!是何言与!昔者,天子有争②臣七人,虽无道,不失其天下;七人者,谓大师、大保、大傅、左辅、右弼、前疑、后丞。维持王者,使不危殆。诸侯有争臣五人,虽无道,不失其国;大夫有争臣三人,虽无道,不失其家;尊卑辅善,未闻其官。士有争友,则身不离于令③名;令,善也。士卑无臣,故以贤友助已。父有争子,则身不陷于不义。故当不义则争之。从父之命,又焉得为孝乎?”委曲从父命,善亦从善,恶亦从恶,而心有隐,岂得为孝乎。

(卷九 孝经)

【注释】①安亲:使父母安宁;孝养父母。②争:音 zhèng / ㄓㄥˋ。通“诤”。诤谏;规劝。③令:善;美好。

【白话】曾子说:“关于慈爱、恭敬、安亲、扬名的道理,学生已经听您讲过了,请问为人子的一切都听从父母的命令,可以说是孝吗?”孔子说:“这是什么话!这是什么话!在古时候,天子有七位直言谏诤之臣,即便天子无道,还不会失掉其天下;诸侯有五位直言谏诤之臣，即便诸侯无道，还不会失掉其国；卿大夫有三位直言谏诤之家臣，即便大夫无道，还不会失掉其家；士人若有直言规劝的朋友，则自己不会失掉美好的名声；如果父母有以道义劝谏自己改过的儿女，自身就不会陷于不义。所以面对父母、领导、朋友不合道义的思想言行，应当要劝谏。一味盲从父母的号令，怎么能够称为孝呢？”

108. Zengzi said: “Teacher, I have attended your lectures on kindness, respectfulness, caring for our parents, and glorifying their names. May I know whether sheer obedience to our parents is considered filial piety?”

Confucius said: “What nonsense is this! What nonsense is this! In the ancient times, if the Son of Heaven (the ruler) had seven ministers who would remonstrate with him, although he did not abide by the *Dao*, he would not lose his kingdom. If the lord of a state had five such ministers, although he did not abide by the *Dao*, he would not lose his state. If a bureaucrat had three such ministers, although he did not abide by the *Dao*, he would not lose the headship of his clan. If an officer had friends who would remonstrate with him, he would not lose his good name. Parents whose children used to remonstrate with them to correct their faults would not ruin the reputation of the family. Therefore, as far as the inappropriate conducts of parents, leaders or friends are concerned, we should by all means remonstrate with them in order to rectify their shortcomings. So, how could listening blindly to our parents' instructions be considered filial piety?"

Scroll 9: *Xiao Jing*

109. 夫兄弟者，左右手也。譬人将斗而断其右手，而曰我必胜，若是者可乎？夫弃兄弟而不亲，天下其孰亲之？

（卷二十五　魏志上）

【白话】兄弟之间就像人的左右手。比如有人将要打斗时，却砍断自己的右手，反而说我一定能取胜，像这样可能吗？抛弃亲兄弟而不亲近，天下人还有谁可以亲近呢？

109. Siblings are like the left and right hands of a man. For instance, if a man about to engage in a fight were to cut off his right hand and claim that he can win the fight, does this make sense? Will a man who abandons and distances himself from his siblings be able to befriend anyone?

Scroll 25: *Wei Zhi*, Vol. 1

仁义
Benevolence and Righteousness

110. 所谓仁者，爱人者也。爱人，父母之行也。为民父母，故能兴天下之利也。所谓义者，能辨物理[①]者也。物得理，故能除天下之害也。兴利除害者，则贤人之业也。

（卷五十　袁子正书）

【注释】①物理：事物的道理、规律。

【白话】所谓“仁”，就是爱人。爱人，是为人父母的品行。能像父母一样爱护人民，所以能兴办有利于天下百姓的事。所谓“义”，是能辨别事物的道理。做事合情合理，所以能为天下百姓消除灾害。兴利除害，是贤人的事业。

110. Being Benevolent (*Ren*) 仁 means showing loving-kindness to others. Loving-kindness is the moral character of parents. If the rulers care for the people with this parental love, they will implement plans that will benefit the people greatly. Being Righteous (*Yi*) 义 means having the ability to discern right from wrong

and carrying out appropriate actions at the right time, which eliminates disasters for everyone. Doing what is beneficial for the people and eliminating disasters are meant to be the mission of men of virtues.

Scroll 50: *Yuan Zi Zheng Shu*

111. 凡人所以贵于禽兽者，以有仁爱，知相敬事也。

（卷二十一　后汉书一）

【白话】人比禽兽可贵的地方，就是因为有仁爱之心，知道互相尊敬对待。

111. In comparison to animals, the noble truth about human beings is that they are capable of showing loving-kindness and mutual respect for one another.

Scroll 21: *Hou Han Shu*, Vol. 1

112. 仁者行之宗，忠者义之主也。仁不遗旧，忠不忘君，行之高者也。

（卷二十二　后汉书二）

【白话】仁厚是德行的根本，忠诚是道义的要素。仁厚的人不会遗弃疏远故旧，忠诚的人不会忘记领导（的恩德），这是高尚的品行。

112. Benevolence is the root of all virtues, and faithfulness is the key to righteousness. A benevolent person will never distance himself from old friends, and a faithful person will never disregard his superiors. This is the noble virtue.

Scroll 22: *Hou Han Shu*, Vol. 2

113. 周家忠厚，仁及草木，故能内睦于九族，外尊事黄耇①。养老乞②言，以成其福禄焉。乞言，从求善言，可以为政者也。

（卷三　毛诗）

【注释】①黄耇：指年老的人。耇，音 gǒu / ㄍㄡˇ。老年人。②乞：祈求；请求。

【白话】周室王族忠厚治国，仁爱延及草木，所以对内能使九族和睦，对外能尊敬老人。恭敬供养老人并虚心请教，所以才积累了绵长的福报。

113. Members of the imperial household of the Zhou dynasty were honest and tolerant, so much so that they would even shower kindness on every plant and every tree. Thus, they were able to keep peace among their clans and show due respect to other elders. They provided for the elders and humbly sought advice from them, and so accumulated long-lasting blessings for the Zhou dynasty.

Scroll 3: *Mao Shi*

114. 圣人之于天下也，譬犹一堂之上也。今有满堂饮酒者，有一人独索然向隅而泣，则一堂之人皆不乐矣。圣人之于天下也，譬犹一堂之上也，有一人不得其所者，则孝子不敢以其物荐进①也。

（卷四十三　说苑）

【注释】①荐进：进献。荐，进献；送上。进，进奉；奉献。

【白话】圣人治理天下就如同处在厅堂之上，假如满堂的人都在饮酒，但有一个人独自对着墙角哭泣，那么满堂的人都会不愉快了。圣人治理天下就好像处在厅堂之上，哪怕只有一个人还未得到适当的安置，那么即使是身为孝子也不敢将他的物品即刻就进献上来。

114. As a wise ruler, presiding in the imperial court can be likened to a chairman sitting in an assembly hall. If there is one person sobbing in a corner, all the people in the hall would stop rejoicing. As the role of presiding in

the imperial court is no different from a chairman in an assembly hall, a wise ruler would see that everyone in the hall is appropriately seated before a filial son could come forward to present gifts to his father.

Scroll 43: *Shuo Yuan*

115. 咎繇曰："帝德罔愆①。临下以简，御众以宽；愆，过也。善则归君，人臣之义也。罚弗及嗣，赏延于世；嗣亦世也。延，及也。父子罪不相及也。而及其赏，道德之政也。宥过②无大，刑故③无小；过误所犯，虽大必宥。不忌故犯，虽小必刑也。罪疑惟轻，功疑惟重；刑疑附轻，赏疑从重，忠厚至也。与其杀弗辜，宁失不经④。"

（卷二　尚书）

【注释】①愆：音 qiān / ㄑㄧㄢ。古同"愆"。罪过，过失。②宥过：宽恕别人的过错。③刑故：处罚故意罪犯。④经：常道。指常行的义理、准则、法制。

【白话】咎繇说："舜帝您品德高尚，没有过失。以简要、不烦扰的方式对待下属，以宽缓的方式管理人民；惩罚不株连子孙，赏赐却延及后代；误犯之罪再大也可以宽赦，故意犯罪再小也必定惩罚；处罚犯罪有疑虑时宁可从轻，奖赏立功有疑虑时宁可从重；与其错杀无罪之人，宁可失之于不守常规。"

115. Minister Gao Yao[17] expressed his opinions to Emperor Shun: "Your Majesty has a moral conduct that is noble and has not committed errors so far. You give simple but precise instructions to your subordinates and govern the people with leniency. Punishments will not be imposed on the offspring of the offenders, whereas rewards will be given to the descendants of the award recipient. Crimes committed out of mistake could be pardoned, but intentional offenses, no matter how minor, would be punished. When doubtful of deciding a sentence, you choose to impose lighter punishment; when doubtful of presenting a meritorious award, you choose to reward handsomely. You would rather be blamed for disrupting investigation procedures than to put innocent people to death by mistake."

Scroll 2: *Shang Shu*

---

[17] Gao Yao 皋陶 served the legendary emperors Yao 尧, Shun 舜 and Yu 禹 dated as far back as 2350 BC. He was appointed Chief Justice by Emperor Shun and considered to be the originator of Chinese judiciary law.

116. 子贡问曰："有一言①而可终身行者乎？"子曰："其恕乎！己所不欲，勿施于人。"

（卷九 论语）

【注释】①言：此处指一个字。

【白话】子贡问孔子说："有没有一个字可以终身依之而行呢？"孔子说："那就是恕字吧！自己不愿接受的事，不要加在别人身上。"

116. Zigong said: "Is there a word that one can hold permanently to one's heart?" Confucius said: "It is this word, *Shu*[18] (forgiveness)—What you do not want done to yourself, do not do to others."

Scroll 9: Lun Yu

[18] *Shu*, 恕

117. 圣人以仁义为准绳，中绳者谓之君子，弗中者谓之小人。君子虽死亡，其名不灭；小人虽得势，其罪不除。左手据天下之图，而右手刎其喉，愚者不为。身贵乎天下也，死君亲之难者，视死若归，义重于身故也。天下大利，比（比下有之仁二字）身即小；身所重也，比义即轻。此以仁义为准绳者也。

（卷三十五　文子）

【白话】圣人以仁义作为心行的准则，符合仁义标准的人就是君子，不符合的就是小人。君子虽然去世，但他的声名不会消失；小人虽一时得势，但他的罪恶却难以消除。左手掌握天下的版图（大权），而右手自割其喉咙，即使愚昧的人也不会这样做，因为生命比天下更为宝贵。为君王和父母的危难而牺牲的人，能视死如归，是把“义”看得比生命还重要的缘故。拥有天下是极大的利益，但同生命相比也是渺小的；生命是极其宝贵的，但同道义相比也是轻微的。以仁义作为准则的人就是这个样子。

117. The sages regard benevolence and righteousness to be the norm of a noble person (*Junz*i)—one who meets this norm is a *Junzi*, whereas one who does not is a scoundrel. Although a *Junzi* might die, his reputation lives on. A scoundrel might hold important positions, but the crimes he committed will never be easily eliminated. Holding a vast territory with the left hand and slitting his own throat with the right hand is something not even a fool would do, for human life is much more precious than winning over the world. However, a man who could sacrifice his life to save the ruler and his own parents from danger values righteousness more than his own life. Owning the whole kingdom has immeasurable benefits, but it is insignificant when compared to one's life. Life is precious, but it is insignificant as compared to righteousness. Such is the behavior of people who regard benevolence and righteousness as their norm in life.

Scroll 35: *Wen Zi*

118. 孔子曰："不义而富且贵，于我如浮云。"

（卷四十八　体论）

【白话】孔子说："用不合乎道义的手段得到的富与贵，对于我，就如同天上聚散不定的浮云一样，不值得花费心思去追逐。"

118. Confucius said: "Riches and honor acquired through unscrupulous means are like the unpredictable floating clouds, which to me are never worth going after."

Scroll 48: *Ti Lun*

119. 子曰："君子无终食之间违仁。造次[1]必于是，颠沛[2]必于是。"造次，急遽也。颠沛，僵仆也。虽急遽僵仆不违仁也。

（卷九　论语）

【注释】①造次：仓猝；匆忙。②颠沛：仆倒。比喻世道衰乱或人事挫折。

【白话】孔子说："君子即便是一顿饭这样短的时间，也不会离开仁。仓促不暇之时，他的心一定在仁；危险困厄之际，他的心一定在仁。"

119. Confucius said: "A man of noble character (*Junzi*) would never act contrary to benevolence, even in between a short meal interval. In moments of haste, he sticks fast to it; in times of danger, he sticks fast to it."

Scroll 9: *Lun Yu*

120. 孟轲称："杀一无辜以取天下，仁者不为也①。"

（卷二十五　魏志上）

【注释】①杀一无辜以取天下，仁者不为也：语出《孟子·公孙丑》，"行一不义，杀一不辜，而得天下，皆不为也。"

【白话】孟子说："即使杀一个无辜的人便能够获得天下，仁德之人也是不会做的。"

120. Mengzi said: "A benevolent person will never kill an innocent man, even if it is the way to win the throne."

Scroll 25: *Wei Zhi*, Vol. 1

121. 未有仁而遗其亲者也，未有义而后其君者也。

（卷三十七　孟子）

【白话】不会有讲求仁爱，却遗弃自己父母的人；也不会有讲求道义，却不以国君作为优先考量的人。

121. There has never been a benevolent person who would abandon his own parents, and a righteous person who does not honor his ruler with due respect.

Scroll 37: *Meng Zi*

122. 有功离仁义者，即见疑；有罪不失仁心（不失仁心作有仁义）者，必见信。故仁义者，事之常顺①也，天下之尊爵也。虽谋得计当，虑患而患解，图国而国存，其事有离仁义者，其功必不遂矣。

（卷三十五　文子）

【注释】①常顺：指自然之性。

【白话】有功劳却丧失了仁义之心，就会被怀疑；有罪过却没有丧失仁义之心，一定会得到信任。所以，仁义是做任何事都要依循的常道，是天下最为尊贵的品德。虽然计谋得当，事先考虑预防祸患而祸患也得以消除，谋划着立国而国家也得以建立，但是如果所做的事有违背仁义的地方，其功业一定不会圆满实现。

122. Those who made contributions but disregarded benevolence will cause doubts and suspicions in others' minds. Those who committed offenses but upheld benevolence and righteousness can gain the trust of others. Therefore, benevolence and righteousness should

be the moral guidelines in everything we do, as they are the noblest virtues. Although cautious strategies can be devised to prevent disasters from happening, and nation building can materialize in a given time, a government that goes against benevolence and righteousness will not achieve a complete success in its undertakings.

Scroll 35: *Wen Zi*

诚信
Be Sincere and Trustworthy

123. 开至公之路，秉至平之心，执大象[①]而致之，亦云诚而已矣。夫任诚，天地可感，而况于人乎？

（卷四十九　傅子）

【注释】①大象：大道，常理。

【白话】开辟极其公正的进贤之路，秉持至为平等的心，把握治国大纲而自然招感贤才，说的也就是真诚而已。真正有了诚意，天地都能被感动，何况人呢？

123. Provide equal opportunities for worthy people to join the government and uphold fairness and principles in governmental administration. In this way, worthy people will naturally be keen to join the government. With utmost sincerity, heaven and earth will be moved, let alone human.

Scroll 49: *Fu Zi*

124. 夫为人上，竭至诚开信以待下，则怀信者欢然而乐进；不信者赧然而回意矣。

（卷四十九　傅子）

【白话】在上位者，若竭尽至诚至信来对待在下者，则有诚信的人就会欢喜并乐于效劳；缺少诚信的人，也会羞愧而回心转意。

124. If a man in high position could treat his subordinates sincerely and earn their trust, trustworthy persons will be keen to serve him while insincere people will feel regretful and change to respect him instead.

Scroll 49: *Fu Zi*

125. 夫信之于民，国家大宝也。仲尼曰：“自古皆有死，民非信不立。”

（卷二十五　魏志上）

【白话】取信于民，是一个国家非常宝贵的财富。孔子说：“自古以来人都免不了死亡，如果失去了百姓的信任，国家便无法安立。”

125. The trust placed by the people on their government is the most valuable asset of any country. Confucius said: “Since the dawn of time, death is inevitable to everyone; but if the people have lost faith in their rulers, there will be no peace in the country.”

Scroll 25: *Wei Zhi*, Vol. 1

126. 君之任臣，如身之信手；臣之事君，亦宜如手之系①身。安则共乐，痛则同忧。其上下协心，以治世事，不俟②命而自勤，不求容③而自亲。何则？相信之忠著也。

（卷四十八　典语）

【注释】①系：联缀；归属。②俟：音 sì／ㄙˋ。等待。③求容：取悦。

【白话】领导人任用下属，就像身体信任自己的手；下属服务于领导人，也应当像手归属于身体。安适则共同欢乐，疼痛则一起忧愁。上下协同一心，治理国家事务，不须命令就自能勤奋，不为取悦而自然亲近。为什么会这样呢？这是彼此信任非常深厚的表现。

126. The manner a ruler delegates duties to his officials can be likened to the body entrusting jobs to its hands; and the way the officials serve their ruler can be likened to the hands that belong to the body—both sharing joy in times of comfort, and sharing sorrow in times

of suffering. When the ruler and his officials work together to cope with administrative issues, the latter will naturally work hard and share delightful moments with him. Why is this so? This is due to the unwavering mutual trust binding them.

Scroll 48: *Dian Yu*

127. 子张问行。子曰："言忠信，行笃敬，虽蛮貊[①]之邦行矣。言不忠信，行不笃敬，虽州里[②]行乎哉？"行乎哉，言不可行也。子张书诸绅[③]。绅，大带也。

（卷九　论语）

【注释】①蛮貊：音 mán mò /ㄇㄢˊ ㄇㄛˋ。古代称南方和北方未开化的部族。亦泛指四方未开化的部族。②州里：古代二千五百家为州，二十五家为里。本为行政建制，后泛指乡里或本土。③绅：古代士大夫束于腰间，一头下垂的大带。

【白话】子张问做事情怎样才能行得通。孔子说："一个人只要说话忠实守信，行为厚道恭敬，即使到了边远的未开化的部族，也无往而不可行。假如说话不忠实守信，行为不厚道恭敬，即使在自己的家乡，难道就能行得通吗？"子张把孔子的话恭恭敬敬地写在衣带上，以便随身记诵，依照实行。

127. Zizhang asked his teacher how a man should conduct himself. Confucius said: "Let his words be honest and truthful, and his actions be earnest and respectful. Such conduct will be appreciated even among the uncivilized tribes. If his words are not honest and truthful, and his actions are not earnest and respectful, will he, with such conduct, be appreciated in his neighborhood?" Zizhang respectfully wrote this advice on the end of his sash to remind himself.

Scroll 9: *Lun Yu*

128. 子曰："人而无信，不知其可也！无信，其余终无可也。大车无輗，小车无軏，其何以行之哉？"大车，牛车。輗，辕端横木以缚轭者。小车，驷马车。軏，辕端上曲钩衡者也。

（卷九　论语）

【白话】孔子说："一个人若无信用，不知他除信以外还有哪一条不错？正如牛拉的大车没有了连接牛与车的木头，马拉的轻车没有了钩住马和车的钩子，如何使车子行走呢？"

128. Confucius said: "If a person is not trustworthy, what other virtues could he possess? How could a bullock cart operate without the crossbar for yoking the oxen, or a small cart without the axle for yoking the horses be made to go?"

Scroll 9: *Lun Yu*

129. 信不可知，义无所立。

（卷五　春秋左氏传中）

【白话】如果信不能明显可见，义就失去了依之而立的基础。

129. If trustworthiness is not upheld, there are no grounds for righteousness to be established.

Scroll 5: *Chun Qiu Zuo Shi Zhuan*, Vol. 2

正己
Righting Oneself

130. 君子敬以直内，义以方外，敬义立而德不孤。

（卷一　周易）

【白话】君子以恭敬持重来端正自己的内心，以正当适宜来规范外在的事物。能够做到内心恭敬、处事适宜，他的德业就广博而不孤立（众人也会以敬、义回应他）。

130. A man of noble character (*Junzi*) upholds respectfulness to correct his mind, and display righteousness in all his actions. As such, he will never be isolated (as his exemplary role to others earns the due respect from people around him).

Scroll 1: *Zhou Yi*

131. 子曰："苟正其身，于从政乎何有？不能正其身，如正人何？"

（卷九　论语）

【白话】孔子说："果真能够端正自己本身，从事政治何难之有？若不能正己，如何正人？"

131. Confucius said: "If a minister can make his own conduct correct, what difficulty will he have in government? If he cannot rectify himself, how can he rectify others?"

Scroll 9: *Lun Yu*

132. 天覆之,地载之,圣人治之。圣人之身犹日也,夫日圆尺,光盈[①]天地。圣人之身小,其所烛远[②],圣人正己,而四方治矣。

(卷三十六　尸子)

【注释】①盈:充满。②烛远:光照远方。比喻泽及远方。

【白话】上天覆盖万物,大地承载万物,圣人治理万物。圣人就好像太阳一样,太阳看起来只像圆周一尺那么大的圆,却能光明普照天地万物。圣人的身体虽小,却能光照千里,恩泽远方。圣人端正自己的思想、言行,天下就能得到治理。

132. Heaven encompasses all things; earth sustains all things; the sages govern all things that come their way. Sages can be likened to the sun, despite seemingly a foot in circumference, it can illuminate all things under heaven and earth. The sages' physique may be small and yet their kindness can spread far and wide. For as long as the sages' thoughts, speech and actions are upright, the world will enjoy peace and order.

Scroll 36: *Shi Zi*

133. 孔子，匹夫①之人耳，以乐道正身不懈之故，四海之内，天下之君，微②孔子之言，无所折中③。

（卷十九　汉书七）

【注释】①匹夫：古代指平民中的男子。亦泛指平民百姓。②微：如果没有。③折中：取正，用为判断事物的准则。

【白话】孔子，不过是个普通百姓，因为不懈地追求圣贤之道端正自身的缘故，如今四海之内，天下的君主，如果没有孔子的言论，就没有办法调和太过与不及，以使处事得当合理。

133. Confucius was but a common man who kept on learning from the sages and aligned his conduct with their teachings. Without the teachings of Confucius, rulers of the four seas would have no basis to gauge the performance of their administration.

Scroll 19: *Han Shu*, Vol. 7

134. 故不仁爱则不能群，不能群则不胜物，不胜物则养不足。群而不足，争心将作。上圣[1]卓然，先行敬让博爱之德者，众心悦而从之。从之成群，是为君矣；归而往之，是为王矣。

（卷十四　汉书二）

【注释】①上圣：犹前圣。指前代的帝王与圣贤。

【白话】所以不仁爱，就不能形成和睦的群体，不能形成和睦群体就无法善用外物，不能善用外物，人们生活所需就会不足。组成了群体而生活所需不足，争斗之心就会产生。前代的圣人高远地率先躬行敬让博爱之德，人民就心悦诚服地跟随他。跟随他的人愈来愈多，形成了群体，这个人就成了首领；远近的人都争着前来归附他，这个人就成为王者了。

134. If there is no compassion there will not be harmonious communities. If there are no harmonious communities, resources will not be utilized properly and this will create a shortage in the supply of daily necessities. With

the shortage in daily necessities, rivalry among the people will be provoked. Thus in ancient times, a man of virtues would cultivate respectfulness, forbearance and loving-kindness to win the support of the people. As his supporters increased, communities were formed, and this man became their leader. As people from far and wide came to pledge their allegiance to him, this leader hence became a ruler.

Scroll 14: *Han Shu*,Vol. 2

135. 修厥身，允德①协②于下，惟明后。言修其身，使信德合于群下，惟乃明君。先王子惠③困穷，民服厥命，罔有弗悦。言汤子爱困穷之人，使皆得其所，故民心服其教令，无有不欣喜也。奉先④思孝，接下思恭。以念祖德为孝，以不骄慢为恭也。视远惟明，听德⑤惟聪。言当以明视远，以聪听德。

（卷二　尚书）

【注释】①允德：诚信之德。②协：协和。③子惠：慈爱；施以仁惠。子，待如己子，慈爱。④奉先：祭祀祖先。⑤听德：谓听用有德之言。

【白话】注重自身修养，以诚信之美德谐和民众，这才是英明的帝王。先王像爱护子女一样爱护困苦贫穷之人，人民都顺从他的命令，没有不高兴的。奉祀祖先，必心存孝敬；接近臣民，必心存谦恭。能够看得长远，才叫做眼明；能够听从有德之人的善言，才叫做耳聪。

135. A wise ruler is one who is mindful of self-cultivation and inspires his people through honesty and sincerity. Ancient wise rulers loved and cared for the poor as if they were their own children. Thus, people obeyed their orders, and everyone was happy. When making offerings to their ancestors, the ancient rulers were filial and respectful. When working closely with their subordinates and people, they were humble and considerate. So, if a wise ruler could see far and wide he was said to have "good vision"; and said to have "good listening skills" if he could heed constructive advice from wise subordinates.

Scroll 2: *Shang Shu*

136. 未有身治正而臣下邪者也。……未有闺门[1]治而天下乱者也。……未有左右正而百官枉者也。……未有功赏得于前,众贤布于官而不治者也。……未有德厚吏良而民畔[2]者也。

（卷二十　汉书八）

【注释】①闺门:宫苑、内室的门。借指宫廷、家庭。②畔:通“叛”。违背;背离。

【白话】不曾有君主自身修治中正而臣下奸邪的。……不曾有君主宫廷内修整而天下混乱的。……不曾有左右近臣正直而百官不正的。……不曾有论功行赏实行在前,众多有才智的人安置在官位上而国家不太平的。……不曾有君主德行淳厚、官吏贤良,而百姓叛乱的。

136. There would not be any unrighteous ministers serving under a virtuous ruler… there would not be disorder in the country if the ruler could run his administration with law and order…there would not be

corrupted officials around if senior officials are stern and upright… there would not be chaos and unrest after the ruler has bestowed rewards according to merits and appointed worthy people to high positions… and there would not be any rebellion by the peasants if the ruler is virtuous and his subordinates are noble.

Scroll 20: *Han Shu*, Vol. 8

137. 救寒莫如重裘①，止谤莫如自修，斯言信矣。

（卷二十六　魏志下）

【注释】①重裘：厚毛皮衣。重，音chóng／ㄔㄨㄥˊ。

【白话】谚语说：要防止寒冷，没有比穿上厚皮衣更有效的了；要止息谤言，没有比修养自己的德行更好的了。这话真是不虚啊！

137. An idiom says: "To fight the freezing cold, nothing is more effective than putting on a thick fur coat; to stop rumors from spreading, nothing is more effective than cultivating one's virtues." These are indeed words of wisdom!

Scroll 26: *Wei Zhi*, Vol. 2

度量
Magnanimity

138. 君子己善，亦乐人之善也；己能，亦乐人之能也。君子好人之为善而弗趍①（趍作趣，音促也），恶人之为不善而弗疾也，不先人以恶，不疑人以不信，不说②人之过，而成人之美。

（卷三十五　曾子）

【注释】①趍：音 cù／ㄘㄨˋ。同“趋”。催迫；催促。②说：后作“悦”。喜悦；高兴。

【白话】君子自己德行良善，也欢喜别人德行良善；自己有才能，也欢喜别人有才能。君子喜欢别人行善却不催促逼迫，讨厌别人作恶却不嫉恶如仇，不先料想别人品行不好，不怀疑别人不守信用，不对别人的过错感到幸灾乐祸，而是成全别人的善心善行。

138. A man of noble character (*Junzi*) is virtuous and he delights in others who are virtuous. He is competent and he delights in others who are competent. Although he appreciates the practice of good deeds, he will never force others to do so. He despises deviant individuals

but he will not detest them as if they were his enemies. He will neither presume the conduct of others to be indecent, nor suspect others to be untrustworthy. He does not take pleasure in others' mistakes but assists others in accomplishing acts of kindness.

Scroll 35: *Zeng Zi*

139. 故曰："记人之功，忘人之过，宜为君者也①。"人有厚德，无问其小节；人有大誉，无訾②其小故。自古及今，未有能全其行者也。

（卷四十八　体论）

【注释】①记人之功，忘人之过，宜为君者也：语出《周书》。②訾：音 zǐ / ㄗˇ。诋毁；指责。

【白话】所以说："记住人的功绩，忘记人的过错，这样的人适合当君主。"一个人如果具有淳厚的美德，就不要追究他的小节；一个人如果拥有很大的声誉，就不要指责他的小过失。从古自今，没有品行十全十美的人。

139. Thus it is said: "Those who remember the contributions of others and forgive their mistakes can become good leaders." To a man of great virtues, do not investigate the small matters concerning his personal life. To a man of great reputation, do not criticize his minor faults. From ancient times until today, there has never been a person whose moral conduct is perfect.

Scroll 48: *Ti Lun*

140. 汉高祖山东之匹夫[①]也，起兵之日，天下英贤奔走而归之，贤士辐凑[②]而乐为之用，是以王天下，而莫之能御。唯其以简节宽大，受天下之物故也。

（卷五十　袁子正书）

【注释】①匹夫：普通人。②辐凑：车辐会聚于毂。形容人物的聚集和稠密。

【白话】汉高祖原是崤山以东的一个普通人，起兵之时，天下的英雄豪杰争先恐后地归顺他，贤良之人群聚而乐于为他所用，所以能够统一天下，没有人能够阻挡他。只因他法令简略，心量宽大，能包容天下各类人才（让他们各自发挥所长）。

140. Emperor Gaozu of the Han dynasty was a civilian from a region east of Xiaoshan. When he decided to raise an army, magnificent men from all parts of the kingdom immediately joined him, while able and virtuous men came to serve him. Under his leadership, no one could stop him from winning the throne because the laws and

regulations he created were brief and clear, and he was a man of great tolerance who could accept all competent people to serve under him.

Scroll 50: *Yuan Zi Zheng Shu*

谦虚
Humility

141. 夫自足者不足，自明者不明。日月至光至大，而有所不遍者，以其高于众之上也。灯烛至微至小，而无不可之者，以其明之下，能照日月之所蔽也。

（卷四十七　刘廙政论）

【白话】自以为完备的人其实并不完备，自以为聪明的人其实并不聪明。太阳和月亮极其明亮巨大，但是也有照不到的地方，因为它们高悬于万物之上。灯烛的火焰极小极微弱，但没有不能去照的东西，因为它在下面照，所以能照到阳光、月色照不到的地方。

141. Those who think they are perfect are in fact inadequate. Those who think they are intelligent are in fact mediocre. While the sun and the moon may be bright, they cannot light up every dark corner of the world for they are too high up in the sky. The glow of a candle may be weak, but it can light up any dark corner beyond the reach of the sun and the moon, for the source of glow is close to the ground.

Scroll 47: *Liu Yi Zheng Lun*

142. 子曰："劳而不伐，有功而不德，厚之至也！语以其功下人者也。"

（卷一　周易）

【白话】孔子说："辛勤付出而不自我夸耀，有功绩而不自认为有功，这是敦厚到了极点啊！这是说君子虽有功勋而能谦下对人。"

142. Confucius said: "He contributes assiduously but does not boast of it; he achieves merits but takes no credit from it. This is honest and sincerity at the greatest height. It means that a man of noble character (*Junzi*) has achieved great merit yet places himself below others."

Scroll 1: *Zhou Yi*

143. 子路进曰："敢问持满有道乎？"子曰："聪明睿智，守之以愚；功被[1]天下，守之以让；勇力振世，守之以怯；富有四海，守之以谦。此所谓损之又损之[2]之道也！"

（卷十　孔子家语）

【注释】①被：覆盖；遍布。②损之又损之：日益去除华伪以归于纯朴无为。引申指尽可能谦抑。损，降抑；克制。

【白话】子路上前问道："请问夫子，想要保持盈满却不倾倒，有办法吗？"夫子说："聪明睿智，而又能保持敦厚若愚的态度；功盖天下，而又能保持礼让不争的态度；勇力足以震撼世界，而又能保持小心畏惧的态度；拥有四海的财富，而又能保持恭敬谦逊的态度。这就是古人所说的'损之又损之'之道啊！"

143. Zilu drew near and asked Confucius: "Dear Teacher, may I ask if there is a method of holding something full without spilling it?"

Confucius said: "While he is intelligent and wise, he appears to be slow-witted. While he has surpassed the world in his contributions, he is forbearing and non-confrontational. While his bravery is strong enough to astound the world, he remains careful and vigilant. While he owns a world of wealth, he remains respectful and humble. This is what the ancients described as the Way of Great Humility!"

Scroll 10: *Kong Zi Jia Yu*

144. 盖劳谦虚己，则附之者众；骄慢倨傲，则去[1]之者多矣。附之者众，则安之征也；去之者多，则危之诊[2]也。

（卷五十　抱朴子）

【注释】①去：离开。②诊：症状。

【白话】大凡有功劳却仍谦逊的人，归附他的人就多；骄狂傲慢的人，背离他的人就多。归附的人多，是平安的征兆；背离的人多，是危险的信号。

144. He who has made great contributions but remains humble and modest will win the support of many people. He who is proud and arrogant will lose the support of many people. The increase in pledges of allegiance is a good sign, but the increasing rate of abandonment is a sign of danger.

Scroll 50: *Bao Pu Zi*

145. 知其荣，守其辱，为天下谷①。知己之有荣贵。当守之以污浊。如是则天下归之。如水流（流下有入字）深谷也。

（卷三十四　老子）

【注释】①谷：水流汇聚的地方。

【白话】知道自己高贵光荣之处，却能守住谦虚卑下的态度，善尽本分，这样，自然成为众望所归，如世间百川所汇的深谷一般。

145. A leader understands his noble status and expertise, and keeps a very low profile while performing his duties. Thus, he has everyone readily pledging their allegiance to him, just like a huge valley that could contain hundreds of streams.

Scroll 34: *Laozi*

146. 夫以贤而为人下，何人不与？以贵从人曲直，何人不得？

（卷三十一　六韬）

【白话】自身贤德而能谦恭待人，谁会不跟随他呢？地位尊贵而能听从接纳他人的是非判断，又有什么人才不能感召到呢？

146. If a man cultivates virtues and treats others respectfully, will anyone refuse to follow him? If a person with noble status accepts and heeds the advice of others, will any worthy man refuse to serve under him?

Scroll 31: *Liu Tao*

147. 夫能屈以为伸，让以为得，弱以为强，鲜不遂[①]矣。

（卷二十六　魏志下）

【注释】①不遂：不顺利。

【白话】人如果能够以屈为伸，以让为得，以弱为强，“天之道，损有余以补不足”，只有这样做，才合于大道，才能长久，所以就很少会有不顺利的。

147. If a man can retreat instead of advancing; forbearing instead of demanding; keeping a weak image instead of a strong one; then he is actually practicing the heavenly way, which “takes away the surplus and replenishes it to the insufficient.” Everything existing according to the law of nature would be lasting and is rarely unsuccessful.

Scroll 26: *Wei Zhi*, Vol. 2

148. 自尊重之道，乃在乎以贵下贱，卑以自牧[①]也，非此之谓也。乃衰薄之弊俗，膏肓[②]之废疾，安共为之？可悲者也！

（卷五十　抱朴子）

【注释】①自牧：自我修养。②膏肓：古代医学以心尖脂肪为膏，心脏与膈膜之间为肓。比喻难以救药的失误或缺点。

【白话】自尊自重之道，就在于以尊贵的身分谦虚对待低贱的人，用谦卑来修养自己，而并非这种骄傲的态度。这种（骄傲的）做法，乃是衰败的弊俗、是严重的社会弊病，怎么能大家都做这样的事呢？真是可悲啊！

148. In cultivating self-respect and self-esteem, a man of nobility should keep a low profile and respect people of inferior status as a way to humble oneself instead of being boastful and arrogant. Arrogance is a corrupt custom and a serious social illness that erodes moral values. Is this not lamentable when everyone likes to be boastful? How sad indeed!

Scroll 50: *Bao Pu Zi*

149. 德盛弗狎侮①。盛德必自敬，何狎易侮慢之有也。狎侮君子②，罔以尽人心；以虚受人，则人尽其心矣。狎侮小人③，罔以尽其力。以悦使民，民忘其劳，则尽力矣。

（卷二 尚书）

【注释】①狎侮：轻慢侮弄。②君子：此处指官员。③小人：此处指百姓。

【白话】君王德行隆盛就不会轻忽侮慢他人。轻忽侮慢官员，就没有人替您尽心；轻忽侮慢百姓，就没有人替您尽力。

149. A virtuous ruler will not despise others. If he despises his officials, they will not serve him wholeheartedly; if he despises his people they will not offer support to him.

Scroll 2: *Shang Shu*

150. 能自得师者王，求圣贤而事之。谓人莫己若[①]者亡。自多足，人莫之益，己亡之道。好问则裕，自用[②]则小。问则有得，所以足也；不问专固，所以小也。

（卷二　尚书）

【注释】①莫己若：以为别人都不如自己。②自用：自行其是，不接受别人的意见。

【白话】能自己去寻求圣贤并以之为师者可以称王，认为没有人能比得上自己的人终究会灭亡。谦虚好问，才智就充足；自以为是，见识就狭隘。

150. He who seeks the virtuous as his teacher will win the throne one day. He who assumes no one else can be better than him will meet his downfall. By being humble and keen to learn, a person's wisdom grows. By being conceited, a person will become narrow-minded.

Scroll 2: *Shang Shu*

151. 是故聪明广智守以愚，多闻博辨[1]守以俭，武力勇毅守以畏，富贵广大守以狭，德施[2]天下守以让。此五者，先王所以守天下也。

（卷三十五　文子）

【注释】①博辨：从多方面论说；雄辩。辨，通“辩”。②德施：德泽恩施。

【白话】所以聪明多智之人应以愚钝自守，博闻善辩之人应以收敛自守，勇武刚毅之人应以畏怯自守，富贵地广之人应以狭小自守，恩德施及天下之人应以谦让自守。这五点，就是古代圣明君王守住天下的原因。

151. An intelligent and witty man should carry with him a dull image. A learned and eloquent man should carry with him a soft-spoken image. A valiant and firm man should carry with him a timid image. A rich landlord should carry with him a meager image. A man who contributed to the good of mankind should carry with him a modest approach. These five factors contributed greatly to the stability of ancient kingdoms under wise rulership.

Scroll 35: *Wen Zi*

谨慎
Be Discreet

152. 人心惟危，道心惟微，惟精惟一，允执厥中。危则难安，微则难明，故戒以精一，信执其中也。无稽之言勿听，弗询①之谋勿庸②。无考无信验也，不询专独也。终必无成，故戒勿听用也。

（卷二　尚书）

【注释】①询：问。②庸：用。

【白话】人心（人的欲望）是危险的，道心（伦理道德）是微妙的，只有勇猛精进，住于一心，才能真正把握中正（无过之、无不及）之道。没有经典为根据的话不要听信，没有征求过贤明之人的谋略不要采纳。

152. Human craving is dangerous, while mindful cultivation of morality is subtle. Only through diligent cultivation and single-mindedness can one pursue the middle path. One should never trust beliefs that are unfounded (in classical works) and should never adopt strategies that are yet to be approved by men of virtues.

Scroll 2: *Shang Shu*

153. 子曰："君子居其室，出其言，善则千里之外应之，况其迩者乎？居其室，出其言，不善则千里之外违之，况其迩者乎？言出乎身加乎民，行发乎迩见乎远。言行，君子之枢机，枢机，制动之主。枢机之发，荣辱之主也。言行，君子之所以动天地，可不慎乎？"

（卷一　周易）

【白话】孔子说："君子处在自家的庭院中，发出言论之后，如果言论是美好的，那么千里之外都能得到回应，何况是近处呢？处在自家的庭院中，发出言论之后，如果不是美好的，那么千里之外也会背弃它，何况近处呢？言论从他本身发出来，影响到民众；行动发生在近处，却显现在远处。言论和行动，对君子来说好比是门户的转轴或弓箭上的机关一样，门轴和机关的发动，关系到的是得到称赞还是羞辱。言论和行为，是君子能够影响天地万物的因素，怎能不慎重呢？"

153. Confucius said: "When a man of noble character *(Junzi)* made a meaningful speech at home, his words might spread to places more than a thousand miles away, and what's more in the neighbourhood? On the other hand, if he made an inappropriate speech at home, his words might provoke others more than a thousand miles away, and what's more in the neighbourhood? His speech has a telling effect on the people, and what he does at home might have an impact on others from faraway places. The speech and actions of a *Junzi* are like the hinges of the door and the spring of a crossbow. Their speedy movement brings about glorious or disgraceful consequences. Being so influential his speech and actions, how could a *Junzi* not be vigilant?"

Scroll 1: *Zhou Yi*

154. 无竞①维人，四方其训之。有觉德行，四国顺之。无竞，竞也。训，教也。觉，直也。竞，强也。人君为政，无强于得贤人。得贤人，则天下教化于其俗。有大德行，则天下顺从其政。言在上所以倡道之。敬慎威仪②，维民之则。则，法也。慎尔出话，敬尔威仪，无不柔嘉。话，善言也，谓教令也。白圭③之玷④，尚可磨也；斯言之玷，不可为！玷，缺也。斯，此也。玉之玷缺，尚可磨鑢而平，人君政教一失，谁能反复之也。

（卷三　毛诗）

【注释】①竞：强盛；强劲。②威仪：庄重的仪容举止。③白圭：亦作“白珪”。古代白玉制的礼器。④玷：玉的斑点，瑕疵。

【白话】国家的强盛在于拥有贤德之人，四方之国才都会接受其教化。君王具备了纯正的德行，四方诸侯才能够齐归于麾下。恭敬谨慎、举止庄重，天下百姓都会效法。依循古人的常道把教令来颁布，言行举止务求优美合度。白玉之瑕，尚可琢磨；政令之失，再难弥补！

154. A ruler is strong because he has virtuous ministers in his government. Thus, nations from four corners of the world would come and heed his practices. A ruler exemplifies virtuous conduct so lords from the four corners of the world would submit under his command. People would follow his respectful, discreet and dignified manners. Educational laws are enacted based on the ancients' ethical standards; conducts are expected to be appropriate and pleasant. Carving and polishing can remove the flaws on a piece of white jade, but the harm done by defective laws is difficult to remedy!

Scroll 3: *Mao Shi*

155. 子曰："君子道人以言，而禁人以行，禁，犹谨也。故言必虑其所终，而行必稽其所弊，则民谨于言，而慎于行。稽，犹考也。"

（卷七　礼记）

【白话】孔子说："君子以言语教导人们向善，以身作则防止人们作恶，所以每说一句话之前，必定先想到它的后果，每做一件事之前，必定先考虑到它可能会造成的弊端，这样人民才会说话谨慎而行事小心。"

155. Confucius said: "A man of noble character (*Junzi*) advises people to be kind through his speech, and keeps them away from acts of evil by his exemplary role. Hence, before speaking, he is very mindful of the effects of his words, and extremely careful of the consequence of his actions, so that everyone will be mindful when speaking, and cautious before doing anything."

Scroll 7: *Li Ji*

156. 激电不能追既往之失辞①，班轮（轮作输）②不能磨斯言之既玷。虽不能三思而吐情谈，犹可息谑调以杜祸萌也。

（卷五十　抱朴子）

【注释】①失辞：亦作“失词”，言辞失当。②班输：春秋鲁国的巧匠公输班。一说班指鲁班，输指公输般，“班输”为两人的合称。

【白话】快速的闪电，也追不回说过的错话；鲁班这样的能工巧匠，也磨不去不当言辞留下的污点。一个人即使不能时时做到三思而后言、说出得体的话，但是停止说戏谑嘲弄话语，以杜绝灾祸的萌生，则是完全可以的。

156. Even a speed as swift as lightning can never retract a slip of the tongue; even a man as talented as Lu Ban cannot eliminate the ill effects of an inappropriate speech. A person may not often think thrice before uttering decent words, but it is possible to avoid speaking words of mockery in order to prevent misfortunes from happening.

Scroll 50: *Bao Pu Zi*

157. 言而不可复者，君不言也；行而不可再者，君不行也。凡言而不可复，行而不可再者，有国者之大禁也。

（卷三十二　管子）

【白话】说一次而不可再说的话，君主就不说；做一次而不可再做的事，君主就不做。凡是不可重复的话，不可再做的事，都是君主最大的禁忌。

157. Any speech that is given once but can never be repeated will not be made by a ruler. Anything that is done once but cannot be repeated will not be carried out by a ruler. Words and actions that cannot be repeated are the ruler's main taboos.

Scroll 32: *Guan Zi*

158. 天子之尊，四海之内，其义莫不为臣。然而养三老于大学①，举贤以自辅弼，求修正之士使直谏。故尊养三老，示孝也；立辅弼之臣者，恐骄也；置直谏之士者，恐不得闻其过也。

（卷十七　汉书五）

【注释】①养三老于大学：三老，古代设三老五更之位，天子以父兄之礼养之。大学，即太学，我国古代设于京城的最高学府。大，音 tài／ㄊㄞˋ。“太”的古字。

【白话】以天子的尊贵，在全国之内，按道理来说，没有人不是他的臣子。然而天子还在太学（以尊敬父亲之礼）奉养三老，选拔贤能之人来作为自己的辅佐，访求修身正行之人（让他们）直言规谏。所以尊养三老，是显示孝道；设立辅助之臣，是担心自己骄纵；设置直言劝谏的官员，是担心听不到自己的过失。

158. Being a royal dignity of the highest order, a ruler would assume command of everyone in the kingdom. However, when the ruler was in the *Tai Xue* (Imperial University), he showed great respect for the Three Elder Teachers in the manner of a filial son serving his parents. He also appointed men of virtues to be his ministers and sought the assistance of righteous people to remonstrate with him. The respect and care for the Three Elder Teachers demonstrated filial piety. The virtuous ministers were appointed to prevent him from being arrogant, and the remonstrating officials were employed to remind him of his faults.

Scroll 17: *Han Shu*, Vol. 5

159. 夫为政者，轻一失而不矜[1]之，犹乘无辖[2]之车，安其少进，而不睹其顿踬之患也。夫车之患近，故无不睹焉；国之患远，故无不忽焉。知其体者，夕惕若厉[3]，慎其愆[4]矣。

（卷四十七　刘廙政论）

【注释】①矜：谨守，慎重。②辖：音 xiá / ㄒㄧㄚˊ。车轴两头的金属键，用以挡住车轮，不使脱落。③夕惕若厉：朝夕戒惧，如临危境，不敢稍懈。若，如；厉，危。④愆：过错，罪过。

【白话】治理政事的人，轻忽一个错误而不慎重对待，就犹如乘坐没有车轴两头金属键的车子，满足于少许的前进，而看不到颠仆的祸患。车子的祸患很近，所以谁都看得到；国家的祸患很远，所以人们就都疏忽了。了解了这种情形，就会终日朝夕戒惧，如临危境，时刻谨慎，不敢犯丝毫错误。

159. If a minister overlooks an error and does not manage it cautiously, it is like sitting in a carriage whose axle has lost the two linchpins on both ends. By being easily satisfied with minor progress, he does not see the disasters that will cause him to stumble. The dangers caused by the defective carriage can be easily discovered by anyone, but disasters that loom in the distance are not readily felt. Be aware of this and remain on guard day and night as if danger is imminent, and stay vigilant to prevent committing the slightest mistake.

Scroll 47: *Liu Yi Zheng Lun*

交友
Making Friends

160. 方[①]以类聚，物以群分，吉凶生矣。方有类，物有群，则有同有异，有聚有分也。顺其所同则吉，乖其所趣则凶，故吉凶生矣。

（卷一　周易）

【注释】①方：品类。

【白话】天下人各行其道而以类聚集，物各有其群而以类相分，同于善同于君子的就吉，同于恶同于小人的就凶，这样，吉祥与凶险也就产生了。

160. People alike tend to group together, and things are divided according to their classes. Associating oneself with the virtuous brings good fortune, while associating oneself with the evil brings misfortune. This is how good fortune and misfortune come into being.

Scroll 1: *Zhou Yi*

161. 孔子曰：“居而得贤友，福之次[①]也。”

（卷四十六　中论）

【注释】①次：泛指所在之处。

【白话】孔子说：“所居之处有贤德之人为友，这是福气之所在。”

161. Confucius said: “Good fortune presides in a neighborhood where one can befriend virtuous people.”

Scroll 46: *Zhong Lun*

162. 夫人虽有性质美[1]而心辨智[2]，必求贤师而事之，择贤友而友之。得贤师而事之，则所闻者尧舜禹汤之道也；得良友而友之，则所见者忠信敬让之行也。身日进于仁义而不自知者，靡[3]使然也。

（卷三十八　孙卿子）

【注释】①质美：纯朴美善。②辨智：明辨事理，有才智。③靡：引申为潜移默化，沾染。

【白话】人虽然有纯朴美好的禀性和清醒明白的智慧，但一定要选择贤师学习，选择善友而交往。得到贤师而去学习，则所见闻的都是尧舜禹汤的圣王之道；得到善友而交往，则所见闻的都是忠诚信实恭敬礼让之善行。自身日益进步于仁义之道而自己并不觉知，这就是因为潜移默化的影响使其如此。

162. Even a person with good character and the ability to discern right from wrong must seek virtuous teachers to guide him. He should also associate with worthy friends. From honorable teachers, he learns about the virtues

of emperors Yao, Shun, Yu and Tang. From worthy friends he learns about faithfulness, trustworthiness, respectfulness and forbearance. In this way, making steady advancement along the virtuous path is natural to him.

Scroll 38: *Sun Qing Zi*

163. 人之交士也，仁爱笃恕、谦逊敬让，忠诚发乎内，信效著乎外，流言无所受，爱憎无所偏，幽闲[1]攻人之短，会友述人之长。有负我者，我又加厚焉；有疑我者，我又加信焉。患难必相及，行潜德而不有，立潜功而不名。孜孜为此，以没其身，恶有与此人交而憎之者也？

（卷四十五　昌言）

【注释】①闲：防止；限制。

【白话】人与人交往，要做到仁爱、宽恕、谦逊、礼让，忠诚发自内心，信用显扬于外，不听信流言蜚语，爱憎没有偏私，私下相处谨防指责别人短处，聚会多说别人长处。有负于我的人，我对他更加宽厚；怀疑我的人，我对他更加诚信。别人有祸患灾难一定相帮，暗中施恩于人而不图回报，暗中成就好事而不求人知。勤勉不懈于此，终身不改，哪有与这样的人结交还憎恶他的呢？

163. When interacting with one another, we must show loving-kindness, forgiveness, humility and forbearance. Sincerity comes from the bottom of our hearts, and trust is shown to others. We should not listen to gossips, and should never be biased and criticize the shortcomings of others; instead, we should try to compliment people for their good deeds openly. For those who betrayed us, we would show leniency to them; for those who doubted us, we should prove ourselves to be even trustworthier. We would secretly help those in need without expecting anything in return and make contributions without craving to be acknowledged. When these principles are never abandoned and diligently practiced, would there be anyone who still hates us?

Scroll 45: *Chang Yan*

学问
The Art of Learning

164. 今人皆知砺其剑，而弗知砺其身。夫学，身之砺砥[①]也。

（卷三十六　尸子）

【注释】①砺砥：磨砺。本为磨刀石。粗者为砺，细者为砥。

【白话】今天人们都知道磨砺自己的剑，却不知磨砺自己的身心。修学，就是对自己身心的磨砺。

164. Nowadays people merely think of sharpening their swords instead of spiritual advancement. Spiritual cultivation is actually sharpening one's body and mind.

Scroll 36: *Shi Zi*

165. 君子博学，而日三省①乎己，则知②明而行无过矣。故不登高山，不知天之高也；不临③深溪，不知地之厚也；不闻先王④之遗言⑤，不知学问之大也。

（卷三十八 孙卿子）

【注释】①省：音 xǐng / ㄒㄧㄥˇ。反省；检查。②知：同“智”。聪明；智慧。③临：由上看下，居高面低。④先王：指上古贤明君王。⑤遗言：犹古训。

【白话】君子要广泛学习圣贤教诲，而且要（效法曾子那样）每日多次反省自己的身心行为有无过错，照这样下去，就能够成为一个智慧明达而行为没有过失的人了。所以不登上高山，就不知道天有多高；不俯视深谷，就不会知道地有多厚；没有听闻古圣先王的教诲，就不知道圣贤学问之道的博大。

165. A man of noble character *(Junzi)* should learn from the saints and sages, self-reflecting several times a day to check on his faults. If he can persist in this practice, he will become a wise man who seldom makes mistakes.

Thus, one will never know how high the sky is if he has never climbed up a mountain; without looking down onto a deep valley, one will never know how deep the earth goes. Without learning the wisdom from the ancient sage-rulers, one will never know how profound and great their teachings could be.

Scroll 38: *Sun Qing Zi*

166. 古之学者耕且养，三年而通一艺，存其大体①，玩②经文而已。是故用日约③少而蓄德④多，三十而五经立也。

（卷十四　汉书二）

【注释】①大体：重要的义理。②玩：反复体会。③约：少，省减，简约。④蓄德：修积德行。

【白话】古代的学者一面耕作劳动，一面修养自己的品德学问，三年通晓一部经，一般是掌握其中的要义，反复体会经文罢了。所以花费的时间少而蓄养的德行却多，到三十岁就能通达五经了。

166. The ancient scholars toiled in the farms while cultivating their intellect and character. In the span of three years they had familiarized themselves with one classic, grasping its essence through repeated study of the same text. Hence, they spent little time in this aspect while accumulating virtues. By the time they reached the age of thirty, these scholars would become proficient in the *Five Classics*[19].

Scroll 14: Han Shu, Vol. 2

[19] The *Five Classics* include the *Book of Odes*, *Book of History, Book of Rites, Book of Changes,* and the *Spring and Autumn Annals.*

167. 君子既学之,患其不博也;既博之,患其不习[①]也;既习之,患其不知[②]也;既知之,患其不能行也;既能行之,患其不能以让也。君子之学,致此五者而已矣。

(卷三十五　曾子)

【注释】①习:复习。②知:省悟。这里指理解。

【白话】君子学习圣贤教诲后,唯恐自己所学不渊博;所学的教诲渊博了,唯恐自己不能时时温习;已经温习了,唯恐自己不能够理解;已经理解了,唯恐自己不能按照道理去落实;已经按照道理落实了,又唯恐自己做不到谦虚退让。君子求学,若能做到这五个方面就行了。

167. A man of noble character (*Junzi*) is overcome by the fear of not acquiring profound knowledge after learning from the sages. Having acquired profound knowledge, he is yet overcome by the fear of being unable to allot time for revision. Having revised the lessons over and over

again, he is yet overcome by the fear of being unable to fully understand the lessons. After understanding the lessons, he is yet overcome by the fear of being unable to practice what he was taught. After practicing what he was taught, he is yet overcome by the fear of being unable to conduct himself humbly. If a *Junzi* can put these five requirements into practice, that would suffice.

Scroll 35: Zeng Zi

有恒
Perseverance

168.《彖》曰：天地之道，恒久而不已也。得其所久，故不已也。日月得天而能久照，四时变化而能久成，圣人久于其道，而天下化成。言各得所恒，故皆能久长也。观其所恒，而天地万物之情可见矣。天地万物之情，见于所恒也。

（卷一　周易）

【白话】《彖传》说：天地的运行规律是永恒运行，没有停息。日月得到天的承载，而能长久照耀天下；四季往复变化，所以能永久生成万物；圣人长久地推行其道义，所以能教化天下以成盛世。观察其所以长久之理，天地万物的情况便可以知道了。

168. The book of *Tuan Zhuan* said: "Heaven and earth move eternally according to the law of nature. The sun and the moon, being encompassed by heaven, shine perpetually. The endless revolving of the four seasons enables all things to thrive under the sun. Men of virtues persistently advocate good morality and righteousness so as to lead their country toward lasting peace and prosperity. Observing what they have been doing, we realize that the same rules apply to the ceaseless thriving of all things under the sun."

Scroll 1: *Zhou Yi*

169. 圣人贵恒，恒者德之固也[1]。圣人久于其道，而天下化成[2]。未有不恒而可以成德，无德而可以持久者也。

（卷五十　袁子正书）

【注释】①恒者德之固也：出自《易经·系辞传下》。②圣人久于其道而天下化成：出自《易经·恒卦》。

【白话】圣人贵有恒，有恒方能使德行坚固。圣人长久坚持德教，天下的教化才可成功。没有不长久坚持而可以成就德教的，也没有无德而可以长治久安的。

169. The sages are known for their perseverance because without it, virtues could not be firmly established. Persisting in their moral and righteous cause, they were successful in teaching and transforming the world. Without perseverance, virtues cannot be established; without virtues, long-lasting stability cannot be found.

Scroll 50: *Yuan Zi Zheng Shu*

170. 夫节士①不能使人敬之，而志不可夺②也；不能使人不憎之，而道不可屈也；不能令人不辱之，而荣在我也；不能令人不擯③之，而操之不可改也。

（卷五十　抱朴子）

【注释】①节士：有节操的人。②夺：用强力使之动摇、改变。亦谓由于强力而动摇、改变。③擯：音 bìn／ㄅㄧㄣˋ。排斥；弃绝。

【白话】有节操的人，不能使人尊敬自己，但他的志向不会受强迫而动摇；不能使人不厌恶自己，但他的道德准绳不会被折服；不能令人不侮辱自己，但人格的尊荣永远保存在自身；不能令人不排斥自己，但他的节操始终不变。

170. When a man of integrity cannot make others respect him, he will not give up his aspirations. If he cannot make others approve of him, he will not compromise his moral standards. If he cannot stop others from insulting him, he will not lose his noble personality. If he cannot prevent others from rejecting him, his integrity remains unchanged.

Scroll 50: *Bao Pu Zi*

处世
Conducting Oneself in Life

171. 君子体仁，足以长人；嘉[①]会，足以合礼；利物，足以和义；贞固，足以干事。

（卷一　周易）

【注释】①嘉：善，美好。

【白话】君子体察并践行仁道，就足以领导众人；妥善成就美好的聚会，就发挥礼的教化；施利于他物，就合乎道义；坚守正道，就可以办好事务。

171. A man of noble character (*Junzi*), by virtue of his benevolence, is fit to become a leader. He facilitates propitious meetings or feasts in accordance with propriety, thereby enabling propriety to be promoted. He provides benefits for others in accordance to the way of righteousness, and by such righteous acts and firmness, he is able to accomplish all tasks.

Scroll 1: *Zhou Yi*

172. 子谓子产,有君子之道四焉。子产,公孙侨也。其行己也恭,其事上也敬,其养民也惠,其使民也义。

(卷九　论语)

【白话】孔子评论子产,说:“他有四种德行,皆是君子之道:他自己做人很谦恭,他事奉君主能敬其事,他用恩惠养民,他使用民众(为公家之事服务)能得其宜。”

172. Confucius commented that Zichan has four of the characteristics of a *Junzi*: In his conduct, he is humble; in serving his superiors, he is respectful; in providing assistance for the people, he is kind; and in deploying the people to carry out public services, he is just.

Scroll 9: *Lun Yu*

173. 子曰:“同声相应,同气相求,水流湿,火就燥,云从龙,风从虎,圣人作而万物睹。”

（卷一　周易）

【白话】孔子说:“这是比喻同样的声音能够产生共鸣,同样的气味会相互交感,水总是流到湿地上,火总是先烧干燥处,龙吟然后景云就会腾升,虎啸之处就会有谷风相随,圣人兴起,万民都来仰望他、亲近他,接受他的引导和教化。”

173. Confucius said: “Similar sounds resonate well with one another while similar scents attract each other. Water flows toward the wetland and fire burns at a dry place. Auspicious clouds rise with a dragon’s cry; the valley winds tail a tiger’s roar. When a sage appears, all men will look up to him, adore him, and follow his guidance and teachings.”

Scroll 1: *Zhou Yi*

174. 艮，君子以思不出其位。各止其所。不侵官也。

（卷一　周易）

【白话】艮卦，君子体察此卦的现象，而抑制内心欲望，所思所虑不超越其身分（安守本分，尊重主事者职权）。

174. The oracle of *Gen* 艮 [20] denotes that a man of noble character (*Junzi*) acts according to its divination puts a restraint on his desires and does not go in his thoughts beyond the duties called for by his positions. (He respects the authority of the person-in-charge.)

Scroll 1: *Zhou Yi*

---

[20] The hexagram *Gen* 艮 ䷳

175. 贵而下贱，则众弗恶也；富能分贫，则穷乏士弗恶也；智而教愚，则童蒙者不恶也。

（卷八　韩诗外传）

【白话】地位高的人能够谦虚对待地位低的人，那么众人就不会厌恶他；有钱的人能经常接济贫穷的人，那么贫穷的人就不会厌恶他；有智慧的人能够教导愚昧的人，那么愚昧的人就不会厌恶他。

175. If the nobility could treat the lowly people with humility, no one would dislike them. If the wealthy could assist the poor and needy, no poor people would dislike them. If wise men could provide guidance to the ignorant, no ignorant people would dislike them.

Scroll 8: *Han Shi Wai Zhuan*

176. 孔子曰："以富贵而下人，何人不与？以富贵而爱人，何人不亲？发言不逆，可谓知言矣。"

（卷十　孔子家语）

【白话】孔子说："身处富贵而能待人谦下，这样的人谁不喜欢和他在一起呢？身处富贵而真心关爱他人，又有谁不愿亲近他呢？说话不违背事理人情，可以说是会说话的人了。"

176. Confucius said: "If a noble and wealthy person is humble, would anyone dislike his company? If a noble and wealthy person could love and care for others, would they distance themselves from him? If one's speech is reasonable and does not contradict humanity, then he is regarded as an eloquent person."

Scroll 10: *Kong Zi Jia Yu*

177. 一朝之忿，忘其身以及其亲，非惑与？

（卷九　论语）

【白话】难忍一时之怒，便忘记了自身的安危和父母家人的祸福所系，不是太糊涂了吗？

177. Is it not too foolish to put our lives and the lives of our parents and family members at stake just because of a fit of anger?

Scroll 9: *Lun Yu*

178. 故有理而无益于治者，君子不言；有能而无益于事者，君子弗为。君子非乐有言，有益于治，不得不言；君子非乐有为，有益于事，不得不为。

（卷三十七　尹文子）

【白话】自己的想法虽有道理，但对治理国家没有益处的，君子绝对不说；自己虽有能力，但对成就事业没有好处的，君子也绝不去做。君子并不喜欢多话，因为对治理国家有好处，所以不得不谏言；君子并不喜欢多事，因为对成就事业有好处，所以不得不去做。

178. If a man of noble character (*Junzi*) has a reasonable plan yet not beneficial to the country, he will not express his idea. If he has a talent, yet not constructive for the country, then he will never make use of it. A *Junzi* does not talk much, but he will always try his best to remonstrate for the benefit of his country. He dislikes assuming too many responsibilities, but he will take on certain tasks for the sake of his country.

Scroll 37: *Yin Wen Zi*

为

政

Chapter Four

ON THE SUBJECT OF ADMINISTRATION

务本
Engaging the Principles

179. 楚庄王①问詹何曰："治国奈何？"詹何盖隐者也。詹何对曰："何（本书何作臣）明于治身，而不明于治国也。"楚王曰："寡人得奉宗庙②社稷③，愿学所以守之。"詹何对曰："臣未尝闻身治而国乱者也，又未尝闻身乱而国治者也。故本在身，不敢对以末。"楚王曰："善。"

（卷三十四　列子）

【注释】①楚庄王：又称荆庄王。楚穆王之子，春秋五霸之一。②宗庙：祭祀祖宗的屋舍。③社稷：社，土地神；稷，谷神。土地与谷物是国家的根本，古代立国必先祭社稷之神，后"社稷"成为国家的代称。

【白话】楚庄王问詹何说："请问该如何治理国家？"詹何回答说："我只明白修身的道理，不明白治国的道理。"楚王说："寡人得以供奉宗庙、掌管国家，希望学到保住它的方法。"詹何回答说："我不曾听说君主自身修养很好而国家却混乱的，也不曾听说君主自身修养不好而国家却大治的，所以治国的根本在于君主自身的修养，至于别的细枝末节我就不敢跟您讲了。"楚王说："你讲得很好。"

179. King Zhuang of the state of Chu asked Zhan He[21]: "Please tell me how could one govern a country?"

To which Zhan He replied: "I only know about self-cultivation but not governing."

King Chu asked again: "I have the honor of enshrining our ancestral temples and rule over my country. I wish to learn the ways to keep peace and order."

Zhan He replied: "I have never heard of a chaotic country that has a ruler who is wise and virtuous, nor have I heard of a peaceful country that has a ruler who is not virtuous. Therefore, the key factor of governing is the ruler's self-cultivation. I am afraid I am not able to advise you further on this matter."

King Chu said: "That was an excellent explanation."

Scroll 34: *Lie Zi*

---

[21] Zhan He 詹何 , a Daoist recluse who used rod and line made from flexible and supple materials to fish effortlessly, drew the attention of King Chu 楚 王 (6th century BC), who received this counsel from him: "This is how I am able to use weak things to control strong ones, light things to bring in heavy ones. If Your Majesty is really able to rule [your] state in the same way, [you] can turn the Empire within the span of [your] hands; what can give you troubles?" (Littlejohn and Dippman 2011)

180. 民心莫不有治道，至于用之则异矣。或用乎人，或用乎己。用乎己者，谓之务本；用乎人者，谓之追（追作近，下同）末。君子之治之也，先务其本，故德建而怨寡；小人之治之也，先追其末，故功废而仇多。

（卷四十六　中论）

【白话】每个人心里都有治理的措施，至于怎样使用，就各不相同了。有人用于修治他人，有人用于修治自己。用于治己，叫做务本；用于治人，叫做逐末。君子处理事情，首先是先致力于根本（治己），所以能够建立德行、功业而很少与人结怨；小人处理事情是先追求末节（治人），所以不能建立功业且又很多怨仇。

180. Everyone may have constructive ideas about governance but how these ideas are put into practice will differ from one another. Some will choose to rectify the shortcomings of others, whereas some will choose to rectify their own shortcomings. Correcting one's own shortcomings is addressing a problem at its source, whereas correcting the shortcomings of others

is addressing a problem at its closing stages. A man of noble character (*Junzi*) tackles a problem at its source, thus shaping a noble character and contributing greatly to the society. So, he rarely holds grudges against anyone. A scoundrel aims at tackling a problem at its closing stages, thus he is unable to serve others while making many enemies.

Scroll 46: *Zhong Lun*

181. 为治之本务，在于安民。安民之本，在于足用。足用之本，在于勿夺时。勿夺时之本，在于省事。省事之本，在于节欲。节欲之本，在于反性。

（卷四十一　淮南子）

【白话】治理国家的根本，在于使百姓安定。安定百姓的根本，在于使百姓衣食丰足。百姓衣食丰足的根本，在于不使其失去农时。不使百姓失去农时的根本，在于减少徭役。减少徭役的根本，在于君主节制物欲。节制物欲的根本，在于返归其清净无欲的天性。

181. The principal function of a government is to provide stability for the people. Stability comes from having abundant food and clothing available for the people, and this abundance comes from uninterrupted farming activities, which are made possible by minimizing the frequency of statute labor on farmers imposed by the government. To achieve this, the ruler must restrain himself from extravagant spending and revert to his original nature that is pure and untainted.

Scroll 41: *Huai Nan Zi*

182. 能成霸王者，必得胜者也。能胜敌者，必强者也。能强者，必用人力者也。能用人力者，必得人心者也。能得人心者，必自得①者也。能自得者，必柔弱者也。

（卷三十五　文子）

【注释】①自得：自得其道。

【白话】老子说："能成就霸业的人，一定是获得胜利的人。能胜敌的人，一定是强者。能成为强者的人，一定是能运用别人力量的人。能运用别人力量的人，一定是赢得人心的人。能够赢得人心的人，一定是符合道义的人。符合道义的人，一定是心地柔和谦顺的人。"

182. Laozi said: "The one who has risen to become an overlord is no doubt a winner. A winner who can defeat his rivals is no doubt a powerful figure. To be able to become powerful no doubt one has to know how to utilize the strength of others effectively. To be able to use the strength of others effectively no doubt one has to

win over their hearts, and to do so he must be a man who can act according to the principles of virtue. In the end, a virtuous man is without doubt, a caring and modest person."

Scroll 35: *Wen Zi*

183. 圣王宣德流化[①]，必自近始。朝廷不备，难以言治；左右不正，难以化远。

（卷十九　汉书七）

【注释】①流化：流布教化。

【白话】圣王宣扬仁德推行教化，必然要从身边近处开始。朝廷还不具备德义，难以谈治理好天下；左右的臣子不够端正，难以使教化远播。

183. When a sage-ruler promotes moral and virtuous values and devise policies to put them into practice, he must start from his immediate company. A government that has no righteous principles will not rule well, and when the ministers are not upright they cannot exert great influence.

Scroll 19: *Han Shu*, Vol. 7

184. 凡为天下治国家，必务其本也。务本莫贵于孝。人主孝，则名章荣，天下誉。誉，乐。人臣孝，则事君忠，处官廉，临难死。士民孝，则耕芸疾，守战固，不疲北。夫执一术而百喜至，百邪去，天下从者，其唯孝乎！

（卷三十九　吕氏春秋）

【白话】大凡人君统治天下、治理国家，一定要致力于根本。致力于根本，没有比孝更重要的。君主孝敬父母，名声就显扬荣耀，天下就安乐。臣子孝敬父母，事奉国君就会忠诚尽责，居官就会清正廉洁，临难就能拼死效命。士人和百姓孝敬父母，耕种便会努力，守卫作战则能意志坚定，不会败逃。掌握一种方法而能使百善皆至，百邪皆去，天下顺从，这种方法大概只有孝道了！

184. To govern a country and earn the respect of the world a ruler must uphold some fundamental principles. Among these principles, nothing can surpass the principle of "being filial to one's parents." When a ruler

respects his parents, he not only gains fame and glory but also contributes to world harmony and happiness. When a minister is filial to his parents, he will be honest and dutiful in serving his leader, as an officer he will serve with integrity and even sacrifice his life when the country is in trouble. When scholars and civilians are filial to their parents, they will work harder on their farms and will never run away from fighting a war to defend their country. If there is one way that can accumulate hundreds of blessings, eliminate hundreds of misfortunes, and win the support of the people, it is none other than the propagation of filial piety!

Scroll 39: *Lü Shi Chun Qiu*

185. 治之本仁义也，其末，法度也。先本后末，谓之君子；先末后本，谓之小人。法之生也，以辅义。重法弃义，是贵其冠履，而忘其头足也。

（卷三十五　文子）

【白话】治国的根本是推行仁义，其次才是施行法度。以根本为先、以枝节为后的人，称为君子；以枝节为先、以根本为后的人，称为俗人。法律的产生，是为了辅助道义的推行。如果重视法律而抛弃仁义，这如同重视帽子和鞋子，却忘记了自己的头和脚。

185. The principal task of a government is to promote the virtues of benevolence and righteousness, followed by the enforcement of laws. One who gives the highest priority to promoting virtues is known as a man of noble character (*Junzi*), otherwise, he is only an ordinary man. The purpose of legislating laws is to facilitate the promotion of justice and righteousness. If one puts too much emphasis on the laws and abandons benevolence and righteousness, it is akin to paying attention to hats and shoes with no consideration for one's head and legs.

Scroll 35: *Wen Zi*

186. 政以得贤为本，理①以去秽②为务。

（卷二十三　后汉书三）

【注释】①理：治理，整理。②秽：恶人，丑类。

【白话】为政以得到贤能之人为根本，治国以去除奸邪之人为要务。

186. It is most important that the government employs virtuous and able people to serve the country, while eliminating evil and malicious people as its most pressing tasks.

Scroll 23: *Hou Han Shu*, Vol. 3

187. 有乱君，无乱国；有治人[1]，无治法。羿之法未亡也，而羿不世中；禹之法犹存，而夏不世王。故法不能独立，得其人则存，失其人则亡。法者，治之端[2]也；君子者，法之源也。故有君子，则法虽省，足以遍矣；无君子，则法虽具，足以乱矣。故明主急得其人，而闇主急得其势。急得其人，则身逸而国治，功大而名美；急得其势，则身劳而国乱，功废而名辱。

（卷三十八　孙卿子）

【注释】①治人：指能治理国家的人才。②端：开始。

【白话】有造成国家混乱的昏君，没有本来就混乱的国家。有能治理好国家的人才，没有不需人治就可以使国家安定的方法。后羿的射法没有亡失，但后羿不能让世世代代的人都百发百中；禹王的治国之法仍然存在，但夏朝不能世世代代称王天下。所以治国之法不能独自存在，得到了能施行的人才能存在，失去了能施行的人就亡失了。治国之法，是治理国家的开端；君子，是治国之法的本源。所以有君子，则法令虽然简略，也足够治理好一切；没有君子，即使法令非常完备，也足以使得社会混乱。所以贤明的君主急于得到能治国的君子，而昏庸的君主急于得到权势。急于得到能治国的君子，于是自身安逸而国家大治，功业伟大而且声名美好；急于得到权势，就会身劳心累而国家混乱，功业毁坏而且名声败坏。

187. There are no such things as chaotic countries, but just countries with corrupted rulers. There are no such things as efficient policies that can keep a country safe and peaceful without the wise rulership of worthy people. The archery skill of Hou Yi is remembered but he could not make every future generation achieve his state of excellence. The governing laws of King Yu remained but these laws could not make the Xia dynasty retain its power forever. Therefore, governing laws cannot exist by themselves. The presence of worthy people who can execute the laws will keep the laws alive. Without these worthy people the laws will be rendered useless. The laws of governance provide the basis while men of noble character (*Junzi*) put them into practice. Their presence

will ensure social order although laws are sparse and few. Without them, not even well-designed laws can prevent social upheavals. Thus, a virtuous leader is eager to find a *Junzi* who can help him to govern well, while an unwise leader is only eager to gain power. With *Junzi* serving in his administration, the ruler is able to relax and enjoy a peaceful and orderly country. He would also gain great reputation for being a good ruler. On the other hand, a ruler who is eager to gain power will exhaust his energy and throw the country into chaos, not only will he jeopardize his career but also bring disgrace to himself.

Scroll 38: *Sun Qing Zi*

188. 君之所慎者四：一曰大位（位作德）不至仁，不可授国柄；二曰见贤不能让，不可与尊位；三曰罚避亲贵，不可使主兵；四曰不好本事，务地利，而轻赋敛，不可与都邑。此四务者，安危之本也。

（卷三十二　管子）

【白话】君主所应谨慎对待的问题有四：一是标榜道德但却做不到仁，这样的人不可授予国家大权；二是见到贤者而不能谦让，这样的人不可赐予高贵的爵位；三是执行刑罚时却避开亲戚、权贵，这样的人不可让他统率军队；四是不重视农业、不注重地利，而随意征收赋税，这样的人不可让他担任地方长官。这四条要务是国家安危的根本。

188. A leader should be cautious about the following four instances: First, a man who flaunts his moral prowess but fails to act benevolently should not be given power to govern the country. Second, a man who is not ready to make way for a virtuous man cannot be conferred a noble position. Third, a man who avoids punishing his relatives

and the powerful nobles should not be allowed to lead an army. Fourth, a man who attaches no importance to farming and infrastructure projects but collects taxes without any justification should not be given the post of a district governor. These four instances are crucial factors in maintaining national security.

Scroll 32: *Guan Zi*

189. 食者民之本也，民者国之本也，国者君之本也。

（卷四十一　淮南子）

【白话】粮食，是人民生存的根本；人民，是国家存在的根本；国家，是君主立身的根本。

189. Food constitutes the basic needs of the people; People constitute the backbone of a country; Country is the ground on which a ruler establishes his destiny.

Scroll 41: *Huai Nan Zi*

190. 夫君尊严而威，高远而危；民者卑贱而恭，愚弱而神。恶之则国亡，爱之则国存。御民者必明此要。

（卷四十八　体论）

【白话】为君者，尽管庄重严肃而威慑天下，但是却居高处远而充满危险；为民者，虽然地位卑下而对人恭顺，愚钝软弱却有难以预测的力量。君主不尊重百姓，国家就会灭亡；君主爱护百姓，国家就会生存发展。治理民众的人一定要明白这个道理。

190. Although a ruler appears noble and majestic, his high and isolated position could land him in danger. Although a civilian has a low status and remains humble, this apparently slow-witted person could have unbelievable power. When a ruler does not respect his people, his country will be destroyed. When a ruler loves and protects his people, his country will thrive and prosper. Those who govern should be aware of this principle.

Scroll 48: *Ti Lun*

191. 案①今年计，子弟杀父兄，妻杀夫者，凡二百二十二人。臣愚以为此非小变也。今左右不忧此，乃欲发兵报纤介②之忿于远夷，殆③孔子所谓“吾恐季孙之忧，不在颛臾，而在萧墙之内④者也”。

（卷十九　汉书七）

【注释】①案：通“按”，依据，按照。②纤介：细微。③殆：大概。④吾恐季孙之忧，不在颛臾，而在萧墙之内：颛臾，鲁附庸国。萧墙，古代宫室内作为屏障的矮墙。藉指内部。萧，通“肃”。此处引用《论语·季氏》中，冉有、子路向孔子报告季氏将伐颛臾，孔子的答话。

【白话】据今年的统计，子弟杀死父兄、妻子杀死丈夫的事情，就有二百二十二人，我认为这不是小变故啊。现在在皇帝身边的臣子不忧虑这样的情况，却打算发兵报复边远地方微小的怨恨，这大概就是孔子所说的“我恐怕季孙氏的忧患不在颛臾，而在自己内部”的道理吧。

191. According to this year's statistics, the number of cases of children who killed their fathers, younger brothers who killed their elder brothers, and wives who killed their husbands was a total of 222. In my humble opinion this is by no means a small incident. Officials close to Your Majesty are not worried by this situation, but instead they are planning to deploy troops to settle minor scores at the faraway borders. This situation is reminiscent of a comment by Confucius: "My concern is that the misery of Baron Ji Sun is not caused by foreign unrest occurring in the region of Zhuan Yu but by affairs in his family."

Scroll 19: *Han Shu*, Vol. 7

192. 夫用天之道，分地之利，六畜生于时，百物取于野，此富国之本也……故为政者，明督工商，勿使淫伪；困辱游业①，勿使擅利；宽假②本农，而宠遂③学士。则民富而国平矣。

（卷四十四　潜夫论）

【注释】①游业：流动的职业。如行商等。②宽假：宽容；宽纵。③宠遂：使之尊荣显达。

【白话】利用自然的时节，分清土地的高下优劣（加以利用），各种牲畜的生长符合时令，万物收获于田野，这就是使国家富强的根本……因此执政者应明确监督工匠与商人，不要让他们弄虚作假；限制贬低商业等流动的行业，不要让他们独占利益；宽待务农之人，使博通圣贤学问之士尊贵荣显。这样，就会使百姓富足、国家太平了。

192. By making full use of the natural cycles of seasonal changes and maximizing the use of lands, livestocks can be raised and bountiful crops can be harvested from the fields. This is the basis upon which a prosperous nation is founded. Thus, the government must make sure that craftsmen and businessmen should maintain the quality of their products and should not control or monopolize trading. The government should be lenient to farmers and also ensure that wise scholars achieve noble and honorable status. In this way, the populace will prosper and the country will become peaceful.

Scroll 44: *Qian Fu Lun*

知人
Good Judge of Character

193. 咎繇曰：都！亦[①]行有九德。言人性行有九德，以考察真伪，则可知也。宽而栗[②]，性宽宏而能庄栗也。柔而立，和柔而能立事。愿[③]而恭，悫愿而恭恪也。乱[④]而敬，乱，治也。有治而能谨敬也。扰[⑤]而毅，扰，顺也。致果为毅也。直而温，行正直而气温和也。简[⑥]而廉[⑦]，性简大而有廉隅也。刚而塞[⑧]，刚断而实塞也。强而义。无所屈挠，动必合义。彰厥有常[⑨]，吉哉。彰，明也。吉，善也。明九德之常，以择人而官之，则政之善也。

（卷二　尚书）

【注释】①亦：助词，无义。②栗：庄敬，严肃。③愿：质朴；恭谨。④乱：治，治理。⑤扰：安抚，和顺。⑥简：简易，不苛求小节。⑦廉：廉隅，棱角。比喻端方不苟的行为、品性。⑧塞：音 sè／ㄙㄜˋ，笃实。⑨常：规律，通例。这里指道德标准。

【白话】咎繇说："啊！人的德行有九种类型：一是秉性宽宏而不失庄敬有度；二是性格柔和而能建功立业；三是老实忠厚而又谦恭严肃；四是精于治事而又恭谨敬慎；五是为人柔顺而能勇敢有为；六是言行正直而又态度温和；七是性情平易而有操守；八是性格

刚断而笃实稳健；九是坚强不屈而所作所为又都能够合乎道义。表彰符合这九种道德标准的人，天下就会吉祥！”

193. Gao Yao said: “Well, kindly consider this norm. Human virtues can be classified into nine characteristics:

1. Generous and respectful;
2. Gentle and accomplished;
3. Honest and humble;
4. Skilful in handling matters but remain unassuming;
5. Submissive yet decisive;
6. Upright yet approachable;
7. Good-natured and ethical;
8. Indomitable yet practical and stable;
9. Tenacious yet benevolent and righteous.

Auspicious indeed is a country if there are officials who possess these nine characteristics!”

Scroll 2: *Shang Shu*

194. 故论人之道：贵即观其所举，富即观其所施，穷则观其所不受，贱即观其所不为。视其所患难，以知其勇；动以喜乐，以观其守；委以货财，以观其仁；振[1]以恐惧，以观其节。如此即人情[2]得矣。

（卷三十五　文子）

【注释】①振：通“震”。震慑。②情：实情。

【白话】所以评价人的方法是：高贵的人要看他所推举的是什么人，富有的人要看他所施予的是什么人，贫穷的人要看他不接受什么，地位低下的人要看他不做什么。观察他处在困难面前的举动，来了解他勇敢的程度；用欢乐之事触动他，来了解他的操守；把财物交给他，来考察他的仁德；用恐惧震慑他，来了解他的气节。这样就可以知道他的真实情况了。

194. As far as the appraisal of someone's character is concerned, let us take these observations into consideration: if he is a man of noble status observe who he nominates as officials; if he is rich observe to whom he will donate for

charity; if he is poor observe what he will not accept, and if he is a man of low status observe what he refuses to do. Observe his behavior when he is in trouble to find out the extent of his bravery; entice him with entertainment to find out whether he can stick to his principles; give him money and goods and observe whether he can uphold his virtues; use fear and intimidation to find out the depth of his moral integrity. In this way we will be able to find out the truth about this person.

Scroll 35: *Wen Zi*

任使
Appointing Officials

195. 正臣进者，治之表也；正臣陷者，乱之机[1]也。

（卷十五　汉书三）

【注释】①机：先兆，征兆。

【白话】忠正之臣得到任用，这是治世的表现；忠正之臣遭到陷害，那就是混乱的先兆。

195. When a loyal and upright minister is assigned important tasks this is evidential of a good government. If such a minister can be brought down because of false charges, this is an early sign of chaos and disorder.

Scroll 15: *Han Shu*, Vol. 3

196. 故夫处①天下之大道而智不穷，兴天下之大业而虑不竭，统齐群言之类而口不劳，兼听古今之辨而志不倦者，其唯用贤乎。

（卷五十　袁子正书）

【注释】①处：定夺；决断。

【白话】所以定夺天下的重大决策而智慧不会穷尽，兴办天下的大业而思想不会枯竭，统一百家之言而口舌不会劳累，兼听古今言论而心志不会疲倦，只有使用贤才这一个办法。

196. Whether a government can make critical decisions with inexhaustible wisdom, execute great plans with inexhaustible ideas, unify a hundred schools of thought with untiring persuasions, and maintain an unyielding spirit while learning from ancient or contemporary views—there is no other way to achieve these except to employ virtuous and competent individuals to serve in the government.

Scroll 50: *Yuan Zi Zheng Shu*

197. 古之圣王，所以潜处①重闱②之内而知万里之情，垂拱③袵席④之上而明照八极⑤之际者，任贤之功也。

（卷二十八　吴志下）

【注释】①潜处：深居。②重闱：重重宫门，指深宫。③垂拱：垂衣拱手，不亲理事务。多指帝王的无为而治。④袵席：床褥与莞簟，引申为寝处之所。袵，音 rèn/ㄖㄣˋ。卧席，指床褥。⑤八极：八方极远之地。

【白话】古代的圣王之所以居住在深宫之内，就知道万里之外的事情；垂衣拱手安坐在袵席之上，而能明察八方最远地区的情况，是因为任用贤才的结果。

197. Ancient sage-rulers could live in the inner chambers of the imperial palace and were knowledgeable of matters from thousands of miles away; sit on their mattress with hands clasped in ease and were knowledgeable of the state of affairs at the furthest corners of his kingdom, all because they had virtuous and competent men to work for them.

Scroll 28: *Wu Zhi*, Vol. 2

198. 遭良吏，则皆怀忠信而履仁厚；遇恶吏，则皆怀奸邪而行浅薄。忠厚积则致太平，奸薄积则致危亡。

（卷四十四　潜夫论）

【白话】百姓遇到好的官吏，就都会心怀忠信而品行仁厚；碰到不良官吏，就都会心怀奸邪而行为浅薄。积累忠信仁厚就会实现天下太平，积累奸邪刻薄就会导致天下危亡。

198. The presence of virtuous officials will transform people into becoming honest and kind. The presence of wicked officials will transform people into becoming evil and mean. When honesty and kindness prevail, there will be peace and prosperity; when evilness and selfishness prevail, the fate of the nation would be at stake.

Scroll 44: *Qian Fu Lun*

199. 贤主必自知士，故士尽力竭智，直言交争[1]，而不辞其患。士为知己者死，故尽力竭智，何患之辞也。

（卷三十九　吕氏春秋）

【注释】①交争：交相谏诤。

【白话】贤主之所以成为贤主，一定是由于能赏识和任用贤士，这样贤者就能竭尽心力和智慧，直言相谏，也不怕招来祸患。

199. A sage-ruler will surely recognize the contributions of virtuous individuals and appoint them to undertake important tasks so that they can serve him wholeheartedly and wisely and remonstrate with him without the fear of being persecuted.

Scroll 39: *Lü Shi Chun Qiu*

200. 非独臣有不尽忠，亦主有不能使也。百里奚愚于虞，而智于秦；豫让苟容中行，而著节①智伯。斯则古人之明验矣。

（卷二十五　魏志上）

【注释】①著节：彰显其节操。

【白话】（治国成效不彰）不仅仅是因为臣子不尽忠，君主不善用人也是原因之一。百里奚在虞国时显得愚钝，在秦国时显得很有智慧；豫让在中行氏手下只是苟且容身，而在智伯手下却显示出他的节操。这都是古人中很明显的例证。

200. An inefficient government may not only be due to treacherous ministers but also due to a ruler's inability to use the right people to do the right tasks. For instance, Baili Xi appeared foolish when he served in the state of Yu but performed brilliantly when he served in the state of Qin. Another example was Yu Rang who led a contemptible life when he served in the household of nobleman Zhong Hang, but showed high moral integrity when he served the nobleman Zhi Bo. These are obvious examples attested by the ancients.

Scroll 25: *Wei Zhi*, Vol. 1

201. 圣主者，举贤以立功，不肖主举其所与同。

（卷四十一　淮南子）

【白话】圣明的君主任用贤人来建立功业，不贤的君主只任用习气爱好与他类同的人。

201. A wise ruler will appoint competent and virtuous people to help him accomplish great missions. An unwise leader will appoint people with similar personalities and preferences to himself.

Scroll 41: *Huai Nan Zi*

202. 明主任人之道专，致人之道博。任人道专，故邪不得间[①]。致人之道博，故下无所壅。任人之道不专，则谗说起而异心生。致人之道不博，则殊涂塞而良材屈。

（卷四十九　傅子）

【注释】①间：音 jiàn/ㄐㄧㄢˋ。挑拨离间，使人不和。

【白话】明智的君主，用人之道专一，招揽人才的途径宽广。用人之道专一，所以邪恶之徒不能离间。招揽人才的途径宽广，进才之路才不会被壅塞。用人之道不专一，谗言就会出现，异心就会产生。招揽人才的途径不宽广，则各条管道都会堵塞，而人才也会被埋没。

202. A wise ruler is consistent when it comes to appointing the right candidates to serve in the government, and the recruitment process that he employs is thorough and extensive. By being consistent he prevents treacherous people from sowing discords; and when the recruitment

process is extensive the channels for recruiting virtuous candidates are never blocked. If appointments are done in an inconsistent manner, false charges will arise and disloyalty will follow. If the recruitment process is not extensive, all channels will be blocked and virtuous candidates will be neglected.

Scroll 49: *Fu Zi*

203. 选举莫取有名，名如画地作饼，不可啖[①]。

（卷二十六　魏志下）

【注释】①啖：音 dàn／ㄉㄢˋ。吃。

【白话】选拔人才时不要只知道选取有名气的人，名气如同画在地上的饼，是不能吃的。

203. Do not select a candidate based solely on his popularity. Popularity is like the picture of a biscuit sketched on the ground that cannot be eaten.

Scroll 26: *Wei Zhi*, Vol. 2

204. 故构①大厦者，先择匠，然后简材；治国家者，先择佐②，然后定民。

（卷四十九　傅子）

【注释】①构：音 gòu／ㄍㄡˋ。架屋；营造。②佐：辅佐的大臣。

【白话】所以，建筑大厦的人，必先选择工匠，然后准备材料；治国的君主，须先选择良臣，然后才能治理好百姓。

204. Thus, before a builder can commence construction he must first select good craftsmen and then prepare the materials needed. Likewise, a ruler must first select good ministers before he can run the government well and deliver beneficial results to the people.

Scroll 49: *Fu Zi*

205. 柔远[①]和迩[②]，莫大宁民[③]。宁民之务，莫重用贤。用贤之道，必存[④]考黜[⑤]。

（卷二十三　后汉书三）

【注释】①柔远：安抚远人或远方邦国。②迩：近。③宁民：安民，使人民安定。④存：立；设置。⑤考黜：按一定标准考核以确定官吏的升降。

【白话】安抚远方和睦近处，再没有比使人民安定更重大的了。使人民安定的关键，没有比任用贤人更重要的了。任用贤者的办法，是一定要设立考核与罢免的制度。

205. To appease people or countries from afar and bring harmony to those close at hand, nothing can be more important than winning the hearts of the people. In order to achieve this nothing can be more pressing than hiring virtuous people to serve in the government. To ensure that the ability of the virtuous and able is properly tapped, a proficiency assessment and dismissal system must be established.

Scroll 23: *Hou Han Shu*, Vol. 3

206. 治乱荣辱之端，在所信任。所信任既贤，在于坚固而不移。

（卷十五　汉书三）

【白话】安定与动乱、荣誉与耻辱的发端，就在于君主所相信并任用的人。所信任的人已经是贤才了，那就要坚信他而不动摇。

206. The reasons that lead to stability or chaos, honor or disgrace, begin with the ministers trusted and empowered by the ruler. If the ministers proved to be virtuous, everyone should have full confidence in them and trust them without the slightest doubts.

Scroll 15: *Han Shu*, Vol. 3

207. 昔之狱官，唯贤是任，故民无冤枉。升泰[1]之祚，实由此兴。

（卷二十七　吴志上）

【注释】①升泰：《三国志》通行本作“休泰”。升泰，太平安宁。休泰，安好、安宁。

【白话】从前主持刑狱的官员，只有贤能之人才可担任，所以百姓没有冤屈。安宁太平的福运，其实是由此兴起的。

207. In ancient times, only the capable and virtuous were permitted to preside over criminal and penal matters, and so cases of unjust prosecution could be avoided. The blessings of a peaceful and prosperous nation are, in fact, the result of this key factor.

Scroll 27: *Wu Zhi*, Vol. 1

208. 耳不知清浊[1]之分者，不可令调音；心不知治乱之源者，不可令制法度（无度字）。

（卷四十一　淮南子）

【注释】①清浊：音乐的清音与浊音。

【白话】耳朵不能分辨清浊声调的人，不可以让他调整音律；心里不懂治乱根源的人，不可以让他制定法令。

208. A man who cannot distinguish a pure tone from an overtone should not be allowed to tune a musical instrument. A man who does not know how to eradicate the root cause of unrests should not be allowed to make laws and regulations.

Scroll 41: *Huai Nan Zi*

209. 是故有大略①者，不可责②以捷巧；有小智者，不可任以大功③。

（卷四十一　淮南子）

【注释】①大略：远大的谋略。略，谋略、智谋。②责：要求，期望。③功：事情，事业。

【白话】有雄才大略的人，不能苛求他们敏捷和灵巧；有小小才智者，不可委任他们去做大事业。

209. A man with great talent and bold vision should not be ordered to act quickly and cleverly. A man of minor intelligence should not be appointed to undertake matters of great importance.

Scroll 41: *Huai Nan Zi*

至公
Paramount Impartiality

210. 先圣王之治天下也，必先公，公则天下平。平，和。

（卷三十九　吕氏春秋）

【白话】从前圣王治理天下，一定要把公正无私放在首位，处事公正无私，则天下太平安和。

210. The sage-rulers of ancient times placed justice as a priority in governing. When governing was done without selfish motives, peace and harmony could be achieved.

Scroll 39: *Lü Shi Chun Qiu*

211. 见人有善，如己有善；见人有过，如己有过。天无私于物，地无私于物，袭[①]此行者，谓之天子。

（卷三十六　尸子）

【注释】①袭：继承，沿袭。

【白话】见到别人有善行，就像自己有善行一样；见到别人有过错，就如同自己有过错一样。天对万物无私无求，地对万物也无私无求，能秉承天地这种无私行为的人，才称之为天子。

211. When we see others perform good deeds we should be joyous as if we have done the same. When we see faults in others we should consider these faults as if they are ours. Heaven and earth give life to everything without expecting anything in return. Hence, only the one who could uphold this demeanor and offer himself to serve selflessly is deemed the Son of Heaven.

Scroll 36: *Shi Zi*

纲纪
The Basis of Principles

212. 先王之政:一曰承天,二曰正身,三曰任贤,四曰恤民,五曰明制,六曰立业。承天惟允,正身惟恒,任贤惟固,恤民惟勤①,明制惟典②,立业惟敦,是谓政体。

（卷四十六　申鉴）

【注释】①勤:尽心尽力,无所吝惜。②典:常道。

【白话】古圣先王的政治:一是顺应自然规律,二是自己端正自身以身作则,三是任用贤德之人,四是体察民情,五是制定合理的法律制度,六是成就国泰民安的事业。忠诚信实地遵循天道,坚持不懈地修正自己,坚定不移地任用贤明,尽心尽力地体恤民情,依照常道来制定律法,敦厚笃实地建立功业,这就是古圣先王为政的要领。

212. The governing principles of the ancient sage-rulers are as follows:

1. Honor the law of nature;
2. Discipline oneself and teach by exemplary roles;

3. Appoint able and virtuous people to hold office;
4. Experience and observe the living conditions of the people;
5. Develop a reasonable legal system;
6. Accomplish peace and prosperity for the country and its people.

Be honest and faithful and act in accordance with the law of nature; persevere diligently with self-cultivation; be tenacious in appointing the able and virtuous to hold office; experience and observe the living conditions of people mindfully; follow the natural law to establish the legal system; and be resolute and pragmatic in striving for achievement. These are the essential governing principles of the ancient sage-rulers.

Scroll 46: *Shen Jian*

213. 武王问太公曰："吾欲以一言与身相终，再言与天地相永，三言为诸侯雄，四言为海内宗[1]，五言传之天下无穷，可得闻乎？"太公曰："一言与身相终者，内宽而外仁也；再言与天地相永者，是言行相副，若天地无私也；三言为诸侯雄者，是敬贤用谏，谦下于士也；四言为海内宗者，敬接不肖，无贫富，无贵贱，无善恶，无憎爱也；五言传之天下无穷者，通于否泰[2]，顺时[3]容养也。"

（卷三十一　阴谋）

【注释】①宗：指宗主。②否泰：《易》的两个卦名。天地交，万物通谓之"泰"；不交闭塞谓之"否"。后常以指世事的盛衰，命运的顺逆。③顺时：顺应时宜；适时。

【白话】武王问太公："我希望能有一句话使我终身铭记，第二句话能与天地长存，第三句话能使我成为诸侯中的杰出者，第四句话能使我成为天下的宗主，第五句话可以将天下代代相传无有穷尽，我可以听您讲讲吗？"太公说："第一句可以使您终身铭记的话，就是要内心宽宏，对外仁爱；第二句可以与天地共存的话，就是要言行相符，像天地那样公正无私；第三句可以让您成为诸侯中杰出者的话，就是要尊敬贤者，虚心纳谏，还要谦卑地礼待士人；第四句让您可以成为天下宗主的话，就是要恭敬谨慎地对待不肖之人，不分贫富、贵贱、善恶、爱憎；第五句可以使您将天下代代相传无有穷尽的话，就是要通达吉凶盛衰的规律，顺应时宜，包容天下，涵养万物。”

213. King Wu of the Zhou dynasty asked Tai Gong: “If I wish to have one saying that I can remember forever; a second saying to show me how I can live eternally alongside heaven and earth; a third saying to enable me to become the leader of all lords; a fourth saying to enable me to become the leader of the world; and a fifth saying to enable my government to last for generations; can you tell me what these sayings are?”

To these questions Tai Gong replied: “The first saying that you wish you can remember forever is: ‘Be generous at heart and act benevolently toward others.’ The second saying that enables you to live eternally alongside heaven and earth is: 'Your actions must correspond to your words and be as upright and selfless as heaven and earth.' The third saying that enables you to become the leader of the lords is: 'Respect the able and virtuous, listen to their advice with an open mind, and with great humbleness, treat them with courtesy.' The fourth saying that enables you to become the leader of the world is: 'Treat the unworthy men, the rich or the poor, the noble or the lowly, good or evil, those you love or disdain, with equal respect and caution.' The fifth saying that enables your government to last for generations is: 'Master the law of good and ill fortune as well as the pattern of rise and decline, and go with the flow to tolerate differences and be accommodating to all things.'"

Scroll 31: *Yin Mou*

214. 礼节民心，乐和民声[①]，政以行之，刑以防之。礼乐刑政，四达[②]而不悖[③]，则王道[④]备矣。

（卷七　礼记）

【注释】①民声：民众的声音。指人民的思想感情。②达：通行。③悖：违背，乖谬。④王道：古圣先王以仁义治天下的政治主张。

【白话】用礼节制人们内心的欲望，用乐调和民众的思想感情，用行政的力量来推行教化，用刑罚的力量防止越轨。礼、乐、刑、政这四者都得到实现而不相违背，那么王道政治就完备了。

214. Propriety can restrain human desires, and music can regulate people's emotions and sentiments. The introduction of effective government policies can achieve the goal of educating and transforming the people, and the enforcement of corporal punishment can deter criminal offenses. Thus, making full use of these four factors—propriety, music, corporal punishment, and government policies that are not contradictory to one another, the formation of a benevolent administration is deemed complete.

Scroll 7: *Li Ji*

215. 仁者爱也，义者宜也，礼者所履也，智者术之原也。致利除害，兼爱无私，谓之仁；明是非，立可否，谓之义；进退有度，尊卑有分，谓之礼；擅杀生之柄，通壅塞之涂[1]，权轻重之数，论得失之道，使远近情伪[2]必见[3]于上，谓之术。凡此四者，治之本。

（卷十八　汉书六）

【注释】①涂，通“途”，道路。②情伪：真假。③见：“现”的古字，显现，显露。

【白话】仁，就是爱人；义，就是合宜；礼，是所践行的准则；智，是策略的本原。求利除害，兼爱无私，就叫仁；明辨是非，确定可否，就叫义；进退有法度，尊卑有区别，就叫礼；拥有生杀的大权，疏通壅塞的任贤进言之路，权衡商品流通的法则，探讨事情得失的道理，使远近真伪的情况必能显现于君主，就叫策略。凡此四个方面，是治国的基础。

215. The foundation of governing is built upon these four factors:

1. Benevolence—to love and care for the people;
2. Righteousness—to do what is right;
3. Propriety—to conduct oneself according to the norms of civility;
4. Wisdom—the basis of strategies.

To bring benefits and eliminate what is harmful to the people, and to love all with no selfish motives is Benevolence. To be able to distinguish right from wrong and to know what is the right thing to do is Righteousness. To be able to conduct oneself decently and to be fully aware of the status of seniority and juniority is Propriety. To know when to exercise the power for passing life or death sentences, to make way for worthy men to serve in the government, to regulate laws concerning commercial transactions, to discuss the advantages and disadvantages of different issues so that the ruler can be fully aware of the actual state of matters is Strategy. These four factors are indispensable elements in ruling a country.

Scroll 18: *Han Shu*, Vol. 6

216. 礼以行义，信以守礼，刑以正邪。舍此三者，君将若之何？

（卷四　春秋左氏传上）

【白话】礼是用来推行道义的，信是用来维护礼的，刑法是用来纠正邪恶的。抛开这三者，国君将怎么办？

216. Propriety is intended to put righteousness into effect, Trustworthiness is intended to put the practice of propriety into effect, and Corporal Punishment is intended to deter acts of evil. Can a ruler manage without these three vital factors?

Scroll 4: *Chun Qiu Zuo Shi Zhuan*, Vol. 1

217. 曾子曰："先王之所以治天下者五：贵贵，贵德，贵老，敬长，慈幼。"

（卷三十九　吕氏春秋）

【白话】曾子说："上古贤明君王用以治理天下的方略有五个：尊重显贵之人，崇敬有德之人，敬爱老人，尊敬长者，慈爱孩童。"

217. Zengzi said: "There were five approaches that the ancient sage-rulers employed to rule their country: Respect the nobles, revere the virtuous, cherish the aged, honor the elders, and be tender to the children."

Scroll 39: *Lü Shi Chun Qiu*

218. 盖善治者，视俗而施教，察失而立防，威德①更兴，文武迭用，然后政调于时，而躁人②可定。

（卷二十二　后汉书二）

【注释】①威德：声威与德行；刑罚与恩惠。②躁人：《后汉书集解》惠栋曰："《周易》云躁人之辞多。躁人，谓私议国政之人也。"

【白话】善于处理政务的人，观察风俗而施行教化，考察过失而设置预防制度，刑罚与恩惠交替使用，文德教化和武备防御轮流施用，然后才能做到政治和时势相适应，而不安于本分的人才可以安定。

218. Good administrators will observe established social customs before implementing policies that can teach and transform the people. They will also examine past errors and set up systems to rectify them, using the penalty and reward measures, moral education as well as the military defence mechanism alternately. Only with these implementations can a government adapt to contemporary times and reconcile people who are discontented with the current state of affairs.

Scroll 22: *Hou Han Shu*, Vol. 2

219. 天地之大德曰生，圣人之大宝曰位。何以守位？曰仁。何以聚人？曰财。财所以资物生也。理财正辞，禁民为非，曰义。

（卷一　周易）

【白话】天地最大的德性在生养万物，圣人最宝贵的在于有崇高的地位。何以保全名位？要靠“仁”。何以聚集人民？用资财。理好财物，节约用度，端正辞令，出之以理，教化民众不要为非作歹，不让他们作恶，这就是“义”。

219. The great virtue of heaven and earth is the giving and maintaining of life. What is most precious for the sage is to get to a prestigious position in which he can exert his influence. What will guard this position for him? Benevolence. How shall he gather a large population around him? By the power of his wealth. The right administration of that wealth, correct instructions to the people, and prohibitions against wrongdoing constitute his Righteousness.

Scroll 1: *Zhou Yi*

220. 文王问师尚父曰："王人者何上何下，何取何去，何禁何止？"尚父曰："上贤下不肖，取诚信，去诈伪，禁暴乱，止奢侈。"

（卷三十一　六韬）

【白话】文王问老师尚父（即太公）："为人君者，应推崇何人，斥退何人？应选拔何人，摒弃何人？应禁止什么，防止什么？"尚父说："应推崇有德才的人，斥退不肖之人；应选用诚实守信之人，摒弃巧诈虚伪之人；应禁止暴乱之事，制止奢侈之风。"

220. King Wen sought this advice from his teacher, Tai Gong: "In my capacity as a ruler, whom should I respect or ignore, whom should I appoint or reject, and what are the things I should prohibit and guard against?"

Tai Gong answered: "You should respect people who are virtuous and competent, ignore people who are unworthy, appoint people who are trustworthy, and reject people who are deceitful and hypocritical. You should prohibit riots and discourage extravagant practices."

Scroll 31: *Liu Tao*

221.《诗》曰："窈窕淑女，君子好仇①。"言能致其贞淑，不贰其操，情欲之感无介乎容仪，宴私②之意不形乎动静，夫然后可以配至尊而为宗庙主。此纲纪之首，王教之端也。

（卷二十　汉书八）

【注释】①仇：配偶。《诗经》原文为"逑"，"逑"通"仇"。②宴私：亲昵，昵爱。

【白话】《诗经·周南·关雎》篇说："温柔娴静、品行端庄的淑女，才是君子的好配偶。"讲的是能够保持贞洁、端庄的品行，没有三心二意的行为，情欲的感触不会在容貌仪表中显露，亲昵的私情不会在举止言谈中表现。只有这样，才配得上拥有至尊地位的君主，才能负责祭祀宗庙。这是社会秩序和国家法纪的首要，也是圣王教化的开端。

221. *Shi Jing* (the Book of Poetry) said: "A gentle and elegant maiden will make a good spouse for a man of noble character (*Junzi*)." This refers to a maiden

who is chaste and composed, loyal and devoted. Her sensuality is not revealed in her demeanor and she never discloses intimate moments in her conversations. Thus she is fit to be the spouse of the noblest ruler, and bears the responsibility of honoring the rites of the ancestral shrines. This is most important among the principles of social order and the laws of the state, and it also serves as the beginning of any lessons given by the sage-rulers.

Scroll 20: *Han Shu*, Vol. 8

222.《易》称："男正位于外，女正位于内，男女正，天地之大义也。"

（卷二十五　魏志上）

【白话】《周易》上说："男子主其位于外（承担家庭生计），女子主其位于内（负责相夫教子），男女各自安于自己的本分，这是天地间的大道理。"

222. The book of *Zhou Yi* said: "A husband has his correct place in the outer (trigram, providing financial support to the family), and a wife has her correct place in the inner (trigram, taking care of her husband and children). That husband and wife occupy their correct places is the great righteousness of heaven and earth[22]."

Scroll 25: *Wei Zhi*, Vol. 1

---

[22] 家人，女正位乎内，男正位乎外，男女正，天地之大义也。家人有严君焉，父母之谓也。父父，子子，兄兄，弟弟，夫夫，妇妇，而家道正；正家而天下定矣。This quote was extracted from the *Book of Changes* that depicts the social roles played by members of a family: In the oracle of *Jia Ren* 家人 (family), "the wife has her correct place in the inner (trigram), and the man his correct place in the outer. That man and woman occupy their correct places is the great righteousness shown (in the relation and positions of) heaven and earth. In *Jia Ren* we have the idea of an authoritative ruler;—that, namely, represented by the parental authority. Let the father be indeed father, and the son son; let the elder brother be indeed elder brother, and the younger brother younger brother, let the husband be indeed husband, and the wife wife. Then will the family be in its normal state. Bring the family to that state, and all under heaven will be established."—James Legge.

教化
Teach and Transform

223. 上圣不务治民事，而务治民心。故曰："听讼[①]，吾由[②]人也，必也使无讼乎"；"导之以德，齐[③]之以礼"。民亲爱则无相害伤之意，动思义则无奸邪之心。夫若此者，非法律之所使也，非威刑之所强也，此乃教化之所致也。

（卷四十四　潜夫论）

【注释】①听讼：听理诉讼、审案。②由：通"犹"。如同，好像。两段引文均出自《论语》。由，《论语》通行本作"犹"。③齐：整饬，整治使有条理。

【白话】古代的圣王不致力于管理民众的事务，而致力于治理人民的内心。所以孔子说："审理案件，我和别人是一样的，不同的是我希望通过伦理道德的教化使诉讼不再发生"；"用道德来引导百姓，用礼义来整饬百姓"。人民彼此亲爱，就不会有互相伤害的想法；行事想到道义，就不会有奸诈邪恶的念头。像这种状况，不是法律所支配的，也不是严刑所强迫的，这是教化所成就的。

223. The ancient sage-rulers would not lavish time managing the daily affairs of the people but would spend most of their time regulating people's mind. Thus, Confucius said: "In hearing lawsuits, I am no different from everyone else. What is different, however, is that I try to educate the people not to engage in litigations." In addition, "Guide them with virtues and teach them civility." When the people love each other they will not harm one another. If they heed righteousness in all their actions they will not harbor wickedness. All the above will never be rectified by enforcing the law and implementing severe punishment. It can only be achieved through moral education.

Scroll 44: *Qian Fu Lun*

224. 君子以情用，小人以刑用。荣辱者，赏罚之精华[①]也。故礼教荣辱，以加君子，治其情也；桎梏鞭朴[②]，以加小人，治其刑也。君子不犯辱，况于刑乎？小人不忌刑，况于辱乎？若夫中人之伦，则刑礼兼焉。教化之废，推中人而坠于小人之域；教化之行，引中人而纳于君子之涂[③]。是谓彰化[④]。

（卷四十六 申鉴）

【注释】①精华：事物中最精粹、最美好的部分。②鞭朴：用作刑具的鞭子和棍棒。亦指用鞭子或棍棒抽打。朴，音 pū / ㄆㄨ。通“扑”。③涂：通“途”。④彰化：使教化彰明。

【白话】对君子要用情理（来感召），对小人则用刑罚（来威慑）。荣誉和耻辱，是对人的最好奖惩。所以，将礼仪教化和荣誉耻辱，用在君子身上，是以情理来治理；脚镣手铐鞭子棍棒，用在小人身上，是以惩治来管理。君子连受耻辱都不愿意，何况接受刑罚呢？小人连刑罚都不惧怕，何况耻辱呢？介于君子和小人之间的中等人，则要刑罚、礼教并用。如果废弃了伦理道德的教育，就会把中等之人推落到小人的境地；如果施行伦理道德的教化，则可以把中等之人引导上君子的道路。这就叫做"彰化"。

224. When appealing to a man of noble character (*Junzi*) one has to employ reasons. When deterring a scoundrel from wrongful acts, one has to impose punishment. Rewards or punishments are the most ideal means to confer honor or humiliation. Hence, propriety, education, sense of honor or shame are measures that are suitable for dealing with *Junzi*, while fetters, handcuffs and floggings are used on a scoundrel to subdue his wickedness. *Junzi* cannot tolerate humiliation let alone being fettered and handcuffed. A scoundrel is not afraid of physical punishment let alone being humiliated and dishonored. Individuals whose characters stand between these two extremes must be corrected using both propriety and punishment. If we abolish the teaching of moral and ethics, we will drive people toward becoming scoundrels. But if we educate them with moral and ethics

they will become *Junzi*. Such is known as the "evidential transformation."

Scroll 46: *Shen Jian*

225. 得人之道，莫如利之；利之道，莫如教（教之下有以政二字）之。

（卷三十二　管子）

【白话】获得人心的方法，没有比给人民以利益最好的了；让人民得到利益的方法，没有比施行教化更好的了。

225. To win the full support of the people, there is nothing better than to provide benefits for them; to achieve this, nothing is better than an education policy that can transform them into better persons.

Scroll 32: *Guan Zi*

226. 君子之教也，外则教之以尊其君长，内则教之以孝于其亲。是故君子之事君也，必身行之，所不安于上，则不以使下；所恶于下，则不以事上。非诸人，行诸已，非教之道也。必身行之。言恕己乃行之。是故君子之教也，必由其本，顺之至也，祭其是与，故曰祭者教之本也已。教由孝顺生。祭而不敬，何以为也？

（卷七　礼记）

【白话】君子的教化，教导人们在外要尊敬君长，在家中要孝顺父母。因此君子奉事长上，一定首先身体力行，凡是上级的做法让自己感到不安的，就不以此对待下级；凡是下级做的让自己憎恶的事，也不以此来奉事上级。批评别人不该做，自己却这样做，这不合教化的道理。因此，君子的教化必须从自身的孝行做起，最顺乎情理的，大概就是祭祀吧，所以说祭祀是教化的根本。如果对祭祀产生轻慢怀疑，对故去的亲人没有心存孝敬感恩之心，何必还要去祭祀呢？

226. The teaching of *Junzi* begins with honoring the ruler and the elders when away from home, and respecting parents when at home. In serving his ruler, he will honor him through his actions. Whatever he does not like in the behavior of his superiors, he will not do the same to his subordinates; whatever he does not approve of in the behavior of his subordinates, he will not do the same to his superiors. Therefore, *Junzi* proceeds from filial piety, and is this not manifested most appropriately in the ceremonial offerings to gods and ancestors? Hence there is this saying: "The first and greatest teaching is to be found in ceremonial offerings." However, if he has doubts about this ritual and provides offerings without gratefulness for his deceased relatives, what good does it do making these offerings?

Scroll 7: *Li Ji*

227. 古之王者，莫不以教化为大务。立大学①以教于国②，设庠序③以化于邑，渐④民以仁，摩⑤民以义，节民以礼。故其刑罚甚轻而禁不犯者，教化行而习俗美也。

（卷十七　汉书五）

【注释】①大学：即太学，我国古代设于京城的最高学府。大，音 tài / ㄊㄞˋ。"太"的古字。②国：国都。③庠序：古代的地方学校。颜师古注"庠序，教学之处也，所以养老而行礼焉。"④渐：滋润；润泽。⑤摩：砥砺；勉励。

【白话】古代的君王，没有不把教化当作治国要务的。设立太学在国都推行教化，建立庠序（地方学校）在城邑乡镇开展教化，以仁爱惠及人民，以道义勉励人民，以礼仪节制人民。所以，刑罚虽然很轻，但却没有人违犯禁令，这是因为教化施行而习俗美好的缘故。

227. The ancient kings regarded the promotion of education as the most important task of a government. They set up imperial universities in the capitals to promote education at the national level, and established local schools to promote education at provincial and district levels, emphasizing the teaching of benevolence, righteousness and civility. Consequently, no one would violate the law although the punishments were light, and moral education was prevalent and social customs were refined.

Scroll 17: *Han Shu*, Vol. 5

228. 本行而不本名，责义而不责功。行莫大于孝敬，义莫大于忠信。则天下之人知所以措身矣。此教之大略也。

（卷五十　袁子正书）

【白话】根据行为而不根据名声，要求人合乎道义而不追求其功绩。没有比孝敬更大的德行，没有比忠信更大的道义。这样天下臣民就知道该怎么做了。这是教化百姓的概要。

228. Judge a man by his conduct, not by his reputation; insist that his actions conform to righteousness instead of emphasizing on his contributions. No other virtues can be greater than filial piety and respect, and no other righteousness can be greater than trustworthiness. In this way, all the ministers and the people will learn how to conduct themselves, and this is the outline of education.

Scroll 50: *Yuan Zi Zheng Shu*

229. 圣王修义之柄，礼之序，以治人情。治者，去瑕秽，养精华也。故人情者，圣王之田也。修礼以耕之，和其刚柔。陈义以种之，树以善道。讲学以耨①之，存是去非类也。本仁以聚之，合其所盛。播乐以安之。感动使之坚固。故治国不以礼，犹无耜②而耕也。无以入之也。为礼不本于义，犹耕而不种也。嘉谷无由生也。为义而不讲以学，犹种而不耨也。苗不殖。草不除。讲之以学而不合以仁，犹耨而不获也。无以知收之丰荒也。合之以仁而不安以乐，犹获而不食也。不知味之甘苦。安之以乐而不达于顺，犹食而不肥也。功不见也。

（卷七　礼记）

【注释】①耨：音 nòu / ㄋㄡˋ。用耨除草。喻除秽去邪。②耜：音 sì / ㄙˋ。耒下铲土的部件，初以木制，后以金属制作，可拆卸置换。一说，耒、耜为独立的两种翻土农具。

【白话】圣王遵循义的根本、礼的秩序，来调治人心。因此人心是圣王耕种的土地。用修养礼仪来耕耘，用倡导道义来播种，用讲习学问（存是去非）来除草，根据仁爱来加以收获，用乐的教化来安定人心。因此治理国家如果不用礼，就如同没有农具而去耕田。制定礼仪规范而不以义为宗旨，就好比只耕田而不播下谷物的种子。推行道义而没有人来讲学以辨明是非，就好比只播种而不锄草。只讲学而不契合仁爱的存心，就好比虽然有人除草但也不会有好的收成。契合仁爱而不以乐的教化来安和人心，就如同虽有收成而没能享用成果。用乐教来使人心安定却不能达到和顺自然的境界，就如同享受了成果而没有得到健康。

229. The sage-rulers cultivated righteousness along with propriety to regulate the human mind. Thus, the human mind could be likened to the field where the kings performed his cultivation—propriety was used for plowing; righteousness was used for sowing the seeds; education was used for weeding; benevolence was used for harvesting; and lastly, music was broadcast to ease the minds of the people. A government that does not observe propriety is like a farmer who has no tools to work with. If propriety does not set righteousness as its purpose, it is as if no seeds are sown in the plowed fields.

If righteousness is not justifiably applied because lessons have not been conducted to explain its applications, it is as if weeding is not done after the seeds are sown. And if teaching is not conducted in line with benevolence, it is as if the fields are weeded but they do not yield good crops. When benevolence is incorporated in the lessons without giving repose to the human minds, it is as if the harvested crops are gathered but not eaten. When music cannot educate and transform the human mind to achive a state of tranquility, it is as if harvested crops are eaten but they do not bring health benefits.

Scroll 7: *Li Ji*

230. 春秋入学，坐国老[1]，执酱而亲馈[2]之，所以明有孝也。行以鸾和[3]，鸾在衡，和在轼。步中采齐[4]，趍[5]中[6]肆夏[7]，乐诗也，步则歌之以中节。所以明有度也。其于禽兽，见其生，不食其死；闻其声，不食其肉。故远庖厨[8]，所以长恩，且明有仁也。

（卷十六　汉书四）

【注释】①国老：指告老退职的卿、大夫、士。②亲馈：亲自奉进食物。③鸾和：鸾与和，古代车上的两种铃子。④采齐：即采荠，古乐曲名。一说，逸诗名。⑤趍：同“趋”。疾行。⑥中：音 zhòng／ㄓㄨㄥˋ。符合。⑦肆夏：古乐章名。⑧庖厨：厨房。

【白话】太子在春、秋入学时，请国老上坐，手里捧着酱，亲自奉上，这是用来教导天下人子当尽孝道。出行时在车上配以鸾铃、和铃，步行（慢行）时符合《采齐》的节奏，疾行时则合于《肆夏》的节奏，这是用来教导天下之人凡事都要合乎礼节法度。对于禽兽，见到它们活着，就不忍心杀死它们来吃；听到它们的叫声，就不愿意去吃它们的肉。所以远离厨房，为的是增长内心的恩义，且显明人是有仁爱之心的。

230. During spring and autumn, the crown prince would enrol in school. At the beginning of the school term, retired senior ministers and scholars were invited to sit at their respective honored seats as the prince held a platter of food with both hands to serve these elders. This was a rite to educate the people that all children must perform their filial duties. The carriage that the prince rode on was decorated with bells. As a royal custom, he would stroll rhythmically to the ancient tune of *Cai Qi*, and proceed briskly to the tune of *Si Xia*, indicating (to the people) that everything must be done in accordance with propriety. With regard to animals, he would not kill them for meat, and if he could hear their cries he would not bear to eat their meat. Thus the rule of "distancing oneself from the kitchen" was established as a means to increase one's compassion and to show that human beings are by nature benevolent.

Scroll 16: *Han Shu*, Vol. 4

231. 孔子曰："圣人之治化也，必刑政相参[1]焉。太上以德教民，而以礼齐之。其次以政导民，以刑禁之。化之弗变，导之弗从，伤义败俗，于是乎用刑矣。"

（卷十　孔子家语）

【注释】①相参：相互配合。

【白话】孔子回答道："圣贤治理教化民众，一定是刑罚和政令相互配合使用。最好的办法是用道德来教化民众，并用礼法加以约束。其次是用政令引导民众，并用刑罚加以禁止。如果教育之后还不能改变，引导之后还不听从，以至于违背道义而败坏风俗，在这种情况下才用刑罚来惩处。"

231. Confucius said: "A sage-ruler will use a combination of laws and punishments to govern and transform the people. The best way to achieve this end is to educate people about the values of virtues, and to use propriety to control their desires. Second to this is to enact laws to guide the people, and to use punishment to deter people

from committing crimes. It is only when education fails to transform unbecoming behaviors, and guidance fails to deter a person from committing offenses that punishment will be used to stop the offenders from corrupting society."

Scroll 10: *Kong Zi Jia Yu*

232. 故圣王务教化而省禁防[1]，知其不足恃也。

（卷十八　汉书六）

【注释】①禁防：谓禁止防范。

【白话】所以圣明的君主致力于教化而减省禁防举措，知道凭借禁止、防范是靠不住的。

232. A sage-ruler would devote more efforts to education, rather than prohibitions, for he knew prohibitions and precautions alone could not be relied upon to transform human behavior.

Scroll 18: *Han Shu*, Vol. 6

233. 威辟[1]既用，而苟免[2]之行兴；仁信道孚[3]，故感被之情著。苟免者，威隟[4]则奸起；感被者，人亡而思存[5]。

（卷二十四　后汉书四）

【注释】①威辟：严酷的刑法。②苟免：苟且免罪。③孚：信服，信从。④隟：古同"隙"。空隙；可乘之机。⑤思存：思念，念念不忘。存，铭记在心。

【白话】严酷的刑法一经施用，以不当手段求得免罪的行为便会兴起；落实仁义道德为人信服，所以人心受到感化的效果就很显著。以不当手段希求免罪，刑法有漏洞时，奸邪之事就会发生；人心受到感化，尽管施政者已去世，人们还将他的恩德铭记在心。

233. Once the practice of imposing severe punishment is employed, the custom of resorting to illegal means to escape punishment will spring up. But the practice of humaneness can gain people's trust, thus making the effect of transformation much more noticeable. Using

illegal means and loopholes to escape from punishment will lead to strings of deviant behavior, whereas when people are touched by the humaneness of an official, they will remember the kindness of that official long after his passing.

Scroll 24: *Hou Han Shu*, Vol. 4

234. 治国,太上养化[①],其次正法[②]。民交让,争处卑,财利争受少,事力争就劳,日化上[③]而迁善[④],不知其所以然,治之本也。利赏而劝善,畏刑而不敢为非,法令正于上,百姓服于下,治之末也。

（卷三十五　文子）

【注释】①养化:谓致力于道德教化,转变人心、风俗,使其归于自然。②正法:依法制裁、办理。③化上:受君主感化。④迁善:改过向善。

【白话】治理国家,最上之策是以道德来感化,其次是依据法律治理。使民众互相谦让,争相处于卑下,面对财利争相拿少的部分,面对工作争相做劳累的事情,每天受到君王的教化,在不知不觉中逐渐向善,这是治国的根本。百姓把奖赏当作利益而勉力为善,畏惧刑罚而不敢为非作歹,君王的法令公正严明,百姓服从,这是治理国家的次要之事。

234. In the governing of a country, the best policy is to use virtues to transform undesirable behaviors and customs, with legal proceedings coming second. Encourage the people to be courteous and humble toward one another, and to accept smaller shares in any financial gains and compete with each other for tougher jobs. Being influenced by the ruler's virtues daily, they would eventually become better persons. Such were the primary tasks in governing. When the people saw rewards as the incentives to perform good deeds, and when they did not dare to commit crimes for fear of punishment, and obeyed the laws because their ruler was strict and impartial, these matters would remain the secondary tasks in governing.

Scroll 35: *Wen Zi*

235. 圣王先德教，而后刑罚；立荣耻，而明防禁①；崇礼义之节，以示之；贱货利之弊②，以变之。则下莫不慕义节（节作礼）之荣，而恶贪乱之耻。其所由致之者，化使然也。

（卷四十三　说苑）

【注释】①防禁：防备禁戒。②弊：通“币”。财物。

【白话】圣王先实行德教，而后才使用刑罚；树立荣辱的标准和观念，并明示应当防止和禁戒的事项；崇尚礼义的节操，并给百姓做示范；轻视货物财利，来改变人们的贪婪。那么，臣民就没有谁不喜欢礼义节操的光荣，而厌恶贪婪淫乱的可耻。之所以能使百姓达到这样的原因，都是教化的结果。

235. A sage-ruler would resort to moral education prior to imposing punishment on people. He would establish the standards and perceptions regarding honor and disgrace, and clarify matters that were prohibited. He would honor the practice of civility and serve as a role model for his

people to emulate. He would despise huge profits derived from commercial transactions to discourage people from greed. Thus, no one would belittle honors brought by civility, and people would despise the disgrace brought about by greed. These are the results of transformation through education.

Scroll 43: *Shuo Yuan*

236. 圣人之于法也已公矣，然犹身惧其未也。故曰："与其害善，宁其利淫①。"知刑当之难必②也，从而救之以化，此上古之所务也。

（卷四十八　体论）

【注释】①与其害善，宁其利淫：出自《周书·列传第十五》。②难必：难以肯定。

【白话】圣人治法已经很公正了，可是仍然担心尚有不公之处。所以说："与其伤害贤善之人，宁可利于有罪之人。"他们深知量刑适当与否难以肯定，于是用道德教化来补救，这是上古时期的古圣先王所致力做的事情。

236. Even when a sage can maintain absolute fairness in the execution of the law, he nevertheless fears the possibility of making a wrongful sentence. Thus it was said: "Rather than harming an innocent good man, it is better to give benefit of doubt to the convicted." He knew it was difficult to be absolutely certain about the

appropriateness of the penalty applied, so he would rather use moral education to make up for possible shortcomings. The ancient rulers were all dedicated to governing along this line of thought.

Scroll 48: *Ti Lun*

237. 孔子曰："不教而诛谓之虐①。" 虐政用于下，而欲德教之被四海，故难成也。

（卷十七　汉书五）

【注释】①虐：残暴，凶残。

【白话】孔子说："不先对人民进行教化，而人民犯了罪就将其诛杀，这叫做暴虐。" 使用暴虐的政治对待下民，却想使道德教化普及天下，所以很难成功。

237. Confucius said: "To put people to death without educating them (on the merits of virtues) is called cruelty." If the government intends to promote moral education on the one hand but imposes tyrannical punishments on the other, it would be extremely difficult for people to accept moral education.

Scroll 17: *Han Shu*, Vol. 5

238. 圣王在位，明好憎以示人（人作之），经[1]诽誉以导之，亲贤而进之，贱不肖而退之。无被疮流血之患，而有高世尊显之名，民孰不从？古者法设而不犯，刑措而不用，非可刑而不刑也，百工[2]维时，庶绩[3]咸熙[4]，礼义修而任贤得也。

（卷四十一　淮南子）

【注释】①经：度量；划分。②百工：百官。③庶绩：各种事业。④熙：兴盛。

【白话】圣明的君主居于高位，阐明好恶来昭示国人，通过对善恶行为的批评、称誉来引导人民，亲近贤人并提拔他，鄙弃不贤的人并罢免他。没有受伤流血之苦，而能够享有崇高尊显的名声，百姓谁不愿意学习效法呢？古代制定了法律却无人触犯，设置了刑罚却不施用，不是该施刑而不用刑，是因为百官都能够做好本职工作，各项事业都兴盛成功，礼义得到修治，贤德之人得到了任用。

238. The sage-ruler held a supreme position and disclosed his likes and dislikes to the general public, praising good conduct and criticizing bad demeanor as a guideline for the people to follow. He associated with worthy men and promoted them to office. He rejected unworthy men and dismissed them. He ruled without causing any bloodshed and enjoyed an excellent reputation. Who among the civilians would be unwilling to learn from him and emulate him? The ancient laws were enacted without anyone violating them. Penalties were drawn up without having to enforce them. This was not due to the fact that the officials had chosen not to enforce the penalties, but more so because all government officials were able to perform well in their jobs; success and prosperity were brought to the country; propriety and virtues were widely promoted; and capable and noble men were appointed to serve in the government.

Scroll 41: *Huai Nan Zi*

239. 善御民者，一[①]其德法，正其百官，均齐民力，和安民心。故令不再而民顺从，刑不用而天下化治。是以天地德之，天地以为有德。而兆民怀之。怀，归。不能御民者，弃其德法，专用刑辟[②]，譬犹御马，弃其衔勒而专用棰策[③]，其不可制也必矣。

（卷十　孔子家语）

【注释】①一：统一。②辟：刑罚。③棰策：赶马的鞭杖。

【白话】善于治理百姓的君王，统一道德和礼法规范，明确百官职责，协调均衡地使用民力，和顺安定民心。如此，政令不必三令五申，百姓便会顺从；不用刑罚，就能教化治理好天下。其恩德可以感通天地，亿万百姓都来归顺。不会治理百姓的君王，抛弃道德和礼法，专用刑罚惩治，就好比驾驭马匹时，抛弃嚼子和笼头，而专用鞭子鞭打，这样一来，马车失控就是必然的了。

239. A ruler who is good at governing the country would stipulate the standards for observance of virtues and propriety, designate the duties of each official position clearly, ensure fair deployment of work force and restore peace and order to the country. In this way, civilians would be law-abiding without the need to be forewarned. Thus, peace is maintained without the use of punishment. The acts of virtues of the ruler are able to move heaven and earth, and millions of people would pledge their allegiance to him. On the contrary, a less capable ruler would abandon virtues and propriety, and rely solely on punishment to govern the country. It is like riding a horse carriage but leaving out the halter and bridle, and only whipping the horse to gallop forward. In this way, the chances of driving out of control is inevitable.

Scroll 10: *Kong Zi Jia Yu*

240. 景公问晏子曰："明王之教民何若？"对曰："明其教令，而先之以行；养民不苛，而防之以刑。所求于下者，不务[1]于上；所禁于民者，不行于身。故下从其教也。称事以任民，中听[2]以禁邪，不穷[3]之以劳，不害之以罚[4]，上以爱民为法，下以相亲为义，是以天下不相违也。此明王之教民也。"

（卷三十三　晏子）

【注释】①不务：当作"必务"，此涉上下文诸"不"字而误。②中听：指治狱得当。③穷：尽，完。④不害之以罚：不用刑罚害民。

【白话】景公问晏子："英明的君主是怎样教化人的？"晏子答道："阐明教义和政令，且自己率先履行；养育人民不苛刻严厉，而用刑罚预防犯罪。要求臣民做到的，君王必须要先做到；禁止百姓做的事情，自己绝不能去做。因此，下民就会听从其教导。估量事情的轻重来使用民力，恰当地处理诉讼来禁止邪恶；不使百姓因过度劳役而筋疲力尽，不用惩罚来伤害百姓；在上者以爱护百姓为准则，在下者以相亲相爱为道义。这样，天下之人就不会互相背离。这就是英明的君主教育人民的方法。"

240. Duke Jing of the state of Qi asked Prime Minister Yanzi: “How does a good ruler educate his people?”

To this Yanzi replied: “He makes it very clear to the people about his teachings and decrees, and leads others in implementing these policies. He does not oppress the people, and punishment is imposed only as a way to deter crimes. What he requests of the people he would do the same, and what he prohibits the people from doing he would not commit it himself. Only then will the civilians follow his order. He would evaluate the extent of human labor needed based on the priority of the tasks, and would handle prosecutions fairly to curb acts of evil. He would not exploit the civilians to the point of exhaustion, or use punishment to injure them. Leaders consider showing care to the people as a norm, and his subjects consider caring for one another as moral and righteous practices. If this ideal is achieved, people will not betray one another. This is the way a good ruler governs his people.”

Scroll 33: *Yan Zi*

241. 夫圣人之修其身，所以御群臣也。御群臣也，所以化万民也。其法轻而易守，其礼简而易持。其求诸己也诚，其化诸人也深。

（卷四十八　体论）

【白话】圣人加强自身的修养，是为了领导群臣。领导群臣的目的，是为了教化百姓。圣人制定的刑法宽松而容易遵守，制定的礼制简约而容易受持。圣人凡事都真诚地要求自己，因此，对百姓的感化就很深刻。

241. A sage-ruler enhanced his self-cultivation so that he could lead all his ministers to serve as good examples for the people. He enacted laws that were easy to obey and propriety that was simple to be put into practice. He exercised strict disciplines over himself and put his words into actions. In doing so, the people were deeply touched, thereby making the transformation of their conduct possible.

Scroll 48: *Ti Lun*

242. 故壹野不如壹市，壹市不如壹朝，壹朝不如一用，一用不如上息欲，上息欲而下反[1]真矣。不息欲于上，而欲于下之安静，此犹纵火焚林，而索原野之不雕瘁（瘁旧作废，改之。），难矣！故明君止欲而宽下，急商而缓农，贵本而贱末，朝无蔽贤之臣，市无专利[2]之贾，国无擅山泽之民。

（卷四十九　傅子）

【注释】①反：同"返"。②专利：垄断某种生产或流通以掠取厚利。

【白话】所以，限定民间不如限定集市，限定集市不如限定朝廷，限定朝廷不如限定用度，限定用度不如在上者去除奢欲。在上者去除奢欲，百姓就能返璞归真。在上者不去除奢欲，却想让百姓安稳清静，这就如同纵火焚烧森林，还想使原野不凋零枯败，实在太难了！所以，英明的君主，遏止欲望，宽待百姓，对商业从严，而对农业宽松，重视农桑，不看重商业，朝廷中没有蒙蔽贤能的佞臣，集市上没有专利霸市的商人，国家没有擅自开发山泽的人民。

242. Instead of monitoring business transactions among the people, the government should monitor the markets. Instead of monitoring the markets, the government should monitor the administration. Instead of monitoring the administration, the government should monitor its expenditure. Instead of monitoring the government expenditure, it would be better if the ruler can control his excessive desires in spending. If the highest authority could control his excessive desires in spending, this would encourage the people to revert to a frugal lifestyle. Simply requesting the people to revert to a frugal lifestyle while continuing his irresponsible spendings would be like hoping the forest would remain intact after a raging forest fire. This is practically impossible! If a ruler is wise, he would restrain his desires, be generous to the people, be strict in dealing with the commercial sector but lenient toward the agricultural sector, and would prioritize agriculture above commercial activities. In his government there would not be any dishonest

ministers who could cover up the contributions made by capable and virtuous individuals. Furthermore, there would not be any businessmen who could monopolize a business and make exorbitant profits from it, and no civilians could exploit the mountains and rivers without authorization.

Scroll 49: *Fu Zi*

243. 古之圣王，举孝子而劝之事亲，尊贤良而劝之为善，发宪布令[1]以教诲，赏罚以劝沮[2]。若此则乱者可使治，而危者可使安矣。

（卷三十四　墨子）

【注释】①发宪布令：发号施令。②沮：阻止，禁止。

【白话】古时候圣贤的君王，推崇孝子，以劝导人们侍奉双亲；尊重贤良，以劝导人们做好事；颁布法令，来教育人民；明确赏罚，来对人民进行勉励和劝阻。照这样做，混乱的社会可使其清明，危险的局面可使其稳定。

243. The ancient sage-rulers gave high esteem to filial sons to encourage people to respect and care for their parents. They honored the virtuous in order to encourage people to perform good deeds. They issued laws in order to educate people, and established the rewards and penalty system to encourage good deeds and deter bad ones. In so doing, a chaotic society could be transformed

into a peaceful and orderly one, and dangerous situations could be transformed to become safe and secure.

Scroll 34: *Mo Zi*

244. 教化之流，非家至而人说之也，贤者在位，能者布职，朝廷崇礼，百僚敬让，道德之行，由内及外，自近者始，然后民知所法，迁善日进而不自知。

（卷二十　汉书八）

【白话】教化的普及，并不是要挨家挨户去对每个人进行说教，只要贤德的人处在正位，有才能的人安排到适合的职位，朝廷崇尚礼节，百官互相恭敬谦让，道德教化由内而外，从近处（朝廷内部）开始，然后百姓知道了效法的准则，不知不觉就会日渐改过向善。

244. It is not necessary to go from door to door to promote education. As long as the ruler is virtuous, with competent officials holding the right positions, and propriety being honored at the court, and the officials being courteous to one another, right conducts would begin from the inner circle to the outer circle, starting with the government itself and spreading to the people as they learn to observe the standards of virtues. Unknowingly, people will transform themselves to become better persons.

Scroll 20: *Han Shu*, Vol. 8

245. 盖尧之为教，先亲后疏，自近及远，周之文王亦崇厥化。

（卷二十六　魏志下）

【白话】唐尧施行教化，先亲后疏，由近到远，周朝的文王也遵行这样的教化。

245. Emperor Yao would exemplify the teachings of saints and sages and further extend this practice to his close relatives and then to the distant ones, starting from near to far. King Wen of the Zhou dynasty also followed this practice.

Scroll 26: *Wei Zhi*, Vol. 2

246. 子曰："夫民，教之以德，齐①之以礼，则民有格心②。教之以政，齐之以刑，则民有遯心③。格，来也。遯，逃也。故君民者，子以爱之，则民亲之；信以结之，则民不背；恭以莅之，则民有逊心。莅，临也。逊，犹顺也。"

（卷七　礼记）

【注释】①齐：整饬；整治使有条理。②格心：归正之心。指向善的心。格，来，指至于善。③遯心：逃避刑罚的心。遯，音dùn/ㄉㄨㄣˋ。同"遁"。逃。

【白话】孔子说："对待人民，要用道德来教育，用礼仪来约束，人民才会有向善的心理。如果用政令来教导，用刑罚来约束，人民就会产生逃避政令和刑罚的心。所以治理人民的人，如果能够以爱护儿女的心来爱护人民，人民就会亲附他；能够以诚信朴实来团结人民，人民就不会背叛他；能够恭恭敬敬地深入体察民情，人民就会自然生起归顺敬服之心。"

246. Confucius said: "If the people are guided by virtues and aligned with propriety, their minds would remain untainted. If they are guided by the policies and aligned with punishments, the intention to dodge punishments will exist. Hence, when the ruler loves the people as if they were his children, they will in turn love him dearly. If he can unite them with his integrity, they will not turn away from him. If he can respect and foster better ties with the people, they will naturally pledge their allegiance to him."

Scroll 7: *Li Ji*

礼乐
Propriety and Music

247. 君子曰："礼乐不可斯须[①]去身。致[②]乐以治心，乐由中出，故治心也。致礼以治躬[③]。礼自外作，故治身也。心中斯须不和不乐，而鄙诈之心入之矣。鄙诈入之，谓利欲生也。外貌斯须不庄不敬，而慢易[④]之心入之矣。易，轻易也。故乐也者动于内者也，礼也者动于外者也。乐极则和，礼极则顺[⑤]。内和而外顺，则民瞻其颜色，而不与争也；望其容貌，而民不生易慢焉。"

（卷七　礼记）

【注释】①斯须：须臾、片刻。②致：深远详审。③治躬：治身，调整身体与言行。④慢易：轻忽怠慢。⑤乐极则和，礼极则顺：《礼记》通行本作"乐极和，礼极顺"。

【白话】君子说："人不可片刻离开礼乐。深入于乐，是为了陶冶心性；深入于礼，是为了调整身体与言行。一个人的心中如果有片刻不和顺不喜乐，那贪鄙诈伪的念头就会趁机而入。外貌如果有片刻不庄重不恭敬，那轻忽怠慢的念头就会趁虚而入。所以乐是调理人的内心，礼是调理人外在的行为。音乐至善能使人和畅，礼仪至善能使人恭顺。内心和畅而外貌恭顺，则人们望见他的外貌神情，就不会与他抗争；看见他的仪容风度，便不会有轻视侮慢的态度。”

247. The man of noble character (*Junzi*) said: “Not for one moment can human live without propriety and music. Immersing oneself in music serves to embellish the mind, while immersing oneself in propriety serves to regulate the body and one’s words and deeds. If there is for one moment a hint of dissatisfaction and misery in the mind, vulgarity and hypocrisy will seize this opportunity to creep into the mind. If there is for one moment any loss of dignity and respect in one’s composure, arrogance will seize this opportunity to sneak into the mind. Thus, music regulates the mind and propriety regulates the composure. The most virtuous music can help a person to be decent. When his mind is peaceful and his composure is respectful, no one would provoke a fight with him or despise him.”

Scroll 7: *Li Ji*

248. 礼以导其志，乐以和其声，政以一其行，刑以防其奸。礼乐刑政，其极一也，所以同民心而出治道。

（卷七　礼记）

【白话】用礼仪引导人心，用音乐调和人情，用政令统一人们的行为，用刑罚防止人们的邪恶。礼仪、音乐、刑罚、政令，它们的最终目标是一致的，都是要使民同心（合乎道德），而实现天下大治的理想。

248. Use propriety to regulate the human mind, use music to regulate human sentiments, use law to standardize human behavior and use punishment to deter wickedness. Propriety, music, punishment and law all share the same goal, which is to guide the human mind toward the virtuous path and realize the ideal of a peaceful world.

Scroll 7: *Li Ji*

249. 夫礼之所兴，众之所以治也；礼之所废，众之所以乱也。

（卷十　孔子家语）

【白话】礼乐教化兴盛时，民众就会因此而安定；礼乐教化废弃时，民众就会因此而动乱。

249. The populace will enjoy stability when propriety and music are widely promoted for educational purposes. When propriety and music lose its educational purposes, social unrests will emerge.

Scroll 10: *Kong Zi Jia Yu*

250. 中国所以常制四夷者，礼义之教行也。失其所以教……则同乎禽兽矣。不唯同乎禽兽，乱将甚焉。何者？禽兽保其性然者也，人以智役力者也。智役力而无教节，是智巧日用，而相残无极也。相残无极，乱孰大焉？

（卷四十九　傅子）

【白话】中国能制服四夷的原因，是推行了礼义之教。丧失了礼义教化……也就和禽兽相同了。不仅是与禽兽相同，甚至比禽兽更混乱无序。为何这么说呢？这是因为禽兽保持自己的天性不变，人却是用巧智驾驭体力者。以巧智驾驭体力，而没有礼教加以节制，就会巧智日见使用，而彼此伤害无穷无尽。彼此相互伤害无穷无尽，祸乱哪有比这更大的？

250. The fact that China had managed to control its surrounding foreigners was attributed to the promoting of propriety and music, without which humans are no different from the beasts and may even be worse. Why is this so? Unlike a leopard that cannot change its spots,

humans can use their intelligence to exercise control over their physical bodies. If this intelligence is used without restraints, it will cause endless harm to one another. What can be more detrimental than this?

Scroll 49: *Fu Zi*

251. 礼之可以为国[①]也久矣，与天地并。君令臣恭，父慈子孝，兄爱弟敬，夫和妻柔，姑[②]慈妇听[③]，礼也。

（卷六　春秋左氏传下）

【注释】①为国：治国。②姑：丈夫的母亲，即婆婆。③听：听从、顺从。

【白话】晏婴回答说："礼可以用来治理国家已经（由来）很久了，可以说是和天地并兴。君王美善，臣下恭敬；父亲慈祥，儿子孝顺；哥哥友爱，弟弟恭顺；丈夫和蔼，妻子温柔；婆婆慈祥，媳妇顺从。这些都是礼的内涵。"

251. Yan Ying said: "The practice of using propriety to govern a country existed a long time ago, perhaps as far back as the beginning of heaven and earth. If a ruler is kind and virtuous, his ministers will serve him with great reverence. If parents are kind, their children will be filial. If elder siblings treat their younger siblings with fraternal love, the younger brothers will in return treat

them with respect. If a husband is kind, the wife will be gentle. If a mother-in-law is caring, the daughter-in-law will be obedient. These are all the essential attributes of propriety."

Scroll 6: *Chun Qiu Zuo Shi Zhuan*, Vol. 3

252. 不知礼义，不可以行法①。法能教不孝，不能使人孝；能刑盗者，不能使人廉（廉下无耻字）耻。

（卷三十五　文子）

【注释】①行法：依法度行事。

【白话】百姓不知道礼义，就不能依法办事。法律能够教训不孝之人，却不能使人有孝心；能够惩治盗贼，却不能使人产生廉耻。

252. People who do not understand propriety are unlikely to be law-abiding. Laws can teach a lesson to unfilial children but are unable to make them behave like filial children. Laws can also punish criminals but are unable to make them feel shameful.

Scroll 35: *Wen Zi*

253. 民无廉耻，不可治也。非修礼义，廉耻不立。民不知礼义，法弗能正也。非崇善废丑，不向礼义。

（卷四十一　淮南子）

【白话】民众如果没有廉耻之心，就无法治理好。而不学习礼义，民众的廉耻观念就不会树立。民众不懂礼义，法律也无法使他们行为端正。不推崇善举、废除恶习，民众就不会向往礼义。

253. When people do not have a sense of shame, they cannot be made to obey the law. If propriety is not practiced, their sense of shame cannot be established. Not even the law can make people correct their behavior if the populace does not understand the purpose of propriety. People will not look up to propriety if the government fails to promote good deeds and eliminate bad behavior.

Scroll 41: *Huai Nan Zi*

254. 子曰："礼云礼云，玉帛云乎哉？言礼非但崇此玉帛而已，所贵者乃贵其安上治民。乐云乐云，钟鼓云乎哉？"乐之所贵者，移风易俗也，非但谓钟鼓而已。

（卷九　论语）

【白话】孔子说："礼啊礼啊，仅是指玉帛等礼品吗？乐啊乐啊，仅是指钟鼓这些乐器吗？（礼的可贵之处，在于能够使上位者安于其位，使下位者受到教化而各得其所。乐的可贵之处，在于能改善社会风俗。）

254. Confucius said: "According to the rules of propriety, are gems and silk all that is meant by propriety? According to the rules of music, are bells and drums all that is meant by music?" (The importance of propriety lies in the fact that it can establish the ruler's position and so he can govern the country well, while music is not just about striking bells and drums but it can regulate and bring about refined social practices).

Scroll 9: *Lun Yu*

255. 曾子曰："夫行也者，行礼之谓也。夫礼，贵者敬焉，老者孝焉，幼者慈焉，小者友焉，贱者惠焉。此礼也。"

（卷三十五　曾子）

【白话】曾子说："所谓行，就是实践礼的意思。礼，就是对尊贵之人恭敬，对老人孝顺，对小孩慈爱，对年轻人友爱，对贫贱之人施予恩惠。这些都是礼的表现。"

255. Zengzi said: "When we say 'put into practice,' it means the practice of propriety. Propriety is the respect shown to the nobles, the filial obedience shown to parents, the kindness shown to children, the friendliness shown to young people, and the care and help shown to the poor and needy. These are all the significance of propriety."

Scroll 35: *Zeng Zi*

256. 为男女之礼，妃匹[①]之合，则不淫矣。为廉耻之教，知足之分，则不盗矣。以贤制爵，令（旧令作有，改之）民德厚矣。

（卷五十　袁子正书）

【注释】①妃匹：指婚配之事。

【白话】制定男女间的礼法、夫妻结合的规范，就没有淫乱之事了。施行廉耻的教化，使百姓知足尽分，就不会有盗窃的事了。以贤良为标准授予爵位，就会使百姓道德淳厚。

256. By regulating rules and customs for marriage and proper civility between males and females as well as husbands and wives, issues relating to promiscuity can be prevented. By implementing educational policies that promote integrity and a sense of shamefulness, people will be encouraged to be contented, and thefts and robberies can thereby be prevented. Stressing virtues as the noble norm to acquire royal titles will influence the populace to become honest and kind.

Scroll 50: *Yuan Zi Zheng Shu*

257. 圣王之自为动静周旋[1]，奉天承亲，临朝享臣，物[2]有节文[3]，以章人伦。盖钦翼[4]祗栗[5]，事天之容也；温恭敬逊，承亲之礼也；正躬严恪[6]，临众之仪也；嘉惠和说[7]，飨下之颜也。举错[8]动作，物遵其仪，故形[9]为仁义，动为法则。

（卷二十　汉书八）

【注释】①周旋：古代行礼时进退揖让的动作。②物：事。③节文：礼节、仪式。④钦翼：恭敬谨慎。钦，尊敬，恭敬。翼，恭敬，谨肃。⑤祗栗：亦作“祗慄”。敬慎恐惧。祗，音 zhī / ㄓ。恭敬。栗，畏惧。⑥严恪：庄严恭敬貌。⑦和说：即“和悦”。⑧错：通“措”。⑨形：表现。

【白话】圣王的言行举止，无论奉事上天、侍奉父母、处理政事、任用臣僚，事事都合礼节制度，以彰显人伦大道。恭敬谨慎，敬畏战栗，是奉事上天的礼仪；温和恭顺、敬慎谦逊，是侍奉双亲的礼节；端庄自身，严谨恭敬，是治理百姓的威仪；和颜悦色，慈善仁惠，是对待臣下的礼仪。圣王言行举止，事事都遵循礼仪，所以表现在外的行为都合于仁义，一举一动都可作为众人的榜样。

257. The composure of a sage-ruler, in attending to the rites of heaven, in serving his parents, in managing his administration by working with ministers and advisors, must all be done in accordance to propriety so that the norm of moral and ethics is fully demonstrated. In attending to the rites of heaven, the sage-ruler displays respect and caution, reverence and fear; in serving his parents, he displays gentleness, respect and modesty; in governing the people, he displays regality and respect; in working with ministers and advisors, he radiates generosity, grace and benevolence. In all his demeanors, he stays on course with propriety and everything he does is within the parameter of benevolence and honor, so he is fit to be a role model for the people.

Scroll 20: *Han Shu*, Vol. 8

258. 哀有哭踊[1]之节，乐有歌舞之容。正人足以副[2]其诚，邪人足以防其失。

（卷十四　汉书二）

【注释】①哭踊：古代丧礼仪节。亦称“擗踊”。顿足拍胸而哭，表示极大的悲哀。踊，跳。②副：相称，符合。

【白话】（古礼中）悲痛时会有边哭边顿足的礼节，高兴时会有载歌载舞的仪容。这对正直的人来说，足以与他的真诚相符；对偏邪的人来说，足以提防他的过失。

258. The ancient funeral rites included crying, beating one's chest and stamping one's feet to express extreme grief, while the ancient rejoicing rites included singing and dancing to express one's pleasures. To an upright person, these rites were sufficient to conform to his sincerity, and to an immoral person, these rites were sufficient to guard against his mistakes.

Scroll 14: *Han Shu*, Vol. 2

259. 乐至[①]则无怨，礼至则不争。揖让而治天下者，礼乐之谓也。至，犹达行。

（卷七　礼记）

【注释】①至：指通行无阻。

【白话】乐教通行则人人心情舒畅而无怨恨，礼教通行则人人心存谦让而无冲突。君王只要拱手揖让之间，天下就可以无为而治，说的就是用礼与乐来治理天下。

259. If music is customarily used for educating people to ease their mind, nobody will have any grievances. When propriety is customarily used for educating people to be mindful of humility, there should be no disputes. If a ruler is accommodating and modest, the country will be well governed, and all this means is that the ruler has been successful in promoting propriety and music in governing.

Scroll 7: *Li Ji*

260. 乐以治内而为同，同于和乐也。礼以修外而为异。尊卑为异。同则和亲，异则畏敬。和亲则无怨，畏敬则不争。

（卷十四　汉书二）

【白话】音乐能用来调治人的内心，使人的情志随着音乐一起变得安和调适；礼仪能用来修治外在行为，使人与人之间尊卑有序。内心安和人们就会和睦亲爱，尊卑有别则会使人心存敬畏。和睦亲爱就不会有怨恨，心存敬畏就不会有争斗。

260. Music can be used to regulate the human mind and pacify one's sentiments to a state of inner calmness. Propriety can be used to regulate human behavior and encourage people to respect social ranks and order. When the mind is in a state of calmness, people will begin to care for one another and become sociable; when there is an awareness of orderliness, people will know where they stand in the society. No resentment will arise when the mind is loving and harmonious; no fighting will arise when there is mutual respect for one another.

Scroll 14: *Han Shu*, Vol. 2

261. 人君无礼，无以临①其一（无一字）邦；大夫无礼，官吏不恭；父子无礼，其家必凶。《诗》曰："人而无礼，胡②不遄③死。"故礼不可去也。

（卷三十三　晏子）

【注释】①临：治，治理。②胡：为什么。③遄：音 chuán／ㄔㄨㄢˊ。迅速。

【白话】君主如果不讲礼义，就无法治理国家；大夫如果不讲礼义，底下官吏就会不恭敬；父子之间不讲礼义，家庭就必有灾殃。《诗经》中说："人如果不遵守礼义，不如赶快去死。"所以礼不可以去掉啊！

261. A ruler who is ill-mannered will not be able to govern properly. A minister who is ill-mannered will have disrespectful subordinates. If manners are not observed between parents and children, a family will be ruined. It was forewarned in *Shi Jing* that "a life without propriety is a life not worth living." Hence, we cannot do without propriety.

Scroll 33: *Yan Zi*

爱民
Caring about People

262. 圣人常善救人，圣人所以常教人忠孝者，欲以救人性命也。故无弃人；使贵贱各得其所也。常善救物，圣人所以常教民顺四时者，以救万物之残伤也。故无弃物。不贱石而贵玉。

（卷三十四　老子）

【白话】古代的圣王在位，总是很善于（以教化）挽救人，所以没有被抛弃不管的人；总是善于利益万物并发挥其功效，所以没有被废弃的物品。

262. The sage-ruler in the past was capable of educating his people and no one was forsaken. He was also good at taking care of all things, and so nothing was wasted.

Scroll 34: *Laozi*

263. 天下有粟[1]，圣人食之；天下有民，圣人收之；天下有物，圣人裁之。利天下者取天下，安天下者有天下，爱天下者久天下，仁天下者化天下。

（卷三十一　六韬）

【注释】①粟：粮食的通称。

【白话】太公说："天下的粮食，由圣人分配享用；天下的百姓，由圣人治理；天下的万物，由圣人裁处。为天下谋利益者取得天下，使天下安定者拥有天下，爱护天下百姓者可以长久地统治天下，仁德普施天下者可以化育天下。"

263: Tai Gong said: "The sage will distribute all food under heaven fairly for everyone's consumption. The sage will govern all the people under heaven well, and he will also be the decision maker for the distribution of all things under heaven. He who brings benefits to the world will win the world; he who brings peace to the world will own the world; he who loves and protects all the people in the world will rule the world for a long time; and he who implements benevolent policies will educate and transform the world."

Scroll 31: *Liu Tao*

264. 尧以不得舜为己忧，舜以不得禹、皋陶为己忧。分人以财谓之惠，教人以善谓之忠，为天下得人谓之仁。是故以天下与人易，为天下得人难。

（卷三十七　孟子）

【白话】尧帝以不能得到像舜这样的人而最为忧虑，舜也同样，以不能得到像禹和皋陶这样的人而忧心。把财物分给别人称作惠，用好的道理教诲别人称作忠，为国家求得贤德之士称作仁。所以说，把天下让给别人容易，而为天下找到大公无私的贤能之士就难了！

264. Emperor Yao was most worried that his chosen successor Shun might not accept his offer to be the emperor; likewise, the latter Emperor Shun was most worried that sages like Yu and Gao Yao might not accept his offer to be the emperor. The act of distributing money and properties to others is considered as kindness; the act of educating people to become better persons is considered as faithfulness; the act of searching for competent people to serve in the government is

considered as benevolence. Hence it was said: "Easy it is to forsake the throne to others but difficult it is to find sages who could serve the people selflessly."

Scroll 37: *Meng Zi*

265. 视民如子。见不仁者诛之，如鹰鹯之逐鸟雀也。

（卷五　春秋左氏传中）

【白话】把百姓看作子女一般。见到不仁者就惩治他，就像老鹰、鹯鸟追赶小鸟那样。

265. Treat the people as if they were your children. Punish wicked people like a hawk going after the birds.

Scroll 5: *Chun Qiu Zuo Shi Zhuan*, Vol. 2

266. 古之贤君，饱而知人之饥，温而知人之寒，逸而知人之劳。

（卷三十三　晏子）

【白话】古代的贤明君主，自己吃饱时，便想到贫穷百姓的饥饿；自己穿暖时，便想到贫寒百姓的受冻；自己生活安逸时，便想到天下百姓的劳苦。

266. While the ancient sage-rulers had sufficient food to eat they would remember people who were starving. While they had adequate clothing they would remember people who were freezing in the cold. While they lived in comfort they would remember many people who were toiling hard in the world.

Scroll 33: *Yan Zi*

267. 故古之君人者，甚憯怛[1]于民也。国有饥者，食不重味[2]；民有寒者，而冬不被[3]裘。岁丰谷登[4]，乃始悬钟鼓陈干戚[5]，君臣上下同心而乐之，国无哀人。

（卷四十一　淮南子）

【注释】①憯怛：音 cǎn dá/ㄘㄢˇ ㄉㄚˊ。忧伤，悲痛。憯，忧伤。怛，悲伤、愁苦。②重味：两种以上菜肴。③被：后作“披”。穿着。④登：成熟，丰收。⑤干戚：盾与斧。古代的两种兵器。亦为武舞所执的舞具。

【白话】古时候为人君者，真正为百姓的痛苦遭遇而悲伤。国民中有挨饿的，君主吃饭时就不要第二道菜；民众中有受冻的，君主冬天就不穿裘衣。只有年终五谷丰登、百姓富足的时候，才开始悬挂起钟鼓，陈列起干戚，君臣官民同心欢乐，国内没有悲哀的人。

267. The wise rulers of the ancient times were truly sympathetic toward the suffering of their people. If some people did not have enough to eat, the rulers would not eat a second dish; if some people did not have enough clothing to keep them warm, the rulers would not wear fur coats. Only when the annual harvest was abundant and everyone was prospering were bells and drums hung, and axes and shields displayed[23]. Celebrating together with the officials and the people, no one would feel sorrowful in their land.

Scroll 41: *Huai Nan Zi*

[23] The drums, bells, axes and shields denote that music and dance were performed to celebrate the occasion, since axes and shields were also used in the performance of military dances.

268. 孟子曰："以佚道①使②民，虽劳不怨；谓教民趣农，役有常时，不使失业，当时虽劳，后获其利则逸矣。以生道杀民，虽死不怨杀者。"杀此罪人者，其意欲生人也，故虽伏罪而死，不怨杀者也。

（卷三十七　孟子）

【注释】①佚道：使百姓安乐之道。②使：役使；使唤。

【白话】孟子说："以谋求百姓安乐的出发点使用民力，百姓纵然劳苦也不会怨恨；以保障百姓生存的出发点处死有罪的人，罪人虽被处死也不怨恨杀他的人。"

268. Mengzi said: "Deploying civilian forces for the sake of public interests will not cause discontentment among the people. Sentencing someone to death for the sake of public security will not evoke hatred from the offender."

Scroll 37: *Meng Zi*

269. 敬贤如大宾[①]，爱民如赤子。内恕情之所安，而施之海内。是以囹圄空虚，天下太平。

（卷十七　汉书五）

【注释】①大宾：泛指国宾。

【白话】尊敬贤才就像尊敬国宾一样，爱护百姓如同爱护婴儿一般。自己感到心安理得的事情，才在全国实施。因此监狱空虚，天下太平。

269. Honor the virtuous like you would honor the state guests. Love the people like you would love a child. If your conscience is clear about a decision, you will implement it throughout the nation. In this way, there will be no convicts in prison and there will be peace and order in the world.

Scroll 17: *Han Shu*, Vol. 5

270. 良君养民如子，盖之如天，容之如地。民奉其君，爱之如父母，仰之如日月，敬之如神明，畏之如雷霆。

（卷五　春秋左氏传中）

【白话】贤良的国君养育臣民如同自己的子女，像天一样庇护百姓，像地一样容纳百姓。百姓尊奉国君，热爱他如同热爱父母，敬慕他如同敬慕日月，尊重他如同尊重神灵，畏惧他如同畏惧雷霆。

270. A good ruler will nurture the people like his own children, protect them the way heaven would do and accommodate them the way earth would do. People will accept their ruler as if he were their parent, admire him as if he were the sun and the moon, revere him as if he were a divine being, and be fearful of him as if he were the thunderbolt.

Scroll 5: *Chun Qiu Zuo Shi Zhuan*, Vol. 2

271. 乐民之乐者，人亦乐其乐；忧人之忧者，民亦忧其忧。乐以天下，忧以天下，然而不王者，未之有也。

（卷四十二　新序）

【白话】国君能以老百姓的快乐为快乐，老百姓也会以你的快乐为快乐；国君能忧老百姓所忧愁的，老百姓也会以你的忧愁为忧愁。以天下百姓的快乐为快乐，以天下百姓的忧愁为忧愁，这样还不能够称王天下，是从来没有的事啊！

271. If a ruler regards the happiness of the people as his own, the people will also regard his happiness as their own. If a ruler sees the concerns of the people as his own, the people will also regard his worries as their own. Both the happiness and hardship of the people are inseparable from his conscience. Thus, how would such rulers fail to run their administration successfully?

Scroll 42: *Xin Xu*

民生
The Livelihood of People

272. 民生[①]在勤，勤则不匮。

（卷五　春秋左氏传中）

【注释】①民生：民众的生计、生活。

【白话】民生在于勤劳，勤劳则生计不会困乏。

272. The livelihood of people relies on hard work, and hard work will assure there is no shortage of daily necessities.

Scroll 5: *Chun Qiu Zuo Shi Zhuan*, Vol. 2

273. 筦子[①]曰："仓廪[②]实知礼节。"民不足而可治者，自古及今，未之尝闻。

（卷十四　汉书二）

【注释】①筦子：即管仲。筦，同"管"。②仓廪：贮藏米谷的仓库。

【白话】管子说："仓库里的粮食充实了，才可以教导人们懂得礼节。"人民的衣食不足而能使国家得到治理的，从古到今还没有听说过。

273. Guanzi said: "After the national granary has sufficient food supply, we can educate the people on propriety." From the ancient times until today, it has never been possible to rule a country successfully when the people were starving and did not have enough clothing to keep them warm.

Scroll 14: *Han Shu*, Vol. 2

274. 民贫则奸邪生。贫生于不足,不足生于不农,不农则不地著[1],不地著则离乡轻家。民如鸟兽,虽有高城深池,严法重刑,犹不能禁也。

(卷十四　汉书二)

【注释】①地著:定居于一地。

【白话】人民贫穷,就会有奸诈邪恶的事发生。贫穷是因为物资不足,物资不足是因为人们不致力于农业生产,人们不务农就不会安居在一地,不能定居一地人们就会轻易离开家乡。(如果)百姓像鸟兽般没有固定的衣食来源,又居无定所,即使有高大的城墙和很深的护城河,有严厉的法律和刑罚,仍不能禁止他们做出种种不法行为。

274. When people are impoverished, crimes and acts of evil would occur. Poverty arises due to insufficient supply of resources caused by people unwilling to work in the fields. When agricultural productions are set aside, families will not settle in one place for long and

will migrate from one place to another. If they wander about like the birds and beasts without a regular source of food, clothing and a place to stay, not even high walls with deep moats or harsh laws and corporal punishments could stop them from committing crimes.

Scroll 14: *Han Shu*, Vol. 2

275. 夫治狱者得其情，则无冤死之囚；丁①壮者得尽地力，则无饥馑之民；穷老者得仰食②仓廪，则无馁饿之殍③；嫁娶以时，则男女无怨旷之恨；胎养必全，则孕者无自伤之哀；新生必复④，则孩者无不育之累⑤；壮而后役，则幼者无离家之思；二毛⑥不戎，则老者无顿伏⑦之患。医药以疗其疾，宽繇以乐其业，威罚以抑其强，恩仁以济其弱，赈贷⑧以赡其乏。十年之后，既笄⑨者必盈巷；二十年之后，胜兵⑩者必满野矣。

（卷二十五　魏志上）

【注释】①丁：壮盛；强壮。②仰食：依靠他人而得食。③殍：音 piǎo／ㄆㄧㄠˇ。饿死的人。④复：谓免除徭役或赋税。⑤累：忧患。⑥二毛：斑白的头发。常用以指老年人。⑦顿伏：犹跌倒。⑧赈贷：救济。⑨笄：音 jī／ㄐㄧ。指女子十五岁成年。⑩胜兵：指能充当兵士参加作战的人。

【白话】如果审理案件的人能获得真实的案情，那么就没有冤死的囚犯；健壮的男子能充分利用土地的潜力，那么就没有遭受灾荒的百姓；贫穷年老的人能得到国家救济的粮食，那么就没有被饿死的人；让人们按适婚年龄进行嫁娶，那么男女就不会有无妻无夫的怨恨；胎儿的养育都能保障，那么孕妇就没有自我伤感的哀叹；对有新生儿的家庭一定免除徭役，那么婴儿就没有无人养育的忧患。人到健壮后再服劳役，那么年幼的人就不会有离家的乡思；年迈的人不再从军当兵，那么老年人就不会有跌倒（在行军路上）的担忧。用医药治疗人民的疾病，宽减徭役使百姓安居乐业，用刑罚来抑制豪强，用恩惠、仁爱来帮助弱者，发放救济钱粮来供给贫乏。这样，十年之后，成年的女子必定会充满街巷；二十年之后，能够当兵参战的人必定会遍布乡野。

275. If the prosecutors can gather all the concrete truths behind a crime, no prisoner will be wrongly executed. If healthy and strong men can be allowed to toil in the fields, there will be no famine. If the poor elderly can receive food supply from the government, they will not die from hunger. Let men and women marry at a suitable age and there will be no resentments arising from

someone not having a husband or a wife. If benefits can be provided for raising a child, a pregnant woman will not wallow in self-pity and feel woeful. If families with newborn babies can be spared from mandatory labor for the state, there is no worry about not having anyone to take care of the babies. Wait until a person has grown up to become a healthy and strong adult before summoning him to labor for the state and no young men will feel homesick. Furthermore, if old people are not enlisted in the army there is no worry that they may collapse on the road during a drill. Attend to ill people with medication; reduce the loads of mandatory farm labor to allow people to settle in their lives; use punishment to control exploitations; use benevolence and kindness to help the weak; and extend relief to the poor and destitute. In ten years' time, women who reach the mature age will fill the streets and alleys; in twenty years' time, men who can be enlisted into the army will be all over the country.

Scroll 25: *Wei Zhi*, Vol. 1

法古
Learn from the Past

276. 故为高必因丘陵，为下必因川泽，为政不因先王之法，可谓智乎？言因自然，既用力少，而成功多。是以惟仁者宜在高位，不仁而在高位，是播恶于众也。仁者能由先王之道。不仁者逆道，则播扬其恶于众人也。

（卷三十七　孟子）

【白话】堆高就一定要凭借本来就突起的丘陵，掘深就一定要凭借本来就低陷的川泽，而治理政事却不依据古代圣王之道，能算得上明智吗？因此，只有有仁德的人才能居于高位，如果没有仁德而又居于高位，这样就会把他的祸害传播到民众身上。

276. To go any higher we must first stand on higher grounds or on a hilltop. To dig any deeper we must commence from low-lying streams or marshes. Can a ruler be pronounced competent if he does not govern according to the ways of former wise kings? Therefore, only the benevolent should occupy high positions. A man lacking in benevolence who occupies a high position will only influence the people through his wicked ways.

Scroll 37: *Meng Zi*

277. 昔帝尧，上世之所谓贤君也。尧王[1]天下之时，金银珠玉弗服，锦绣文绮[2]弗衣[3]，奇怪异物弗视，玩好之器弗宝，淫佚之乐弗听，宫垣[4]室屋弗崇，茅茨[5]之盖不剪，衣履不敝尽不更为，滋味[6]重累[7]不食，不以役作之故，留[8]耕种之时，削心约志，从事乎无为，其自奉[9]也甚薄，役赋也甚寡。故万民富乐而无饥寒之色，百姓戴[10]其君如日月，视其君如父母。

（卷三十一　六韬）

【注释】①王：音 wàng／ㄨㄤˋ。统治，称王。②文绮：华丽的丝织物。③衣：音 yì／ㄧˋ。穿。④宫垣：泛指房舍或其它建筑物的围墙。特指皇宫的围墙。垣：音 yuán／ㄩㄢˊ。指墙、城墙。⑤茅茨：茅草盖的屋顶。亦指茅屋。茨，音 cí／ㄘˊ。⑥滋味：美味。⑦重累：犹重迭。相同的东西层层相积。形容多。⑧留：拖延，搁置。⑨自奉：谓自身日常生活的供养。⑩戴：尊奉，拥戴。

【白话】从前的尧帝，上古时代的人们称他是贤君。尧帝统治天下时，不佩戴金银珠玉，不穿着锦绣华美的衣服，不观赏珍贵奇异的物品，不珍藏供玩赏的宝器，不听恣纵逸乐的音乐，不修建高大的围墙和宫室，不修剪茅草覆盖的屋顶，衣服鞋子不破旧就不去更换，美味佳肴过多就不去食用，不因工役劳作的缘故而耽误百姓耕种的农时，去除私心、约束欲望，致力于无为之治。尧帝自身日常生活的供养则很微薄，征用劳役赋税也很少，所以天下万民富足安乐而没有饥寒的面色。百姓尊奉他们的君主如同日月一样，看待他们的君主如同父母一般。

277. The ancients honored Emperor Yao as a virtuous ruler. When Yao was the emperor he did not adorn himself with gold, silver, pearls, and jade. He did not wear brocaded, embroidered, or florid costumes. He did not admire rare and exotic items. He took no interest in collecting treasured wares that were pleasing to the eyes. He did not listen to licentious music, nor did he build lavish enclosing walls and chambers. He did not crop the reeds that grew on the roof of his thatched hut. He did not replace clothes or shoes that were not worn out.

He would not eat if too many dishes were served to him. He did not interfere with the agricultural production by taking farm labors away to work on state projects. Yao was unselfish, moderate, and administered with a policy of non-interference. He lived by little and collected very few taxes. Hence, all the people were rich and happy and none was poor and starving. The people revered their ruler like they would worship the sun and the moon, and looked upon him as if he were their parent.

Scroll 31: *Liu Tao*

278. 五德以时合散（散作教），以为民纪，古之道也。仁义勇智信，民之本，随时而施舍，为民纲纪，古之所传政道也。

（卷三十三　司马法）

【白话】将五德（此指仁、义、勇、智、信）适时地付诸教育，作为人民行为的准则，这是自古以来的法则。

278. The objective of incorporating the five virtues (benevolence, righteousness, courage, wisdom and trustworthiness) into the education system was to enable them to serve as the ethical standards of people's behavior. This has been a customary practice since ancient times.

Scroll 33: *Si Ma Fa*

赏罚
Reward and Punishment

279. 赏在于成民之生，罚在于使人无罪，是以赏罚施民而天下化矣。

（卷三十一　六韬）

【白话】奖赏的目的是成就人民更好的生活，刑罚的目的是使人不会犯罪。因此，赏罚用来治理百姓，天下人心就会受感化了。

279. The purpose of giving rewards is to encourage the people to be kind and to lead a better life, whereas the purpose of punishment is to deter people from committing crimes. Thus, governing the people with a combination of rewards and punishments will transform people to become better persons.

Scroll 31: *Liu Tao*

280. 善治民者，开其正道，因所好而赏之，则民乐其德也；塞其邪路，因所恶而罚之，则民畏其威矣。

（卷四十九　傅子）

【白话】善于治理百姓的人，开辟百姓向善的正道，顺着人好善好德的天性奖赏善人，则百姓自然欢喜地感戴其恩德；杜绝百姓行恶的邪路，顺着人厌恶邪恶的天性惩罚罪行，则百姓自然会畏惧其威严。

280. A well-run government will open up ways to encourage people to walk on the righteous path and award good people based on the human propensity for kindness. As a result, people are thankful for the government's thoughtfulness. At the same time, a good government will stop all evil means that can mislead people to commit crimes and impose punishments based on the human dislike for wickedness. As a result, civilians will be fearful of its authority and abide by the law.

Scroll 49: *Fu Zi*

281. 赏一人而天下知所从，罚一人而天下知所避。明开塞之路，使百姓晓然知轨疏（疏疑迹）之所由，是以贤者不忧，知者不惧，干禄者不邪。

（卷五十　袁子正书）

【白话】奖赏一个人，天下人都知道以他为榜样而跟从；惩罚一个人，天下人都知道以他为教训而躲避。明确能做的和不能做的，使百姓知道应该走什么样的道路，所以贤人就不担心，有才智的人就不害怕，谋求做官的人也不会走上邪路。

281. Reward a person and make him an example for others to follow; punish a person and make him an example for others not to emulate. Clarify what is allowed and what is prohibited so as to make sure that people know the directions they should take. In this way, the virtuous will have no worries, the intelligent will have no fear, and no aspiring officials will risk walking on the path of corruption.

Scroll 50: *Yuan Zi Zheng Shu*

282. 赏足荣而罚可畏，智者知荣辱之必至。是故劝善[1]之心生，而不轨之奸息。

（卷五十　袁子正书）

【注释】①劝善：勉力为善。

【白话】赏赐足以使民众觉得荣耀，惩罚足以让民众觉得畏惧。有才智的人知道荣耀和耻辱必会（伴随着自己善或恶的行为）到来，所以勉力为善的心就产生了，图谋不轨的念头就停息了。

282. Rewards should be evidently sufficient to make people feel honored whereas punishments should be evidently effective to make people dread justice. Intelligent people know that honor comes from good deeds and punishment comes from bad deeds. Therefore, efforts to perform good deeds will increase whereas intentions to do bad deeds will cease.

Scroll 50: *Yuan Zi Zheng Shu*

283. 善赏者，费少而劝多；善罚者，刑省而奸禁。

（卷三十五　文子）

【白话】善于奖赏的人，花费很少而劝勉的人多；善用惩罚的人，刑罚不多而能使奸邪得以禁止。

283. A person who is experienced in giving rewards needs only to spend a little to convince many people to perform good deeds. A person who is experienced in imposing punishment needs only few penalties to stop acts of evil from happening.

Scroll 35: *Wen Zi*

284. 凡爵列①官职，赏庆②刑罚，皆以类相从③者也。一物失称④，乱之端也。德不称位，能不称官，赏不当功，刑不当罪，不祥莫大焉。

（卷十四　汉书二）

【注释】①爵列：爵位。②赏庆：奖赏。③以类相从：按其类别各相归属。④失称：不相当。

【白话】凡是爵位、官职、赏赐和刑罚，都要按功过的等级来相应地施予。一件事做得不恰当，就是混乱的开端。德行与爵位不相符，能力与官职不相符，赏赐与功劳不相当，刑罚与罪过不相当，没有比这样更不吉祥的了。

284. Award noble titles, official positions, rewards or punishments according to one's performance. One wrongly given reward or punishment will mark the beginning of chaos. When one's virtue does not correspond to the requirement of a noble title, or one's ability does not match the requirement of an official

position, or if a reward does not match the contribution made and a punishment does not fit the crime, nothing can be more menacing than this situation.

Scroll 14: *Han Shu*, Vol. 2

285. 若赏一无功，则天下饰诈矣；罚一无罪，则天下怀疑矣。是以明德慎赏，而不肯轻之；明德慎罚，而不肯忽之。

（卷四十九　傅子）

【白话】如果奖赏一个无功的人，天下人就会作伪欺诈；处罚一个无罪的人，天下人就会怀有疑虑。所以贤明者慎于奖赏，不肯轻易实施；贤明者慎于处罚，而不随意执行。

285. If praises and rewards were given to an unworthy person, the whole kingdom would deem this as an excuse for lying. If punishments were imposed upon an innocent person, this would create distrust on the government's part. Thus a good official is most careful in giving out rewards, and he will be equally careful when imposing punishments. He will not carry out both matters indiscriminately.

Scroll 49: *Fu Zi*

286. 废一善则众善衰，赏一恶则众恶多（多作归）。善者得其佑，恶者受其诛①，则国安而众善到矣。

（卷四十　三略）

【注释】①诛：惩罚；责罚。

【白话】废除一桩善行，那么众多善行都会减退；奖赏一桩恶行，那么众多恶行就会增长。善人得到福佑，恶人受到诛罚，国家就会安定，各种善举就会兴起。

286. Abolish one good conduct and the public will be discouraged from doing good deeds. Award one bad deed and criminal activities will increase considerably. If kind people receive blessings and wicked people receive fair punishments from the state, the country will enjoy peace and order, and the practice of doing kind deeds will flourish.

Scroll 40: *San Lüe*

287. 赏不劝，谓之止善；罚不惩，谓之纵恶。

（卷四十六　申鉴）

【白话】奖赏起不到劝勉民众的作用，这叫做“止善”；处罚起不到警戒恶行的效果，这就叫“纵恶”。

287. If a reward system is unable to encourage people to do kind deeds, it is regarded as “hindering virtues.” If a penalty system is unable to deter people from doing unlawful acts, it is regarded as “inducing wickedness.”

Scroll 46: *Shen Jian*

288. 善为国者，赏不僭①而刑不滥。赏僭，则惧及淫人；刑滥，则及善人。若不幸而过，宁僭无滥。

（卷五　春秋左氏传中）

【注释】①僭：音 jiàn／ㄐㄧㄢˋ。犹过分。

【白话】善于治理国家者，赏赐不过分，刑罚不滥用。赏赐过分，就怕赏及恶人；刑罚滥用，就怕伤及好人。如果不幸赏罚过当，那么宁可赏赐过分，也不可滥用刑罚。

288. A good ruler will not give out rewards excessively, and neither will he impose punishments indiscriminately. He makes sure that excessive rewards are not given to undeserving persons and unjust punishments are not imposed on innocent people. In the event that rewards and punishments are not impartially given, it would be better to offer more rewards than to abuse punishments.

Scroll 5: *Chun Qiu Zuo Shi Zhuan*, Vol. 2

289. 赏不遗远[①]，罚不阿[②]近，爵不可以无功取，刑不可以势贵免，此贤愚之所以佥[③]忘其身者也。

（卷二十七　蜀志）

【注释】①遗远：遗弃关系疏远者。②阿：徇私，偏袒。③佥：音 qiān / ㄑㄧㄢ。都；皆。

【白话】奖赏时不遗漏关系疏远的人，惩罚时不袒护亲近的人，没有功劳的人不可以取得爵位，权势显贵的人也不会免掉应受的刑罚，这就是不论贤愚都能忘我为国效劳的原因。

289. Distantly related people will not be ignored in the provision of rewards, and close relatives will not be spared from the imposing of penalties. Those without contributions cannot be granted the rank of nobility, and those who have violated the laws must be sentenced although they belong to the noble class. When such practices are carried out, all officials, whether they are virtuous or unaccomplished, would serve the country selflessly.

Scroll 27: *Shu Zhi*

法律
Law and Statute

290. 德教者，人君之常任也，而刑罚为之佐助焉。

（卷四十五　昌言）

【白话】道德教化，是人君治国的常道，而刑罚只是德教的辅助。

290. Implementing moral education to achieve transformation is the virtuous way of a wise ruler. Punishment is only used to uphold the values of moral education.

Scroll 45: *Chang Yan*

291. 法令者治之具，而非制治[①]清浊之源也。

（卷十二　史记下）

【注释】①制治：犹统治。

【白话】法令是治理天下的一种工具，而不是导致政治清明或污浊的根源。

291. Law and order are merely instruments used in governing a country; they are not the root cause leading to a clean or corrupt government.

Scroll 12: *Shi Ji*, Vol. 2

292. 古者明其仁义之誓，使民不踰。不教而杀，是虐民也。与其刑不可踰，不若义之不可踰也。闻礼义行而刑罚中[①]，未闻刑罚任（任作行）而孝悌兴也。高墙狭基，不可立也；严刑峻法，不可久也。

（卷四十二　盐铁论）

【注释】①中：音 zhòng／ㄓㄨㄥˋ。得当。

【白话】古时候（贤明君王）宣明以仁义修身的誓约，使百姓不逾越礼义。如果不先进行教育，等到百姓犯罪就加以杀戮，这是残害百姓。与其制定刑法使百姓不敢触犯，不如提倡礼义使百姓耻于违反。只听说推行礼义，刑罚就能运用得恰当；没有听说过施行刑罚，孝悌之风就能兴盛起来的。围墙高大，地基狭窄，是不能立得住的；用严厉的刑法治理国家，是不能长久的。

292. The ancient sage-rulers pledged vows to keep themselves aligned with virtues so that the people would not neglect the importance of propriety. If the government did not educate the people but killed them when they violated the law, this would amount to committing atrocity against the people. Rather than imposing severe laws that aimed to deter people from disobedience, it would be better to promote propriety to convince people to be law-abiding. We have heard that promoting propriety could ensure fair punishment, but we have not heard that enforcing punishment could promote the practices of filial piety and fraternity. Walls that are mighty will not stand firm if the foundation is shallow. A government that uses heavy penalties to govern a country will not last long.

Scroll 42: *Yan Tie Lun*

293. 君不法天地，而随世俗之所善[①]以为法，故令出必乱。乱则复更为法，是以法令数变，则群邪成俗，而君沉于世，是以国不免危亡矣。

（卷三十一　六韬）

【注释】①善：喜好。

【白话】如果君主不效法自然常道，而附和世俗的喜好来制定法令，那么这样的法令一旦颁布，必定会引起混乱。出现混乱后再更改法令，所以导致法令被屡次修改，这就使得奸邪的风气流行起来，而君主沉溺于世俗之中，因此国家就免不了危亡了。

293. If a ruler does not rule according to the law of nature but enact laws to satisfy certain quarters, this will bring forth chaos. The unrests will force the government to change the laws repeatedly, and acts of wickedness will begin to happen frequently over time. If the ruler still indulges himself in worldly luxuriating, it is inevitable that his country will be destroyed in time to come.

Scroll 31: *Liu Tao*

294. 善为治者，纲举而网疏。纲举则所罗者广，网疏则小罪必漏。所罗者广，则大罪不纵，则甚泰[①]必刑。微过必漏，则为政不苛；甚泰必刑，然后犯治[②]必塞。此为治之要也。

（卷三十　晋书下）

【注释】①甚泰：过分。泰，同“太”。②犯治：犯法于治世。

【白话】善于治理国家的人，会抓住总纲而让法网稀疏。能够抓住总纲，那么它的涉及面就很广；法网稀疏，则小过失就得以忽略。涉及面广，则大罪不会纵容，大过必会惩罚。小过失得到忽略，那么为政就不会苛刻；大罪一定惩处，则在治世违法乱纪的行为就会被遏制。这就是治理国家的关键。

294. A wise ruler will only enforce the basic principles of the law, but at the same time make allowances (grant leniency) for minor violations. This means that as the net of justice is cast far and wide to enable extensive area

coverage, minor violations are thus ignored. When this net of justice covers an extensive area, serious offenses and crimes will be caught and heavily penalized. Thus, the administration will not be deemed tyrannical as minor offenses or violations are accommodated. When serious crimes are punishable by laws, incidents of law-breaking and social disorder will be kept under control. This is the key to running a good government.

Scroll 30: *Jin Shu*, Vol. 2

295. 一令逆者，则百令失；君令一逆，民不从，故百令皆废也。一恶施者，则百恶结。一恶得施，则百恶结而相从也。

（卷四十　三略）

【白话】一项政令违逆人心，所有的政令就都会失去作用；一件坏事施行了，上百件坏事就会接连发生。

295. When one law betrays the trust of the people, all other laws will lose their effectiveness. With one bad action put into practice, hundreds of immoral practices will come into being.

Scroll 40: *San Lüe*

296. 道径众，民不知所由也；法令众，人不知所避也。故王者之制法也，昭乎如日月，故民不迷；旷乎若大路，故民不惑。幽隐远方，折乎知之；愚妇童[①]妇，咸知所避。是故法令不犯，而狱犴[②]不用也。

（卷四十二　盐铁论）

【注释】①童：愚昧；浅陋。②狱犴：牢狱。犴，音 àn／ㄢˋ。古指乡亭牢狱。

【白话】道路多了，人们就不知道该走哪一条；法令多了，百姓就不知道怎样避免触犯法禁。因此，圣明的君主制定法律，如同日月一样昭明，所以百姓不会迷惘；如同大路一样宽广，所以百姓不会疑惑。连偏僻遥远之地的人，也能清楚了解法令；愚昧无知的妇女，也都知道怎样避免犯法。因此法律和政令没人违犯，监狱也不需要使用。

296. With too many diverging routes ahead, it is hard to know which way to go. With too many codes of laws being regulated, it is difficult to avoid violations. The laws enacted by the sage-rulers were like the sun and the moon lighting up the darkened path so that people would not lose their way, or like a wide and open road that would not lead the people astray. Hence, people living in the remote corners were clear about the laws, and even benighted women knew how to avoid breaking the laws. No one would violate the law, and prisons would not be needed anymore.

Scroll 42: *Yan Tie Lun*

征伐
Military Ethics

297. 夫文，止戈为武。文，字也。武王克商，作《颂》曰："载①戢②干戈，载櫜③弓矢。"戢，藏也。櫜，韬也。诗美武王能灭暴乱而息兵也。夫武禁暴，戢兵，保大，定功，安民，和众，丰财者也，此武七德也。故使子孙无忘其章④。著之篇章，使子孙不忘也。

（卷五　春秋左氏传中）

【注释】①载：语气助词。用在句首或句中，起加强语气的作用。②戢：音 jí / ㄐㄧˊ。收藏兵器。③櫜：音 gāo / ㄍㄠ。纳弓于弓袋。④章：诗歌或乐曲的段落。

【白话】从文字构造看，止戈二字合起来就是"武"字。周武王战胜商纣以后，周人《周颂》说："把干戈收藏起来，把弓矢装进袋子里。"所谓武，是用来禁止暴乱、止息战争、保持太平、建立功业、安定百姓、和睦万邦、丰富资财的，所以要使子孙后代不要忘记这些内容。

297. From the point of morphology, the Chinese character for "military" is Wu 武 , formed by using two words: "Stop"—Zhi 止 , and "Dagger-axe"—Ge 戈 . It was said that after King Wu defeated King Jie of the Shang dynasty, the Zhou people wrote the *Hymn of Zhou* which said: "Store the dagger-axe and put the arrows back in their quivers." Therefore, military was used mainly to stop riots, end wars, maintain peace, establish meritorious achievements, bring peace to the people, maintain harmonious ties with other nations and to enrich resources. The hymn was recorded as a reminder for future generations to take note of this lesson.

Scroll 5: *Chun Qiu Zuo Shi Zhuan*, Vol. 2

298. 是故百战百胜，非善之善者也；不战而屈人之兵，善之善者也。未战而敌自屈服也。

（卷三十三　孙子兵法）

【白话】因此，百战百胜，称不上是最高明的；不交战而使敌兵降服，才是高明中最高明的。

298. Hence to fight and conquer in all your battles is not supreme excellence; supreme excellence consists in breaking the enemy's resistance without fighting[24].

Scroll 33: *Sun Zi Bing Fa*

---

[24] Lionel Giles, "Attack by Stratagem," *Chinese Text Project,* http://ctext.org/art-of-war/attack-by-stratagem.

299. 仁人之兵，所存者神，所过者化①。若时雨②之降，莫不悦喜。故近者亲其善，远者慕其德，兵不血刃③，远迩④来服。德盛于此，施及四极⑤。

（卷三十八　孙卿子）

【注释】①化：从化；归化；归顺。②时雨：应时的雨水。③兵不血刃：兵器上没有沾血，谓战事顺利，未经交锋或激战而取得胜利。④远迩：犹远近。⑤四极：四方极远之地。

【白话】仁人之兵，所驻扎的地方，能得到安定和平；所行经的地方，人们无不从化。就像应时的雨水降临，无不欢欣喜悦。所以近者敬爱他们的美善，远方仰慕他们的道德，不必交战就能胜利，远近都来归服。道德昌盛如此，就会恩泽广施至四方极远之地。

299. Wherever a benign army was stationed there would be stability and peace. Wherever it passed by people would be transformed. Like a rainfall that arrived at the right time and place, none would be displeased.

Immediate neighbors admired their kindness and people from afar praised their virtues. They won the battle even without starting a war and gained the allegiance of those from far and near. When the attainment of virtues could be cultivated to such a high level, blessings would spread far and wide to the four corners of the kingdom.

Scroll 38: *Sun Qing Zi*

300. 圣王之用兵也，非好乐之，将以诛暴讨乱。夫以义而诛不义，若决江河而溉荧火，临不测而挤欲坠，其克之必也。

（卷四十　三略）

【白话】圣明的君主用兵，不是自己喜好用兵，而是用以诛灭凶暴、讨伐叛乱。以正义来讨伐不义，就像决开江河去浇灭如萤虫之火，就像在深渊的边缘去推挤将要坠落之物，其胜利是必然的。

300. A sage-ruler would resort to military armaments not because he liked declaring wars, but to stop horrendous violence and rebellions. Crusading against evil by waging a righteous war is like breaking a dam and pouring water to extinguish a tiny speck of fire, or like pushing an object that is about to fall from the edge of a cliff. Victory is inevitable.

Scroll 40: *San Lüe*

301. 国虽大，好战必亡；天下虽平，忘战必危。

（卷十八　汉书六）

【白话】国家虽大，好战必亡；天下即使太平，忘战必然危殆。

301. However huge a country may be, if it goes on warmongering, it would eventually be destroyed; while peaceful as it may seem, a country that neglects readiness for war will face impending danger.

Scroll 18: *Han Shu*, Vol. 6

302. “军旅之后，必有凶年”，言民以其愁苦之气，伤阴阳之和也。出兵虽胜，犹有后忧，恐灾害之变，因此以生。

（卷十九　汉书七）

【白话】“大的军事行动之后，必定会有灾荒之年”，说的就是战争给百姓带来的愁苦之气，会伤害天地阴阳的和谐。出兵即使取胜，仍然会有战后的忧患，恐怕灾害异变，会因此而发生。

302. The saying that “After a war, bad times will follow” means that war will bring sorrow to the people and upset the harmonious balance between heaven and earth as well as the *Yin* and *Yang* energies. Although a war has been won, the country will still experience hardship, and disasters and abnormal phenomena would follow.

Scroll 19: *Han Shu*, Vol. 7

敬慎

Chapter Five

RESPECTFULLY CAUTIOUS

微渐
Taking Precautions

303. 古者衣服车马，贵贱有章，以褒有德而别尊卑。今上下僭差①，人人自制，是故贪财趍②利，不畏死亡。周之所以能致治③，刑措④而不用者，以其禁邪于冥冥，绝恶于未萌也。

（卷十九　汉书七）

【注释】①僭差：僭越失度。僭，音 jiàn／ㄐㄧㄢˋ。超越本分，冒用在上者的职权、名义行事。②趍：音 qū／ㄑㄩ。同“趋”。追求；追逐。③致治：使国家在政治上安定清平。④刑措：亦作“刑错”或“刑厝”，置刑法而不用。措，搁置。

【白话】古代衣服车马贵贱有规章，用来褒扬有德之人而使尊卑有所区别。而今上下之间有超越本分的错失，人人自行制订而无节度，于是人们贪财谋利，不惜冒生命危险。周朝之所以能达到天下大治，刑罚搁置不用，其原因就是在歪风未显露时就将其制止，在罪恶未萌生时就将其杜绝。

303. Ancient attires and modes of transport were governed by specific regulations to commend virtuous men and to differentiate social status. However, in recent times, everyone is trying to surpass each other in setting up their own rules to pursue monetary or personal gains, even if it means putting their lives at risks. The fact that the Zhou dynasty could enjoy peace and order even though corporal punishment was set aside was because they took preventative measures to stop unhealthy habits from thriving and stopped crimes before they could happen.

Scroll 19: *Han Shu*, Vol. 7

304. 且夫闭情[①]无欲者上也，咈心[②]消除者次之。昔帝舜藏黄金于崭岩[③]之山，抵珠玉于深川之底。及仪狄[④]献旨酒[⑤]，而禹甘之，于是疏远仪狄，纯（纯当作绝）上旨酒。此能闭情于无欲者也。

（卷四十七　政要论）

【注释】①闭情：闭绝欲望。②咈心：违背心意。咈，音 fú／ㄈㄨˊ。违背；违逆。③崭岩：高峻的山崖。元和本作“渐岩”。崭、渐此处读音均为 chán／ㄔㄢˊ。渐，通“巉”，或作“崭”。④仪狄：传说为夏禹时善酿酒者。⑤旨酒：美酒。

【白话】人能够做到闭情无欲可以算是上等人了，刻意违背心意消除欲求的人就要差一等了。过去舜帝让黄金埋藏在险峻的高山之上，将珠玉弃置在深川的谷底。仪狄进献美酒给大禹，大禹品尝后觉得非常甘甜，于是疏远仪狄，杜绝人们进献美酒。这就是能够自我节制而达到无欲的例子。

304. One who is able to abstain from desires can be considered supreme, while one who forces himself to suppress his desires is less so. In the past, Emperor Shun buried gold in the dangerously steep mountains and discarded jewelries at the bottom of a deep gorge. When an expert winemaker presented fine wine to King Yu, the king, upon savoring its sweet taste, distanced himself from the winemaker and decreed the prohibition of wine. These are noble examples of self-control that led to the abstinence from desires.

Scroll 47: *Zheng Yao Lun*

305. 抱朴子曰："三辰①蔽于天，则清景②闇于地；根茇③蹶④于此，则柯条⑤瘁于彼。道失于近，则祸及于远；政缪于上，而民困于下。"

（卷五十　抱朴子）

【注释】①三辰：指日、月、星。②清景：犹清光。③茇：音 bá / ㄅㄚˊ。草木的根。④蹶：音 jué / ㄐㄩㄝˊ。竭尽。⑤柯条：枝条。

【白话】抱朴子说："日、月、星被天上云雾遮住了，地上的光明就会暗淡；植物的根部这里竭尽，枝条那里就会干枯。正道废失于近，则祸患及于深远；政治乖错于上，则百姓穷困于下。"

305. Bao Pu Zi said: "When the sun, the moon and the stars were covered by clouds and mists, the light on earth would grow dim. When the roots of plants decayed, branches and twigs would wither. The principles of righteousness might have been compromised in a local area, but the impact that they caused would be deep and far-reaching. When the rulership of the government became inefficient, the populace would suffer from impoverishment."

Scroll 50: *Bao Pu Zi*

风俗
Social Customs

306. 俗之伤破人伦①，剧于寇贼之来，不能经（旧无经字，补之）久，其所损坏一时而已。

（卷五十　抱朴子）

【注释】①人伦：本于人的天性、符合伦理道德的正常的人际关系，大致为君臣、父子、夫妇、兄弟、朋友五种，故称“五伦”。

【白话】世俗习惯对人伦的破坏，比外敌、强盗的入侵还要厉害，外敌的入侵不能持久，他们的损害只是一时而已。

306. Bad social customs can bring a far greater destruction to the five moral relationships[25] than the invasion of foreign enemies and bandits, as foreign invasions do not last long and their damages are but temporary.

Scroll 50: *Bao Pu Zi*

---

[25] The correct approach to dealing with realationships between parents and children, brothers and sisters, husband and wife, superiors and subordinates, and among friends, is known collectively as the “five moral relationships”.

307. 亲亲[①]以睦，友贤不弃，不遗故旧，则民德归厚矣。

（卷三　毛诗）

【注释】①亲亲：爱自己的亲人。

【白话】君主关爱亲人来保持和睦，友爱贤者而不离弃，不忘故旧，那么百姓的品德就会回归于淳厚了。

307. If a ruler loves and cares for his relatives to preserve harmony, extends his fraternal affection to virtuous men without deserting them, and never forgets his old friends, then the virtue of the people will return to its simple kindness.

Scroll 3: *Mao Shi*

308. 使天下皆背道而趋利，则人主之所最病[1]者。

（卷二十五　魏志上）

【注释】①病：忧虑。

【白话】假使天下的人都违背道义去追逐利益，那便是君主所最为担忧的事了。

308. If everybody in the country contravened codes of morality and righteousness to pursue personal benefits, this should unquestionably be the greatest concern for a ruler.

Scroll 25: *Wei Zhi*, Vol. 1

309. 若夫商①、韩②、孙③、吴④,知人性之贪得乐进,而不知兼济其善,于是束之以法,要之以功,使下(使下作使天下)唯力是恃,唯争是务。恃力务争,至有探汤赴火而忘其身者,好利之心独用⑤也。人怀好利之心,则善端⑥没矣。

(卷四十九　傅子)

【注释】①商:商鞅。姓公孙,名鞅,战国时卫人。少好刑名法术之学,后入秦为相,受封于商。用法严苛,树敌众多,后被车裂而死。或称为"卫鞅"。②韩:韩非。战国时韩国的诸公子之一,法家思想的集大成者。后为李斯所谮,下狱而死。③孙:孙武。齐人,春秋时兵法家。所著《孙子兵法》被誉为"兵学圣典"。④吴:吴起。战国时卫人。政治家、军事家。因招怨贵戚大臣,后被射死。著有《吴子》。⑤独用:单独行世,单独使用。⑥善端:善言善行的端始。

【白话】至于商鞅、韩非、孙子、吴起,知道人有贪求财物、乐于提高地位的一面,而不知同时助长其善的一面，因此，用刑法约束，用功名鼓励，使天下人只依靠强力，只致力于争夺。依仗强力、务求争夺，以至于有人赴汤蹈火而忘记死活，都是争利之心所驱使的。人人都抱着求利之心，人善良的一面就丧失了。

309. While great men like Shang Yang[26], Han Fei[27], Sunzi[28] and Wu Qi[29] knew very well that humans are inclined to acquire material wealth out of greed and are also keen to pursue social status, these great men were not aware that people need to be educated to enhance their morality.

---

[26] Shang Yang 商鞅 , 4th century BC, a legalist philosopher, premier of the State of Qin 秦国 . With the support of Duke Xiao of Qin 秦孝公 , he enacted numerous reforms in Qin in accordance with his legalist philosophy and assisted Qin in its change from a peripheral state to that of a militarily powerful and strongly centralized kingdom. He changed the administration of the state through an emphasis on meritocracy and devolving power from the nobility.

[27] Han Fei 韩非 belonged to the school of Ancient Chinese Philosophy called Legalism. His philosophy became one of the guiding principles of King Zheng of Qin, who became Qin Shi Huang 秦始皇 , the first emperor of China. Despite its outcast status throughout the history of Imperial China, Han Fei's political theory continued to heavily influence every dynasty afterwards.

[28] Sun Wu 孙武, author of *Sun Zi: The Art of War,* a book considered to be the "bible of military expertise."

[29] Wu Qi 吴起 , 5th–4th century BC, was a statesman, a legalist philosopher and a military strategist whose name is often mentioned alongside Sunzi 孙子 . He was appointed Prime Minister by King Dao of Chu 楚悼王 . His reforms made Chu a strong state at that time.

Hence, they used punishment to control the people, conferred honors to motivate them, and encouraged them to rely on sheer power to rival one another. The sole reliance on power to dominate would reach a point when people would defy all odds just for the sake of personal benefits. If everyone adopts this kind of selfish mentality, the innate kindness of mankind would be lost.

Scroll 49: *Fu Zi*

治乱
Conquering Chaos

310. 君之所审者三：一曰德不当①其位，二曰功不当其禄，三曰能不当其官。此三本者，治乱之原②也。

（卷三十二　管子）

【注释】①当：音 dāng / ㄉㄤ。对等，相当。②原：本原，根本。今字作“源”。

【白话】君主所应注意的问题有三个：一是臣子的德行与他的爵位不相称，二是臣子的功劳与他的俸禄不相称，三是臣子的能力与他的官职不相称。这三个根本问题是国家安定与动乱的根源。

310. A leader should observe the following three fundamental factors that can affect the stability of a country:

1. Whether a minister's moral conduct and his noble rank are compatible;

2. Whether a minister's contributions and the stipends he receives are compatible;

3. Whether a minister's ability and his post are compatible.

These three fundamental factors constitute the root cause of a country's stability or disorder.

Scroll 32: *Guan Zi*

311. 夫世之治乱、国之安危，非由他也。俊乂[1]在官，则治道清；奸佞干政，则祸乱作。故王者任人，不可不慎也。

（卷四十八　典语）

【注释】①乂：音 yì/一ˋ。贤才。

【白话】天下的治乱、国家的安危，不是由于其他什么原因。贤能之人做官，国家就会治理得安定太平；奸诈谄媚之人参与政事，灾祸、动乱就会发生。所以君王用人，不能不慎重。

311. There is certainly a reason why there is law and order or chaos in a country. When virtuous and able men are appointed to office, the country will be well governed, peaceful and stable. When treacherous and slanderous men are involved in government administration, disasters and upheavals will arise. Therefore, a ruler has to be extremely cautious when appointing government officials.

Scroll 48: *Dian Yu*

312. 乱之初生，僭[①]始既涵[②]。僭，不信也。涵，同也。王之初生乱萌，群臣之言，信与不信，尽同之不别。乱之又生，君子信谗。君子斥在位者，信谗人言，是复乱之所生。君子信盗[③]，乱是用[④]暴。盗，谓小人。盗言孔[⑤]甘。乱是用餤[⑥]。餤，进也。

（卷三　毛诗）

【注释】①僭：音 jiàn／ㄐㄧㄢˋ。虚伪，不可信。②涵：同。③盗：指谗佞的小人。④是用：因此。用，表示凭借或者原因。⑤孔：甚，很。⑥餤：音 tán／ㄊㄢˊ。进食，引申为增进或加剧。

【白话】追溯动乱的源头，是君王面对伪言，分不清善恶真假。动乱再次出现，那是君王听信谗言，良臣却无辜受压。君王信任小人，才会乱象丛生。小人的甜言蜜语盛行于世，动乱终将逐步升级，直至无法收拾。

312. The original cause of chaos can be attributed to the king's inability to differentiate good from evil and truth from falsehood. The recurrence of chaos can be attributed to the king's fault in believing slanderous advice, resulting in innocent ministers being suppressed. The proliferation of disorder can be attributed to the king's unwise reliance on unscrupulous people. Their clever talks could mislead the whole country, resulting in the escalation of turmoil going beyond control.

Scroll 3: *Mao Shi*

313. 政险失民，田薉[1]稼恶，籴[2]贵民饥，道路有死人，夫是之谓人妖[3]也。政令不明，举措不时，本事不理，夫是之谓人妖也。礼义不修，外内无别，男女淫乱，父子相疑，上下乖离，寇难日至，夫是之谓人妖也。三者错，无安国矣。其说甚迩，其灾甚惨。

（卷三十八　孙卿子）

【注释】①薉：音 huì／ㄏㄨㄟˋ，荒芜。②籴：音 dí／ㄉㄧˊ，买进谷物。③人妖：人事方面的反常现象；人为的灾祸。

【白话】政治险恶失去民心，田地荒芜收成不好，粮价昂贵百姓饥饿，路上有冻饿至死的人，这叫做人为的灾祸。政令不清明，各种举措不符合时机，对农业生产放任不管，这叫做人为的灾祸。不进行伦理道德的教化和学习，内外没有区别，男女淫乱，父子间没有信任，君臣彼此背离，内忧外患一起到来，这叫做人为的灾祸。这三种情况交错发生，国家就无法安宁了。这些道理很浅近，但这些灾难却很惨重啊。

313. When a government is treacherous and the populace loses faith in it; when the fields are not well cultivated and harvest does not meet demands; when there is a hike in the prices of grains and people starve and freeze to death by the roadside—such are man-made disasters. When the code of laws of the government is not transparent and various implementations are ill-timed and agricultural production is left unmanaged—such are man-made disasters. When moral education is not widely promoted, promiscuity between men and women becomes rampant; parents and children do not trust each other; leaders and subordinates betray each other; and so internal turmoil and foreign invasion happen concurrently—such are man-made disasters. With frequent occurrences of the above three situations, the country will no longer be peaceful and stable. The above principles may appear very simple but the disasters are catastrophic indeed!

Scroll 38: *Sun Qing Zi*

鉴戒
Heedful of Troubling Signs

314. 目也者，远察天际，而不能近见其眦①。心亦如之。君子诚知心之似目也，是以务鉴于人以观得失。

（卷四十六　中论）

【注释】①眦：音 zì／ㄗˋ。眼角，上下眼睑的接合处。

【白话】人的眼睛，远望可以看到天的尽头，而近看却看不到自己的眼角。人心也是这样。君子深知人心也像眼睛一样，因此，努力以人为鉴，来了解自己的过失。

314. The human eye can see far across the horizon, yet it is unable to see something as close as its corner. So is the human mind. A man of noble character (*Junzi*) knows that his mind is no different from his eyes and is thus ever ready to learn from others in order to understand his own shortcomings.

Scroll 46: *Zhong Lun*

315. 古之人目短于自见，故以镜观面；智短于自知，故以道正己。目失[1]镜，则无以正须眉；身失道，则无以知迷惑。

（卷四十　韩子）

【注释】①失：违背；离开。

【白话】古时候的人，因为眼睛不足以看见自己，所以用镜子来观察面容；因为智慧不足以认识自己，所以用道德仁义来端正自己的思想言行。眼睛失去镜子，就没有办法端正容颜；身行离开道德仁义，就无法觉察自己的迷惑。

315. As the ancients could not observe their entire physiques, they used mirrors to reflect on their appearances. They also realized that they were not wise enough to understand themselves so they abided by virtues, benevolence, and honor in order to regulate their minds, speech and actions. Without mirrors we will not be able to see our faces clearly, let alone clean and tidy them; without abiding by virtues, benevolence and honor, we will not be able to detect the state of misconception in us.

Scroll 40: *Han Zi*

316. 子曰："由，汝闻六言六蔽[1]乎？"对曰："未。""居[2]，吾语汝。好仁不好学，其蔽也愚；仁者爱物，不知所以裁之，则愚也。好智不好学，其蔽也荡[3]；荡，无所适守。好信不好学，其蔽也贼[4]；父子不知相为隐之辈。好直不好学，其蔽也绞[5]；好勇不好学，其蔽也乱；好刚不好学，其蔽也狂[6]。"狂，妄抵触人也。

（卷九　论语）

【注释】①蔽：壅蔽、覆障、弊端的意思。②居：坐。古人铺席于地，两膝着席，臀部压在脚后跟上，谓之"坐"。③荡：放荡无操守。④贼：伤害。⑤绞：急切。⑥狂：狂妄抵触他人。

【白话】孔子说："由，你听说过六种事有六种壅蔽的道理吗？"子路直起身回答说："没有。"孔子说："坐吧，我告诉你。好仁而不好学，其弊病是不分善恶，如同愚人；好智而不好学，其弊病是放荡不羁而无操守；好信而不好学，其弊病是死守信诺而伤害道义情理；好直而不好学，其弊病是急躁而好揭短；好勇而不好学，其弊病是错乱种种规矩；好刚而不好学，其弊病是狂妄而容易冒犯他人。"

316. Confucius asked his student Zilu: "Have you ever heard of the six sayings and their six ill effects?"

Zilu answered: "No, I have not."

"Come, sit down, and let me explain to you," Confucius said. "The ill effect of longing to be benevolent without the desire to study will create a foolish person who cannot discern right from wrong. The ill effect of longing to be wise without the desire to study will make an outrageous person who cannot be disciplined. The ill effect of longing to be trustworthy without the desire to study will create a stubborn person who would blindly keep his words without regards to morality and rationality. The ill effect of longing to have forthright character without the desire to study will create a quick-tempered person who likes to criticize the shortcomings of others. The ill effect of longing to be bold without the desire to study will create an unaccommodating person. The ill effect of longing to be tough without the desire to study will create an arrogant person with rude conduct."

Scroll 9: *Lun Yu*

317. 孔子曰："士有五：有埶[1]尊贵者，有家富厚者，有资勇悍者，有心智慧者，有貌美好者。埶尊贵，不以爱民行义理[2]，而反以暴傲；家富厚，不以振穷[3]救不足，而反以侈靡无度；资勇悍，不以卫上攻战[4]，而反以侵凌私斗；心智慧，不以端计数[5]，而反以事奸饰诈[6]；貌美好，不以统朝莅民[7]，而反以蛊[8]女从欲[9]。此五者，所谓士失其美质[10]也。"

（卷八　韩诗外传）

【注释】①埶："势"的古字。指权势。②义理：合于伦理道德的行事准则。③振穷：救助困穷的人。④攻战：犹作战、战斗。⑤计数：谋略。⑥饰诈：谓作假骗人。⑦莅民：管理百姓。⑧蛊：诱惑，迷乱。⑨从欲：纵欲。从，"纵"的古字。⑩美质：美好的本质。

【白话】孔子说："士人有五类：有的权势尊贵，有的家境富裕，有的本性勇敢，有的天资聪明，有的容貌美好。权势尊贵的人，不利用他的权位去爱护百姓、依照伦理道德行事，反而利用权势暴戾傲慢、欺压百姓；家境富裕的人，不利用他的财富去救济贫穷困乏的人，反而利用财富来过奢侈糜烂、没有节制的生活；本性勇敢的人，不利用他的勇敢保卫国君、和入侵者战斗，反而凭借勇力来欺侮别人，进行私人间的争斗；天资聪明的人，不利用他的明察来策划政治的措施，反而凭借智谋来从事奸邪的事，作假骗人；容貌美好的人，不利用他的威仪统率朝廷官吏、治理人民，反而用它来诱惑女子，放纵情欲。这五种人，可说是士人中丧失了其美好禀赋的人。”

317. Confucius said: “There are five types of scholars.

1. Some are noble and powerful;
2. Some come from rich families;
3. Some are endowed with bravery;
4. Some are born intelligent;
5. Some are born with attractive faces.

- If the noble and powerful do not use their power to protect the people and administer affairs in accordance to moral virtues, but instead use their power to despotic ends;

– If the rich do not use their wealth to help the needy and the destitute, but instead lead luxuriating and indecent lifestyles;

– If the brave do not offer their service to protect the rulers and defend against invaders, but instead use their power to bully others and wage personal vendetta;

– If intelligent people do not use their insights to draw up government policies, but instead use their intelligence to commit unscrupulous acts and deceptions;

– If attractive people do not use their distinguished countenance to take the lead in governing the country, but instead use their good looks to seduce women and indulge in sexual misconducts;

– People with the aforementioned characters can be deemed to have absolutely lost their natural endowments."

Scroll 8: *Han Shi Wai Zhuan*

318. 动则三思，虑而后行，重慎出入，以往鉴来。言之若轻，成败甚重。

（卷二十六　魏志下）

【白话】一举一动都要反复思考后再行动，出入都要慎重（不放纵个人喜好），用过去的历史教训作为将来的借鉴。这些话说起来好像很轻松，但对于事业成败影响却很重大。

318. One needs to think carefully before moving into action. Whether to advance or to retreat, one should remain very cautious. Use lessons learned from the past as a guide for the future. These words may seem unimportant but they will play a big role in deciding success or failure.

Scroll 26: *Wei Zhi*, Vol. 2

319. 览往事之成败，察将来之吉凶，未有干名[①]要[②]利，欲而不厌[③]，而能保世[④]持家[⑤]，永全福禄者也。

（卷二十六　魏志下）

【注释】①干名：求取名位。干，求。②要：音 yāo／一幺，求取。③厌：通"餍"，满足。④保世：谓保持爵禄、宗族或王朝的世代相传。⑤持家：保持家业。

【白话】观察往事的成败，考察将来的吉凶，还没有追名逐利，贪婪而不知满足，却能保持家道世代相传并长久享有福禄的人。

319. Learn from the cases of success and failure from the past, and examine the good and ill aspects of the future. No one would succeed in keeping their family legacies and enjoying lasting prosperity if they are only after fame and wealth just to satisfy their endless greed.

Scroll 26: *Wei Zhi*, Vol.2

320. 周公曰："吾闻之于政也，知善不行者则谓之狂，知恶不改者则谓之惑。夫狂与惑者，圣王之戒也。"

（卷三十一　鬻子）

【白话】周公说："我听说关于为政方面的事，知道是好事而不施行的叫做狂，知道是恶行而不改正的叫做惑。狂与惑是圣王所戒除的。"

320. The Duke of Zhou said: "I have heard this about governing: Knowing something is good but not putting it into action is referred to as 'arrogance.' Knowing something is bad but not correcting it is referred to as 'in a state of doubts.' Arrogance and doubts are detrimental characters that a sage-ruler should always avoid adopting."

Scroll 31: *Yu Zi*

321. 昔桀纣灭由妖妇，幽厉乱在嬖妾①。先帝览②之，以为身戒，故左右不置淫邪之色，后房无旷积之女。

（卷二十八 吴志下）

【注释】①嬖妾：爱妾。②览：《三国志》通行本作“鉴”。

【白话】从前夏桀、商纣的灭亡是由于迷恋妖艳的妇人，周幽王、周厉王时发生动乱，是因为宠幸爱妾。先帝吸取这些教训，以此作为自身的借鉴，所以身边不安置淫邪的美色，后宫没有积聚多余的女子。

321. In the past, King Jie of the Xia dynasty and King Zhou of the Shang dynasty were both dethroned because they were obsessed with seductive women. King You and King Li of the Zhou dynasty plunged their kingdom into chaos when they spoiled themselves in the comfort of their favored consorts. With these lessons in mind, our ancient kings were cautious not to allow sensual figures to stay near them, nor have unnecessary ladies serving in the imperial chamber.

Scroll 28: *Wu Zhi*, Vol. 2

322. 天下有三危：少德而多宠，一危也；材下而位高，二危也；身无大功而有厚禄，三危也。

（卷四十一　淮南子）

【白话】天下有三种危险情况：缺少德行却倍受尊宠，是第一种危险；才能低下却地位高贵，是第二种危险；自身没有大功却享有优厚俸禄，是第三种危险。

322. There are three risky situations in this world:

1. Less than virtuous people are well-respected and favored;
2. Incompetent people are occupying high positions;
3. Unaccomplished people are enjoying handsome payoffs.

Such are the three risky situations.

Scroll 41: *Huai Nan Zi*

323. 夫与死人同病者,不可生也;与亡国同行者,不可存也。岂虚言哉?何以知人且病?以其不嗜食也。何以知国之将乱?以其不嗜贤也。

(卷四十四 潜夫论)

【白话】与死人患同一种病的人,不能活下来;与亡国之君行为相同的君主,其国家也不能长存。这难道是空话吗?怎么知道人将要生病呢?通过他不爱吃饭就可知晓。怎么知道国家将会动乱呢?通过君主不爱贤才就能看出。

323. A person will not survive if he suffers the same illness as that of a dead man. A country will not survive if its ruler behaves the same as all other deposed rulers. Do you think this does not make sense at all? How do we know that a person is ill? We know that when he has no appetite. How do we know that a country will end up in shambles? We know that when a ruler does not show respect toward the virtuous and able ministers.

Scroll 44: *Qian Fu Lun*

324. 国得百姓之力[①]者富，得百姓之死[②]者强，得百姓之誉者荣。三得（三得旧皆作三德，改之）者具，而天下归之；三得者亡，而天下去之。

（卷三十八　孙卿子）

【注释】①力：勤，尽力。②死：谓为某事或某人而牺牲性命。

【白话】国家若能得到百姓的效力就会富足，若能得到百姓拼命效死就会强盛，若能得到百姓的称誉就会荣耀。三者具备，那么天下的人民都将归顺；三者无一，那么天下的人民就会背离。

324. If a country has the full support of its people it will enjoy prosperity. If people are prepared to die defending the country's interest it will become strong; if a country is widely acclaimed by the people it is worthy of honor. If these three conditions are met, a country will earn the allegiance of all the people. Without these three conditions, the whole populace will turn its back on the country.

Scroll 38: *Sun Qing Zi*

325. 为雕文刻镂，技巧华饰，以伤农事，王者必禁之。

（卷三十一　六韬）

【白话】在器物上刻镂花纹图案、追求精巧的技能和华丽的装饰，而妨害农业，圣明的君主一定会严加禁止。

325. Carving glyptic motifs on the utensils and pursuing exquisite crafts and lavish costumes at the expense of agricultural development is something that a wise ruler would strictly forbid.

Scroll 31: *Liu Tao*

应事
Making Correct Response

326. 凡人之道，心欲小，志欲大，智欲圆，行欲方，能欲多，事欲少。

（卷三十五　文子）

【白话】大凡一个人的处世之道，内心要谨慎，志向要宏大，智虑要周到通达，行为要方正不苟，能力要多，事务要少。

326. In all your ways be discreet but hold on to a great ambition; be thoughtful and thorough, upright and conscientious, resourceful, and focus on only a few things at a time.

Scroll 35: *Wen Zi*

327. 溺者不问隧[1],迷者不问路。譬之犹临难而遽[2]铸兵,噎而遽掘井,虽速亦无及。

(卷三十三　晏子)

【注释】①隧:路,指涉水之路。②遽:音jù/ㄐㄩˋ。仓猝,匆忙。

【白话】被水淹的人事先没有探明涉水的路线,迷途的人事先没有问路。这就好比面临外敌入侵的危难时,才急急忙忙铸造兵器,吃饭噎着以后才急急忙忙去挖井,即使很快,也来不及了。

327. People have drowned because they did not bother to find out a shallower path to wade across the water, and people who lost their way did not bother to find out the directions. This is like casting military weapons out only when the enemies are approaching, or digging a well when we need water to flush down something that is choking us. Even though efforts could commence immediately, it would nevertheless be too late to rectify the impending situation.

Scroll 33: *Yan Zi*

328. 故举重越高者，不慢于药；爱赤子者，不慢于保；绝险[1]历远者，不慢于御。此得助则成，释助则废矣。

（卷三十七　慎子）

【注释】①绝险：越过险阻。

【白话】托负重物跨越高处的人，一定不敢忽视药物；疼爱婴儿的人，一定不敢怠慢保姆；越过险阻游历远方的人，一定不敢怠慢驾御车马的人。这是因为得到帮助才能成功，失去帮助就会失败。

328. Those who journey across high terrains would not forget to bring along medical supplies. Those who love their newborn babies dare not neglect their nannies. Those who need to travel far through rugged terrains dare not neglect their drivers. Getting help from others enables us to achieve success. Without them, we would not succeed.

Scroll 37: *Shen Zi*

329. 圣人居高处上，则以仁义为巢①；乘危履倾，则以圣贤为杖。故高而不坠，危而不仆②。

（卷四十　新语）

【注释】①巢：居所。②仆：向前跌倒。

【白话】圣人身处高位，就以道德仁义作为自己安身的居所；面临险境危难，就把圣贤之人作为自己依靠的拄杖。所以圣人身居高位不会坠落，身临险境也不会跌倒。

329. Virtuous people holding high positions in the government regarded benevolence as the pillars of their conduct. In times of difficulty and crisis they would emulate the meritorious conduct of the sages. This is why virtuous people who hold high positions would not fall from grace, nor would they fall from power in times of crisis.

Scroll 40: *Xin Yu*

330. 夫圣人之屈者以求申也，枉者以求直也。故虽出邪僻之道，行幽昧之涂，将欲以兴大道成大功，犹出林之中，不得直道，拯溺之人，不得不濡①足。

（卷四十一　淮南子）

【注释】①濡：音 rú/ㄖㄨˊ。浸渍，沾湿。

【白话】圣人委屈自己，是为了日后道义的伸展；暂时的弯曲，是追求日后的挺直。所以他虽然从邪僻不直的道路上出发，而走在昏暗不明的路上，是要由此振兴大道、成就大业，就好比要走出丛林就不可能只走笔直的道路，要拯救溺水的人就不能不沾湿双脚一样。

330. A sage will endure humiliation for the sake of spreading justice in the future, and a temporary detour has to be taken so that another straightened road could be reached later. He may have taken a crooked path or a darkened route, but it is all for the sake of reviving the Great Way, so that bigger accomplishments can be achieved in the future. No one can walk out of a forest

by using only a straightened path or rescue a drowning person without getting both his legs wet.

Scroll 41: *Huai Nan Zi*

331. 地广而不德者国危，兵强而凌敌者身亡。虎兕[1]相搏，而蝼蚁得志；两敌相机，而匹夫乘闲。是以圣王见利虑害，见远存近。

（卷四十二　盐铁论）

【注释】①兕：音 sì／ㄙˋ。古代兽名。一说兕就是雌犀。

【白话】土地广阔而不实行德政，国家就会有危险；兵力强大而侵犯他国，自身就会灭亡。猛虎和兕相互搏斗，蝼蛄和蚂蚁就会得志；两个对手相互抗争，平庸之辈就会有机可乘。因此，圣明的君主，看到有利的一面，还会考虑有害的一面；既会考虑未来，也会注意眼前的形势。

331. A vast territory without a good government will place the country in danger. A powerful army that invades other countries will meet with its demise. When ferocious tigers fight among themselves, mole crickets and ants will emerge as the eventual winners. So an

unaccomplished third party would triumph when two competitive parties are involved in bitter rivalries. Hence a brilliant ruler would observe the positive side of any action and weigh the risks and dangers involved. He will be well prepared for the future besides being alert of the present situation.

Scroll 42: *Yan Tie Lun*

332. 服一彩[①]，则念女功之劳；御[②]一谷，则恤农夫之勤；决不听之狱[③]，则惧刑之不中；进一士之爵，则恐官之失贤；赏毫牦之善，必有所劝[④]；罚纤芥之恶，必有所沮[⑤]。

（卷四十七　政要论）

【注释】①彩：光色；花纹。②御：进食；食用。③不听之狱：没有定罪的案子。不听，不定罪。④劝：勉励。⑤沮：阻止；终止。

【白话】穿上一件彩服，就想到织女的辛劳；吃一粒米，就体恤农夫劳作的不易；判决一件还没有定罪的案子，就担心用刑是否适当；晋升一个爵位，就思考自己是否用人失贤；对一个极小善举的赏赐，一定要能起到劝勉人们向善的作用；对一个极微恶行进行处罚，也一定要起到警戒世人不敢作恶的功效。

332. When one puts on a bright and colorful silk garment, he should appreciate the hard work done by the female weavers. When one eats a grain of rice, he should appreciate the hard work of the farmers. Before deciding on the sentence of a prosecution case, be wary of whether the sentence given fits the crime. When awarding a promotion, beware if any worthy individuals have been left out. Every reward given to even a small act of kindness must inspire people to become better persons. Every punishment given to even a small crime must serve as a grave warning to the people not to commit wrongdoings.

Scroll 47: *Zheng Yao Lun*

慎始终
Exercising Caution from the Beginning to the End

333. 事者难成而易败也，名者难立而易废也。千里之堤，以蝼蚁之穴漏；百寻①之屋，以突②隙之烟焚。突，灶突也。

（卷四十一　淮南子）

【注释】①百寻：形容极高或极长。寻，古制八尺为一寻。②突：烟囱。

【白话】事情不易成就却容易失败，名声不易树立却容易摧毁。千里大堤，会因蝼蚁之穴而发生渗漏；百寻高楼，会因烟囱缝隙冒出的火星而焚毁。

333. It is not always easy to accomplish a task, and failures are not uncommon. Reputations are difficult to establish but can be easily brought down. An imposing thousand-mile-long embankment will leak because of some small holes bored by mole crickets and ants, and a tall mansion can be burnt down by a few sparks of fire from the chimney.

Scroll 41: *Huai Nan Zi*

334. 慎厥终，惟其始。靡不有初，鲜克有终。故戒慎终如其始也。殖①有礼，覆昏暴。有礼者封殖之。昏暴者覆亡之。钦②崇天道，永保天命。王者如此上事。则敬天安命之道也。

（卷二　尚书）

【注释】①殖：树立。引申为扶植势力；培养人才。②钦：敬。

【白话】慎重地结束一件事要如开始时一样战战兢兢。对符合礼义的事情大为扶持，对昏乱凶恶的事要严惩禁绝。敬奉上天的意志，才可永保上天赋予的使命。

334. Start and finish a project with the same degree of caution. Support causes that comply with propriety and punish immoral and violent criminals severely. Only by respecting the will of heaven can one implement the mission entrusted by heaven.

Scroll 2: *Shang Shu*

335. 无安厥位，惟危。言当常自危惧。以保其位也。慎终于始。于始虑终。于终虑始。

（卷二　尚书）

【白话】不要自安于天子之位，要想到其危险。慎重地考虑到后果，从开头就要小心谨慎啊！

335. Do not for one moment think that the throne will shield a ruler from danger, but be mindful of the danger that this position will bring. Thorough and cautious plannings must be done right from the beginning.

Scroll 2: *Shang Shu*

336. 能长保国者，能终善者也。诸侯并立，能终善者为长；列士并立，能终善者为师。

（卷三十三　晏子）

【白话】能够保持国家长久者，是能自始至终行善政的人。诸侯并立于世，自始至终能行善政者可为首领；众多士人并立于朝，自始至终能行善事者可以为师。

336. A virtuous ruler is one who can reign long and prosperous by running an ethical government from the beginning till the end. Among the lords who are equal in status, the one who can administer an ethical government will emerge as the leader. Among all the ministers in the imperial palace, the one who can maintain virtuous practices from the beginning till the end will emerge as the teacher.

Scroll 33: *Yan Zi*

337. 劳谦君子，有终，吉。劳谦匪懈。是以吉也。

（卷一　周易）

【白话】有功劳而且懂得谦虚的君子，能够保持谦德至终，凡事都会吉利。

337. A man of noble character (*Junzi*) makes great contributions, and yet he remains humble. He will maintain this virtue until the end and enjoy good fortune along the way.

Scroll 1: *Zhou Yi*

养生
Maintaining Good Health

338. 目之所好，不可从也；耳之所乐，不可不慎（本书不慎作顺一字）也；鼻之所喜，不可任也；口之所嗜，不可随也；心之所欲，不可恣也。故惑目者，必逸容①鲜藻②也；惑耳者，必妍音淫声也；惑鼻者，必芷蕙③芬馥④也；惑口者，必珍羞⑤嘉旨⑥也；惑心者，必势利功名也。五者毕惑，则或承之祸，为身患者，不亦信哉？是以其抑情也，剧乎堤防之备决；其御性也，过乎腐辔⑦之乘奔。故能内保永年，外免衅⑧累也。

（卷五十　抱朴子）

【注释】①逸容：犹美貌。②鲜藻：华丽的装饰。③芷蕙：皆香草名。《抱朴子》通行本作“茝蕙”，茝亦香草名。④芬馥：香气浓郁。⑤珍羞：亦作“珍馐”，珍美的肴馔。⑥嘉旨：指美酒佳肴。⑦辔：音 pèi／ㄆㄟˋ。驾驭马的缰绳。⑧衅：音 xìn／ㄒㄧㄣˋ。罪过；过失。

【白话】眼所喜欢看的，不可依从；耳所喜欢听的，不可顺应；鼻所喜欢闻的，不可放任；口所喜欢吃的，不可随顺；心所贪求的，不可恣意放肆。所以迷惑眼睛的，必是美貌华饰；迷惑耳朵的，必是艳歌俗曲、靡靡之音；迷惑鼻子的，必是芬芳馥郁的香味；迷惑口舌的，必是珍馐佳肴；迷惑心灵的，必是权势利禄与功名。五者全都被迷惑，就可能要遭遇灾祸、危害生命，这不是确信无疑的吗？因此他们抑制自己的欲望，比预防堤防崩溃还更认真严肃；他们制约自己的秉性，比用腐朽的绳索套着奔马还更小心翼翼。所以内则能保持长寿，外则免除世上的祸患。

338. What the eyes love to see do not follow; what the ears love to hear do not comply; what the nose loves to smell do not indulge; what the mouth loves to taste do not pursue; what the heart desires do not gratify. That which can enchant the eyes are beauty and splendors; that which can enchant the ears are sensual songs and decadent music; that which can enchant the nose are sweet smelling fragrance; that which can enchant the mouth are exotic food and delicacies; that which can enchant the heart are power, money and position. When all the five senses are enchanted, one will most likely confront disasters and life threatening danger. Do you

not believe in this? Thus there are people who would restrain their desires more seriously than they would prevent a dike from collapsing; and there are people who would control their characters more vigilantly than they would use a rotten rein to control a galloping horse. On a personal level this approach will secure a longer lifespan for an individual, and on a social level this approach will protect a person from misfortune.

Scroll 50: *Bao Pu Zi*

339. 夫酒醴之近味，生病之毒物，无豪锋之细益，有丘山之巨损。

（卷五十　抱朴子）

【白话】酒类近似于美味，却都是致病的毒药，无丝毫的好处，却有像山一样大的损害。

339. Although alcoholic drinks are enticing they are nevertheless illness-inducing toxics. They are not beneficial to health and the damages they cause are as enormous as a mountain.

Scroll 50: *Bao Pu Zi*

明辨 Chapter Six

DISCERNING

邪正
Good or Evil

340. 夫邪正之人，不宜共国①，亦犹冰炭不可同器。

（卷二十三　后汉书三）

【注释】①共国：同治国事。

【白话】邪恶与正义的人，是不适合共理国事的，就好比冰和炭不能放在同一个容器中一样。

340. Wicked men and righteous men cannot work together to govern a country, just like ice and charcoal cannot be placed in the same container.

Scroll 23: *Hou Han Shu*, Vol. 3

341. 君子非义（义上有仁字，下同）无以生，失义则失其所以生；小人非嗜欲无以活，失嗜欲则失其所以活。故君子惧失义，小人惧失利。观其所惧，知居（居作各）殊矣。

（卷四十一　淮南子）

【白话】君子若没有仁义就不能生存，失去仁义就等于失去生存的基础；小人若没有嗜欲就不能生活，失掉嗜欲也就失去了他生活的依托。所以君子担心失去仁义，而小人害怕失去利益。观察他们所担心的，就能看出君子与小人的不同。

341. A man of noble character (*Junzi*) cannot live without honor[30]; losing it would be like losing the fundamental reason to live. A scoundrel cannot live without desires; losing them would be like losing the means to survive. Thus, a *Junzi* worries about losing his benevolence and righteousness whereas a scoundrel worries about losing his benefits. By observing what they fear, we can discern the difference between a *Junzi* and a scoundrel.

Scroll 41: *Huai Nan Zi*

[30] For a *Junzi*, the notion of "honor" would contain characteristics of benevolence and righteousness.

人情
Human Sentiments

342. 自古有国有家者，咸欲修德政以比隆[①]盛世，至于其治，多不馨香。非无忠臣贤佐，闇于治体[②]也，由主不胜[③]其情，弗能用耳。夫人情惮难而趣[④]易，好同而恶异，与治道相反。

（卷二十七　吴志上）

【注释】①比隆：同等兴盛。②治体：治国的纲领、要旨。③不胜：制伏不住。④趣：趋向，归向。

【白话】自古以来有国的诸侯、有家的卿大夫，都想实施德政来达到与古代盛世同样的兴盛，但是他们治理的成果，大多都不美好。这不是因为没有忠诚贤明的辅臣，以及不懂得治国的要领，而是由于君主不能克制自己的私情，不能任用忠臣及遵从治国正道。人之常情总是害怕困难而趋向容易，喜好别人赞同而厌恶异议，这与治国之道刚好相反。

342. Since ancient times, feudal lords and ministers had wanted to achieve the glorious accomplishments of past dynasties by using virtuous administration. But the results were often not as ideal as they had expected. This was due not so much to the fact that they had no good ministers to assist them, or that they did not understand the important principles of governing; rather, the failings stemmed from a ruler's inability to control his personal feelings, and use faithful ministers to serve the country, or follow the right principles of governing. It is normal for people to prefer easy solutions over difficult ones. They love receiving compliments from others but dislike objections. These, in fact, contravene the principles of good rulership.

Scroll 27: *Wu Zhi*, Vol. 1

343. 夫小臣之欲忠其主也，知爱之而不能去其嫉妒之心，又安能敬有道，为己愿稷契之佐哉。

（卷四十七　刘廙政论）

【白话】那些小臣们想效忠他的君主，只知道偏爱君主，而不能去掉自己的嫉妒心理，又怎能恭敬有德有才之人，愿意自己成为稷、契这样的辅佐之臣呢？

343. If the ministers who pledge allegiance to their ruler could serve him with blind dedication but retain jealousy in their hearts, how can they respect and work with virtuous and able people and make themselves the equal of ministers Ji and Qi[31]?

Scroll 47: Liu Yi Zheng Lun

---

[31] Ji 稷 and Qi 契 helped emperors Yao 尧 and Shun 舜 to establish an agrarian economy and education system based on regulating relationships between parents and children, brothers and sisters, husband and wife, superiors and subordinates, and among friends, known collectively as the "five moral relationships".

才德
Talents and Virtues

344. 释道而任智者必危，弃数①而用材者必困。

（卷四十一　淮南子）

【注释】①数：道理；规律。

【白话】放弃大道而单凭自己的聪明行事一定会很危险，抛弃常理而任用才能必然会陷于困境。

344. People who are not bothered with moral values but rely solely on personal resourcefulness to do things will endanger themselves. Those who abandon the law of nature in exercising their talents will end up in a dilemma.

Scroll 41: *Huai Nan Zi*

345. 弓调而后求劲焉,马服而后求良焉,士必悫[①]而后求智能焉。不悫而多能,譬之豺狼,不可迩也。迩,近也。言人无智能者,虽不悫信,不能为大恶也,不悫信而有智能者,然后乃可畏也。

(卷十　孔子家语)

【注释】①悫:音 què / ㄑㄩㄝˋ。恭敬谨慎;朴实忠厚。

【白话】弓调好后才能进一步要求它有劲,马驯服后才能要求它成为良马,读书人一定要恭谨朴实,然后才要求他聪明能干。不恭谨忠厚而又多才多能,就像豺狼一样,不可以接近。

345. A bow has to be tuned before it can unleash its power; a horse has to be tamed before it can become a fine horse; a scholar has to learn to humble himself before he can become smart and capable. A disrespectful, insincere and capable person is like a cunning wolf that should be avoided.

Scroll 10: *Kong Zi Jia Yu*

朋党
Formation of Cliques

346. 夫乘权席[①]势之人，子弟鳞集[②]于朝，羽翼阴附者众。毁誉将必用，以终乖离之咎。

（卷十五　汉书三）

【注释】①席：凭借；倚仗。②鳞集：群集。

【白话】那些倚仗权势的人，他们的子弟群集于朝廷，左右党羽和私下依附的人非常之多。他们必定使用诋毁和赞誉的手段，最终因背离正道产生灾祸。

346. Those who count on powerful connections have their sons and nephews mustered in the imperial court. Forming factions on the left and right, they will have more than a few henchmen secretly assisting them under their wings. They like to use defamation and compliments in achieving their ambition but will eventually end up in disaster, as the righteous way is being compromised.

Scroll 15: *Han Shu*, Vol. 3

347. 若不笃于至行，而背本逐末，以陷浮华焉，以成朋党焉。浮华则有虚伪之累，朋党[1]则有彼此之患。

（卷二十六　魏志下）

【注释】①朋党：同类的人相互集结成党派，排除异己。

【白话】如果不专注于培养高尚的品行，而背离为人的根本（孝敬仁义），追逐枝末（功名富贵），就会陷入浮华虚荣，就会结帮成伙。追求浮华就会受虚伪所累而内心空虚不安，结成团伙则会有彼此牵连的祸患。

347. If we do not focus on cultivating noble conduct but instead abandon virtue in return for fame and glory, we will become arrogant and vain, and form factions to meet selfish ends. Vanity will blind us with hypocrisy and make it difficult for us to have peace of mind, while factionalism will directly involve everyone even if only one member is caught committing offenses.

Scroll 26: *Wei Zhi*, Vol. 2

辨物
Differences that Matter

348. 知人者智，能知人好恶是智。自知者明。人能自知贤不肖，是为反听无声，内视无形，故为明也。胜人者有力，能胜人者，不过以威力也。自胜者强。人能自胜己情欲，则天下无有能与己争者，故为强也。知足者富，人能知之为（无之为二字）足，则保福禄，故为富也。强行①者则有志。人能强力行善，则为有意于道。不失其所者久，人能自节养，不失其所（所下有受天二字），则可以久也。死而不妄者寿。目不妄视，耳不妄听，口不妄语，则无怨恶于天下，故长寿也。

（卷三十四　老子）

【注释】①强行：勤勉力行。

【白话】能够了解别人是有智慧，能够了解自己才算明白。能够战胜别人是有力量，能够战胜自己的欲望、习气才算强大。知足就是真正的富有，努力行善就是有志。所作所为不离开自己本性的才能持久，身死而精神长存的才是真正的长寿。

348. Understanding others is wisdom. Understanding ourselves is enlightenment. To conquer others is power; to conquer ourselves is deemed formidable. One who knows contentment is wealthy; one who strives to perform kind deeds is purposeful. One who acts according to his innate kindness shall prevail. The physical self may die but the spiritual self lives on, and that is true longevity.

Scroll 34: *Laozi*

349. 耳不听五声①之和为聋，目不别五色②之章③为昧，心不则德义之经为顽，口不道忠信之言为嚚④。

（卷四　春秋左氏传上）

【注释】①五声：指宫、商、角、徵、羽五音。②五色：青、赤、白、黑、黄五种颜色。古代以此五者为正色。③章：彩色；花纹。④嚚：音 yín / 一ㄣˊ。奸诈。

【白话】耳朵听不清五声的唱和是听觉失灵，眼睛辨不明五色的花纹是视觉模糊，心里不效法德义的准则是顽劣，嘴里不说忠信的话是奸诈。

349. Our hearing is impaired if we cannot distinguish the melody produced by the five tones[32], and our vision is blurred if our eyes cannot distinguish the five colors[33]. We are said to be stubborn if our mind refuses to follow the code of virtuous conduct. We are deemed a liar if we do not speak trustworthy words.

Scroll 4: *Chun Qiu Zuo Shi Zhuan*, Vol. 1

[32] Pentatonic scale
[33] The five colors are green, red, white, black and yellow.

350. 所谓为善者，静而无为也；所谓为不善者，躁而多欲也。

（卷四十一　淮南子）

【白话】所谓为善，就是心神宁静，顺应内在的善良本性和外在的发展形势，不任意妄为；所谓为不善，就是浮躁而多欲。

350. To practice what is kind is to attain a state of inner calmness, submitting to the innate kindness that lies within us, and complying with outer circumstances without resorting to acts of arrogance. Doing what is unkind is to be reckless and filled with endless desires.

Scroll 41: *Huai Nan Zi*

351. 有见人之私欲，必以正道矫之者，正人之徒也；违正而从之者，佞人之徒也。自察其心，斯知佞正之分矣。

（卷四十九　傅子）

【白话】看到别人有私欲，就用正确的思想去矫正的人，是正直之人；违背正直之道而顺从对方私欲者，是奸佞之徒。（君主）自己审察他们的内心，就知道佞人和正人的区别了。

351. Those who see the selfish motives of others and correct them with the right frame of mind are upright individuals. Those who compromise virtues to please the selfish motives of others are treacherous flatterers. If rulers could figure out what the people are thinking, they would be able to discriminate between upright and treacherous men.

Scroll 49: *Fu Zi*

352. 夫物之相类者，世主之所乱惑也；嫌疑[①]肖象者，众人之所眩耀[②]也。故狠[③]者类智，而非智也；狠，慢也。愚者类君子（君子作仁一字，下同），而非君子也；戆[④]者类勇，而非勇也。

（卷四十一　淮南子）

【注释】①嫌疑：疑惑难辨的事理。②眩耀：迷惑；迷乱。③狠：当作"狙"，本字为"怚"，骄傲。④戆：音 zhuàng / ㄓㄨㄤˋ。急躁而刚直。

【白话】彼此相似的事物，君王常被迷惑；彼此相像难以辨别的现象，大众常被迷乱。所以傲慢自恃的人看似有智慧，实际上不算智慧（而是独断）；愚钝的人看似宽厚仁慈，而实际上那不是仁慈（而是懦弱）；急躁刚直的人看似勇敢，而实际上那不是勇敢（而是鲁莽）。

352. Things that look alike can fool a ruler. Matters that appear no different from one another can fool the public. A haughty individual may appear wise but in fact he is not. A naive person may look kind and compassionate but in fact he is not. A reckless person may look courageous but in fact he is not.

Scroll 41: *Huai Nan Zi*

353. 使人大迷惑者，必物之相似者也。玉人①之所患，患石之似玉者；贤主之所患，患人博闻辩言而似通者。通，达。亡国之主似智，亡国之臣似忠。似之物，此愚者之所大惑，而圣人之所加虑也。思则知之。

（卷三十九　吕氏春秋）

【注释】①玉人：雕琢玉器的工人。

【白话】使人深受迷惑的，一定是相似的事物。玉匠所担心的，是与玉相似的石块；贤明的君主所担心的，是那些表面上见闻广博、能言善辩，很像是通达治国之道的人。使国家败亡的君主看似聪慧，使国家败亡的臣子看似忠诚。这些相似的事物，是愚者十分迷惑的，却是圣人多加思虑的。

353. Things that look similar can often confuse one's judgment. What a jade craftsman usually worries about is that he might mistake stones that look like jade for genuine jade, while what wise rulers worry about is that they might mistake an officer who appears

knowledgeable and eloquent for someone skillful in governing. A ruler who brings his country to ruin may look wise, while ministers who ruin a country may look honest and faithful. These similarities might confuse unwise people but not the sages who would remain watchful over them.

Scroll 39: *Lü Shi Chun Qiu*

354. 夫美（美疑业）大者深而难明，利长者不可以仓卒[①]形[②]也，故难明长利之事废于世。

（卷四十七　刘廙政论）

【注释】①仓卒：亦作“仓猝”，匆忙急迫，此处指短时间内。②形：流露；显示。

【白话】真正美好的谋略因为道理太深而难以阐明，真正长远的利益很难在短时间内显现，所以难于阐明而有长远利益的事往往就被世人废弃了。

354. It is not easy to clarify a strategic plan that has profound wisdom, and it is also difficult to foresee the long-term effects of something beneficial. Thus, long-term benefits that are hard to clarify are often ignored.

Scroll 47: *Liu Yi Zheng Lun*

355. 吾观其吏，暴虐残贼，败法乱刑而上下不觉，此亡国之时也。夫上好货①，群臣好得，而贤者逃伏②，其乱至矣。

（卷三十一　六韬）

【注释】①好货：贪爱财物。货，财物，金钱珠玉布帛的总称。②逃伏：逃亡隐匿。

【白话】我观察他的官吏，凶狠残忍，败坏法纪，乱施刑罚，而君臣上下还执迷不悟，这是该亡国的时候了。君主贪爱财物，群臣贪得利益，而贤者纷纷逃避隐藏，国家的混乱已经到了。

355. "I observed the behavior of his officials and found that they were cruel and brutal. They violated the legal procedures and imposed punishments indiscriminately. If the rulers and ministers remain oblivious to this madness, it is time for this administration to come to an end. As rulers are greedy for material wealth and officials are greedy for profits, men of virtues will go into hiding. This phenomenon signifies that the country will soon be overcome by chaos and disorder."

Scroll 31: *Liu Tao*

因果
Cause and Effect

356. 山致其高，而云雨起焉。水致其深，而蛟龙生焉。君子致其道，而德泽流焉。夫有阴德①者，必有阳报②。有隐行③者，必有昭名。

（卷三十五　文子）

【注释】①阴德：暗中做的有德于人的事。②阳报：显明的报应。③隐行：犹阴德，谓不为人知的美行。

【白话】山达到了一定的高度，就会兴起云雨。水达到了一定的深度，就会有蛟龙出没。君子达到了高尚的道德修养，其仁德恩惠就会流布四方。暗中施恩于人的人，一定会得到明显的回报。有人所不知的高尚品行的人，日后一定会有显著的名声。

356. When mountains surpass a certain level of height, clouds and rain will hover over them. When water runs deep, the rain dragon will roam about. When a man of noble character (*Junzi*) has achieved high attainments in his cultivation, his benevolence and compassion will spread to the four corners of the world. Those who do kind deeds unassumingly will reap apparent rewards, and those who have hidden virtues will enjoy remarkable reputation over time.

Scroll 35: *Wen Zi*

357. 盖德厚者报美，怨大者祸深。故曰，德莫大于仁，而祸莫大于刻。

（卷四十二　新序）

【白话】道德深厚的人一定会获得吉祥美好的回报，与人结怨太多的人，一定会招来深重的祸患。所以说，没有比仁慈更大的美德，没有比苛刻更大的祸患。

357. People who are virtuous will be blessed with good and auspicious fortune. People who made enemies with others will suffer untold consequences. Thus, no other virtues can replace benevolence, and no other misfortunes can be worse than ruthlessness.

Scroll 42: *Xin Xu*

358. 诗曰："下民之孽①，匪降自天。僔遝②背憎③，职竞④由人。"

（卷四　春秋左氏传上）

【注释】①孽：灾害，灾祸。②僔遝：音 zǔn tà / ㄗㄨㄣˇ ㄊㄚˋ。谓相聚面语。僔，聚。遝，通"沓"。纷多聚积。③背憎：谓背地里憎恨。④职竞：职，只。竞，争。后遂以"职竞"用为专事竞逐之意。.

【白话】《诗经》上说："百姓遭受的灾难，不是老天降下的。当面说说笑笑，背后憎恨攻击，这完全是人们互相争斗造成的。"

358. According to the book of *Shi Jing*: "The disasters suffered by the civilians were not cast upon them from heaven. People might talk pleasantly in front of each other, but behind their backs, they tried all means to bring down one another due to resentment. Thus mutual rivalries were the major cause of all disasters."

Scroll 4: *Chun Qiu Zuo Shi Zhuan*, Vol. 1

359. 和气致祥，乖气[1]致异。祥多者其国安，异[2]众者其国危。

（卷十五　汉书三）

【注释】①乖气：邪恶之气；不祥之气。②异：怪异不祥之事；灾异。

【白话】贤臣在位齐心效力的和谐气氛感召吉祥，奸臣当道排挤忠良的不和气氛招致灾异。祥瑞多国家就安定，灾异多国家就危难。

359. When wise and competent ministers work together, harmony will prevail, leaving an air of auspiciousness. When treacherous officials are in power, abnormal phenomena will prevail, courting calamities to strike. When auspiciousness is prolonged, the nation will enjoy peace and stability. When too many strange disasters continue to strike, the fate of the nation will be at stake.

Scroll 15: *Han Shu*, Vol. 3

360. 及至后世，淫泆衰微，诸侯背叛，废德教而任刑罚。刑罚不中[①]，则生邪气，邪气积于下，怨恶蓄于上，上下不和，阴阳缪戾[②]，而妖孽[③]生矣。此灾异所缘而起也。

（卷十七　汉书五）

【注释】①不中：不适合，不适当。②缪戾：错乱，违背。③妖孽：指物类反常的现象，不祥之兆。

【白话】到了后世，君王恣意逸乐，王道衰败，诸侯背叛，废弃道德教化而任用刑罚。刑罚使用不恰当，就会产生邪恶不良的风气，邪恶风气聚集于下，怨恨憎恶蓄积于上，上下不和，阴阳错乱，那么怪异凶恶的事物或预兆就会产生。这就是天灾人祸发生的原因。

360. Toward the end of any declining dynasty, the rulers indulged in licentious pleasures and degraded the Way of the sage-rulers. The lords revolted, neglected moral teachings and abused corporal punishment. If punishment was not fair, social ills would arise and cause immoral practices to gather momentum, while hostilities and hatred accumulated over time and there were mass discords between the upper and lower societies. The balance of the *Yin* and *Yang* energies was disrupted and a lot of abnormal and menacing phenomena would appear as a result. These are, in fact, the causes and effects of natural and man-made disasters.

Scroll 17: *Han Shu*, Vol. 5

*Glossary**

Bao Pu Zi

Bao Pu Zi 抱朴子 was written in the Eastern Jin dynasty (317 – 420) by Ge Hong 葛洪. He was a believer of Daoism and a medical specialist, and practiced the skill of making pills for immortality.

Chang Yan

Chang Yan 昌言 contains the frank and open advice given by Zhongchangzi 仲长子. Zhongchangzi promotes propriety, righteousness, integrity and moral shame. He advises rulers to deploy able and virtuous people and advocates the adherence to strict laws. The book, which is also known as 仲长子昌言 (*The Frank Advice of Zhong Chang Zi*), mainly discusses how a ruler can rule a country properly. This entire book was still preserved during the Song dynasty (960 – 1279), but now it no longer exists in its entirety.

Chun Qiu Zuo Shi Zhuan

Chun Qiu Zuo Shi Zhuan 春秋左氏传 (*Commentary of Zuo on the Spring and Autumn Annals*) or *Zuo Zhuan* 左传 is sometimes known as the *Chronicle of Zuo*. It is among the earliest Chinese works of narrative history and covers the period from 770 – 476 BC. It is one of the three commentaries to the *Spring and Autumn Annals*. *Zuo Zhuan* was traditionally attributed to Zuo Qiuming 左丘明 from Lu (state) at the end of the Spring and Autumn period** (770 – 476 BC), but the actual compiling time was the mid-Warring States period (475 – 221 BC).

Dian Yu

The author of *Dian Yu* 典语 (*Political Discourse*) is Lu Jing 陆景 (250 – 281). Lu Jing lived for only thirty-one years but he wrote many books, all of which were lost except *Dian Yu*. This book discusses politics and stresses on paying high salaries to government officials to eradicate corruption.

**The references are primarily from wikipedia.org, chinaculture.org, and chinaknowledge.org websites, and Lu et al., Qunshu Zhiyao Kaoyi.*

**The Spring and Autumn Period starts from 770 BC when King Ping of Zhou 周平王 moved the capital of Zhou dynasty east from Haojing 镐京 to Luoyi 洛邑 and ends at 476 BC when the States of Han 韩国, Wei 魏国 and Zhao 赵国 divided the Jin 晋国 territory between themselves (known as the "Three Jin Territories" or "The Partition of the Jin State", the watershed between the Spring and Autumn and Warring States period.)

Fu Zi

Fu Zi 傅子 was written by Fu Xuan 傅玄, who was from the Western Jin dynasty (265 - 317). His book mentions that nature goes according to the flow of *Qi* 气. Generally, Fu Xuan criticizes the existence of gods and mysteries. He proposes that the majority of the people should become farmers rather than scholars, businessmen, and laborers.

Guan Zi

Guan Zi 管子 discusses Legalism, Confucianism, Daoism, as well as military and agricultural aspects. Its abundance of historical information brings about great research value. It is said that the book was produced by Guan Zhong 管仲, who lived in the Spring and Autumn period (770 - 476 BC). However, the existing *Guan Zi*, which was compiled by Liu Xiang 刘向 of the Western Han dynasty (206 BC - 9 AD), only has seventy-six remaining chapters. Its contents are classified into eight categories.

Han Shi Wai Zhuan

Han Shi Wai Zhuan 韩诗外传 is sometimes translated as *Illustrations of the Didactic Application of the Classic of Songs* by Han Ying 韩婴. It is a commentary and complement to the *Shi Jing* 诗经 (*Book of Odes*) by Han Ying.

Han Shu

Han Shu 汉书 is sometimes translated as the *History of the [Former] Han Dynasty* or *Book of Han*. It offers a detailed history of the Western Han dynasty (206 BC - 9 AD), and biographies of many individual figures help to supplement the historical facts. *Han Shu* has 100 chapters. The author, Ban Gu 班固, started to write *Han Shu* based on *Hou Zhuan* 后传 *(Later Traditions*) written by his father Ban Biao 班彪, but Ban Gu died and left the book unfinished in 92 AD. Ban Gu's sister Ban Zhao 班昭 continued working on it. It is regarded as one of the *Four Histories*四史 of the *Twenty-Four Histories* 二十四史 canon.

Han Zi

Han Zi 韩子 is also known as *Han Fei Zi* 韩非子. It is the work of Han Fei 韩非 (280 - 233 BC), who was a great master of the Legalist school during the Warring States period (475 - 221 BC), and was the disciple of Xunzi 荀子. Han Fei inherited the theory from his teacher Xunzi, which says human nature is evil, and proposed to govern a country with punishment and reward.

Hou Han Shu

Hou Han Shu 后汉书 , which is also translated as *History of the Later Han Dynasty* or *Book of the Later Han*, is a second work after *Han Shu*. The book covers the history of the Eastern Han period (25 – 220), and was compiled in the 5th century by Fan Ye 范晔 (398 – 445). Like the *Han Shu*, *Hou Han Shu* is part of the early four historiographies of the *Twenty-Four Histories* canon.

Huai Nan Zi

Huai Nan Zi 淮南子 was compiled by Western Han dynasty's (206 BC – 9 AD) Liu An 刘安 and some of the people who visited and stayed with him. It is also known as *Huai Nan Hong Lie* 淮南鸿烈 . The writings exemplify Daoist thinking of the highest level, although it should be noted that the book also combines Confucianism, Legalist thinking, ideas of Yin and Yang, as well as the Five Elements. It also records many legends and fairytales.

Jin Shu

Jin Shu 晋书 is one of the official Chinese historical works. It covers the history of the Jin dynasty from 265 to 420. It was written by a number of officials who were commissioned by the court of the Tang dynasty (618 – 907). The lead editor was the prime minister Fang Xuanling 房玄龄 . *Jin Shu* draws mostly from the official documents in earlier archives. The book also includes the history of the Sixteen Kingdoms which were contemporaneous with Eastern Jin (317 – 420). Several essays in the biographical volume were composed by Emperor Taizong of the Tang dynasty.

Kong Zi Jia Yu

Kong Zi Jia Yu 孔子家语 is sometimes known as the *Familiar Discourses of Confucius*. It is a book of famous sayings by Confucius compiled by Wang Su 王肃 .

Lao Zi

Lao Zi 老子 (also known as *Dao De Jing* 道德经) is a Daoist philosophical work written in verse. The book has 81 chapters and is divided into two parts, namely *Dao* (the Way) and *De* (virtues). It is regarded as the greatest classic of Daoism.

Li Ji

Li Ji 礼记 is variously translated as the *Record of Rites*, *Classic of Rites*, *Book of Rites*, or *Book of Customs*. It was one of the *Wu Jing* 五经 (*Five Classics*). It describes the social forms, governmental system, and ancient/ceremonial rites of the Zhou dynasty (1046 - 256 BC). The original text is believed to have been compiled by Confucius himself, but sadly, many Confucian classics (including this book) were destroyed during the rule of Qin Shi Huang 秦始皇 , the "First Emperor of Qin dynasty" (221 - 206 BC). Hence, the edition usually referred to today was edited and reworked by various scholars during the Han dynasty (206 BC - 220 AD), including Dai De 戴德 (also called Senior Dai), who reworked the text in the 1st Century BC, and his younger brother Dai Sheng 戴圣 (Junior Dai). The *Record of Rites* known today is attributed to Dai Sheng.

Lie Zi

Lie Zi 列子 is an eight-volume book based on the compilation of ideas from many books. *Lie Zi* discusses politics, economics, military matters, philosophy, customs, and the natural sciences.

Liu Tao

Liu Tao 六韬, or the *Six Strategies*, is a famous book on the art of war in ancient China. It consists of 6 chapters and 60 articles in total, and it is the longest work on military strategies during the pre-Qin days (before 221 BC). After the Western Han dynasty (206 BC–9 AD), *Liu Tao* began to spread widely. After the Tang dynasty (618–907), militarists often quoted from *Liu Tao*. It was regarded as the indispensable book for militarists in the Song dynasty (960–1279).

Liu Yi Zheng Lun

Liu Yi Zheng Lun 刘廙政论 can be translated as *Political Treatise by Liu Yi*. This five scroll book only has eight chapters left at present.

Lü Shi Chun Qiu

Lü Shi Chun Qiu 吕氏春秋 , also known as *Spring and Autumn Annals of Premier Lü Bu Wei*, is an encyclopedic Chinese classic compiled around 239 BC under the patronage of Chancellor Lü Buwei 吕不韦 of the Qin dynasty (221 - 206 BC). Its content is wide-ranging and includes Confucianism, Daoism, as well as musical, military and agricultural aspects. It is an important reference for the research on the history of the early state of Qin. It is known for its collection of anecdotes.

Lun Yu

Lun Yu 论语 (*Analects of Confucius*) was written by the disciples of Confucius during the Spring and Autumn period through to the Warring States period (475 - 221 BC). The *Analects* records the words and acts of Confucius and his disciples as well as the discussions they held. It offers the essential material for studying Confucianism. The chapters in the *Analects* are grouped by individual themes.

Mao Shi

Mao Shi 毛诗 (*Classic of Poetry — Mao's Edition*), is also called *Shi Jing* 诗经 or the *Classic of Poetry*, *Book of Songs*, *Book of Odes*, or sometimes known simply by its original name, *The Odes*. It is the earliest existing collection of Chinese poems and songs. It comprises 305 poems and songs, with many ranging from 10–7 BC. As with all great literary works of ancient China, *Shi Jing* has been annotated and commented on numerous times throughout history. The annotations by the Han dynasty (206 BC–220 AD) scholar Mao Heng 毛亨 and his nephew Mao Chang 毛苌 are most wellknown and are considered authoritative.

Meng Zi

The main content of *Meng Zi* 孟子 (*Book of Mencius*) is the sayings of Mengzi or Mencius 孟子 and his disciples. Mencius proposed a theory of virtuous benevolence. He believes that humans are born with four moral characters: benevolence, righteousness, propriety, and wisdom. Humans would lose these moral characters if they did not maintain or develop them through practice. Hence, he insists that people pay attention to inner cultivation. Mencius proposed to engage benevolence to gain the allegiance of other countries instead of war.

Mo Zi

Mozi 墨子 was the founder of the Mohist School. He lived in the state of Lu 鲁国, between the late Spring and Autumn period (770 - 476 BC) and the Warring States period (475 - 221 BC). Mozi thinks that Confucianism centers too much on proprieties. He believes in serving the interests of others by greatly sacrificing oneself. Further, he opposes invasion and war. The book *Mo Zi* is a philosophical text compiled by Mohists based on Mozi's thoughts.

Qian Fu Lun

Qian Fu Lun 潜夫论 (*Comments of a Recluse*) was written by Wang Fu 王符 during the Eastern Han dynasty (25 - 220). The work was named as such to hide his identity from the public. Wang Fu criticized the contemporary government and revealed the misconduct of government officials, including their extravagance and oppression of the people.

San Lüe

San Lüe 三略 (*Three Strategies*) is divided into three parts: *Shang Lüe* 上略, *Zhong Lüe* 中略, and *Xia Lüe* 下略. The first two parts quote from military writings of the past, *Jun Chen* 军谶 (*Military Prophecies*) and *Jun Shi* 军势 (*Military Power*) and elaborates them, while the third part is the author's own discussion. Some attribute the work to Huang Shigong 黄石公, but in recent research, it is said that this book was written by an anonymous person between the Qin dynasty (221 - 206 BC) and Han dynasty (206 BC - 220 AD).

Shang Shu

Shang Shu 尚书 (*Classic of History*) or *Shu Jing* 书经 is a compilation of documentary records related to events in ancient Chinese history. Other translated titles of the book include *Classic of Documents*, *Book of History*, or *Book of Documents*.

Shen Jian

Shen Jian 申鉴 (*Mirrors of the Past, Lessons for the Future*) was written by Xun Yue 荀悦. Xun Yue was a politician and historian from the late Eastern Han dynasty (25 - 220) who advocated Confucianism. The book *Shen Jian*, which is divided into five chapters, uses historical examples as advice on how to rule a country. It emphasizes benevolence and righteousness as the moral foundation of human beings.

Shen Zi

Shen Zi 慎子 is a legalist text by Shen Dao 慎到 (395 - 315 BC) from the Warring States period (475 - 221 BC). Shen Dao believes in the use of law to govern a country.

Shi Ji

Shi Ji 史记 (*Records of History or Records of the Grand Historian*), written from 109 - 91 BC, was the Magnum opus of Sima Qian 司马迁. Sima Qian recounted Chinese history from the time of the Emperor Huang (2600 BC) until Sima Qian's own time, the Western Han dynasty (206 BC – 9 AD) under the reign of Emperor Wu of Han dynasty 汉武帝 . It covers more than 3,000 years of Chinese history, and is divided into 130 scrolls. When compiling this book, Sima Qian consulted a wealth of literatures as well as archives and ancient books written by ordinary people. Interviews and field investigations were also employed to ensure the accuracy of the content. As the first systematic text on the history of ancient China, *Shi Ji* profoundly influenced Chinese historiography and prose.

Shi Zi

The book *Shi Zi* 尸子 was authored by Shi Jiao 尸佼 (390 – 330 BC) who lived in the state of Jin during the Warring States period (475 – 221 BC). Legend says that he was the teacher of Shang Yang 商鞅 .

Shu Zhi

San Guo Zhi 三国志 (*Records of the Three Kingdoms*) is a sixty-five volume historical record on the three kingdoms of Wei, Shu and Wu (220 – 265). *San Guo Zhi* is divided into three books, and *Shu Zhi* 蜀志 (*Book of Shu* or *Collected Biographies of the Kingdom of Shu*) is one of them. *Shu Zhi* contains 15 volumes. *San Guo Zhi* records the important figures of that period. The histories of the ethnic minorities in China and those of the neighboring countries are also included. It was written mainly as a series of biographies by Chen Shou 陈寿 during the Jin dynasty, (265 – 420) and was annotated by Pei Song Zhi 裴松之 in Song (state) of the Southern dynasty (420 – 589).

Shuo Yuan

Shuo Yuan 说苑 (*The Garden of Stories*) was written by Liu Xiang 刘向 during the Western Han dynasty (206 BC – 9 AD). It contains anecdotes from the ancient Qin dynasty (221 – 206 BC) to the Han dynasty (206 BC – 220 AD), with arguments to publicize political thoughts, ethics, and morality propounded by Confucianism.

Si Ma Fa

Si Ma Fa 司马法 (*The Methods of Sima*) is a book of military systems from ancient times. It summarizes the use of proprieties to manage the army during the Shang (1600 – 1046 BC) and Zhou dynasties (1046 – 256 BC).

Sun Qing Zi

Sun Qing Zi 孙卿子 was also known as Xun Kuang 荀况 or Xunzi 荀子 . He was a famous philosopher and educator from the state of Zhao during the late Warring States period (475 – 221 BC). The work *Sun Qing Zi* revolves around nature, understanding knowledge, logical thoughts, ethical management, and how to rule a country.

Sun Zi

Sun Zi 孙子 or *Sun Zi Bing Fa* 孙子兵法 (*Sun Zi's Art of War*) is the world' s earliest military book extant in China. After the Song dynasty (960 – 1279), it was listed as the first book of the *Seven Military Classics*. This book was written by Sun Wu 孙武 at the end of the Spring and Autumn period (770–476 BC). It has thirteen articles in total.

Ti Lun

Ti Lun 体论 (*A Discourse on the Nature of Being*) was written by Du Shu 杜恕 . There are altogether eight chapters in this book. In *Ti Lun*, Du Shu describes how to use proprieties in the five moral relationships and in politics.

Wei Zhi

Wei Zhi 魏志 (*Book of Wei* or *Collected Biographies of the Kingdom of Wei*) is from *San Guo Zhi* 三国志 (*Records of the Three Kingdoms*). *Wei Zhi* consists of thirty volumes.

Wen Zi

Wen Zi 文子 has twelve volumes and elucidates the doctrine of Daoism. This book is believed to be written around the middle to late Warring States period (475 – 221 BC).

Wu Yue Chun Qiu

Wu Yue Chun Qiu 吴越春秋 (*Spring and Autumn Annals of Wu and Yue*) is a historical record of the states of Wu and Yue during the Spring and Autumn period (770 – 476 BC), and is attributed to Zhao Ye 赵晔 .

Wu Zhi

Wu Zhi 吴志 (*Book of Wu* or *Collected Biographies of the Kingdom of Wu*), is also from *San Guo Zhi* 三国志 (*Records of the Three Kingdoms*). It consists of twenty volumes.

Wu Zi

Wu Zi 吴子 records the discussion of war strategies between the Senior General, Wu Qi 吴起 , and the Marquess Wen of Wei 魏文侯 and the Marquess Wu of Wei 魏武侯 .

Xiao Jing

Xiao Jing 孝经 (*Doctrine of Filial Piety*), is also known as the *Classic of Filial Piety*. It is a Confucian classic giving advice on filial piety. This document probably dates back to 400 BC. Its true authorship is unknown, although the work is often attributed to one of Confucius disciple named Zengzi 曾子, who recorded the conversations between his teacher Confucius and himself.

Xin Xu

*Xin X*u 新序 (*The New Order*) was written by Liu Xiang 刘向 . Its main theme revolves around a benevolent government, as propounded by Confucianists. Liu Xiang saw the Han dynasty (206 BC－220 AD) weakening, so he wrote *Xin Xu* to criticize the ruler and to offer advice to government officials. He mocked feudalism and voiced men's dissatisfaction with a feudal lord. As the focus is on pre-Qin (before 221 BC) experiences, the historical facts were not carefully verified. However, given the frequent use of fables, *Xin Xu* is of great literary value.

Xin Yu

The book *Xin Yu* 新语 (*New Commentaries*) was written by Lu Jia 陆贾 in the early Han dynasty. However, the title *Xin Yu* was not given by Lu Jia himself. This book shows Lu Jia's attempt to help the first emperor of the Han dynasty (206 BC－220 AD), Han Gaozu 汉高祖 , summarize the lessons learned from the Qin (221–206 BC) and Han dynasties. The book promotes the use of *Dao* to govern a country.

Yan Tie Lun

Yan Tie Lun 盐铁论 (*Discourse on Salt and Iron*) was written by Huan Kuan 桓宽 during the Western Han dynasty (206 BC－9 AD). This ten volume, sixty chapter book records the debates between the Han government and more than sixty virtuous scholars and intellectuals in Chang'an. The main debate was on the state monopole over salt and iron production and distribution in 81 BC, but issues of politics, economy, culture, and military matters were also brought up.

Yan Zi

The book *Yan Zi* 晏子 was written by Yan Ying 晏婴 from the Spring and Autumn period (770 – 476 BC). Yan Ying served as a government official for Duke Ling of the state of Qi 齐灵公 , Duke Zhuang of Qi 齐庄公 and Duke Jing of Qi 齐景公 . Yan Ying encourages the thrifty management of the government. He also believes in reducing punishment and taxes.

Yin Mou

Yin Mou 阴谋 (*Secret Strategies*) is a record of the questions and answers between Jiang Tai Gong 姜太公 and King Wu 周武王 of Zhou dynasty (1046 – 256 BC) with respect to the ways of ruling a country and educating its people.

Yin Wen Zi

Yin Wen Zi 尹文子 was written by Yin Wen 尹文 during the Warring States period (475 – 221 BC) is divided into two parts. This philosophical treatise mainly describes the principles of good politics. Yin Wen said: "If one cannot rule by the principles of *Dao*, then use the law. If laws do not work, use tactics. If tactics fail, use authority. Finally, if authority has no effect, use force/influence."

Yu Zi

The author of the book *Yu Zi* 鬻子 is uncertain. The book offers thorough knowledge of kind and compassionate governing of a country. The welfare of the people is considered as the priority. Also, *Dao* is promoted in *Yu Zi*.

Yuan Zi Zheng Shu

Yuan Zi Zheng Shu 袁子正书 was written by Yuan Zhun 袁准 . Yuan Zhun believes that one has to strike a balance between virtues and laws when ruling a country.

Zeng Zi

Zengzi 曾子 , also known as Zeng Sen 曾参 (505 – 436 BC) was a student of Confucius from the state of Lu (1042 – 249 BC). He was famous for his filial piety. The book expounds Zengzi' s thoughts and has 18 chapters.

Zheng Yao Lun

Zheng Yao Lun 政要论 (*A Discourse on the Importance of Politics*)was written by Huan Fan 桓范 from the Three Kingdoms (220 – 265). This book discusses ways to deploy government officials. Huan Fan believes that a country's prosperity is dependent on a leader's humility and receptiveness of the advice given to him.

Zhong Lun

Zhong Lun 中论 (*A Discourse on the Middle Way*) was written by Xu Gan 徐干 , a philosopher and poet. He was among the Jian-an-qi-zi 建安七子 or the seven famous poets in the late Eastern Han dynasty (25 – 220) who upheld Confucianism. Xu Gan was against exegetical studies. He believes that righteousness is of primary importance.

Zhou Yi

Zhou Yi 周易 (*Book of Changes*) or *Yi Jing* 易经 dates back to 2800 – 2737BC, the divinity system developed over time to become the most influential philosophy in the literature and government administration of the Zhou dynasty (1046 – 256BC). Later, during the time of Spring and Autumn period (770 – 476 BC), Confucius is traditionally said to have written the *Shi Yi* 十翼 , *Ten Wings*, a group of commentaries on *Yi Jing*. By the time of Emperor Wu of Han dynasty 汉武帝 of the Western Han dynasty (206BC – 9 AD), *Shi Yi* was often called *Yi Zhuan* 易传 (*Commentary on the Yi Jing*).

Bibliography

Books

Li, Bing Nan. *Lunyu Jiang Yao* [An Explanation on the Main Points of Analects.] Chinese Taiwan: Fufong Press, 2009.

Littlejohn, Ronnie and Jeffrey Dippmann ed. *Riding the Wind with Liezi: New Perspectives on the Daoist Classic*. Albany: State University of New York Press, 2011.

Lu, Xiaozu and Zhao, Baoyu and Zhang,Yaowu. *Qunshu Zhiyao Kaoyi* [Investigations of Discrepancies on Qunshu Zhiyao.] China: Unity Press, 2011.

E-Books

Eno, Robert. trans. T*he Analects of Confucius: An Online Teaching Translation*. version 2.0, 2010. ebook. http://www.indiana.edu/~p374/Analects_of_Confucius_%28Eno-2012%29.pdf (PDF version updated to 2.1).

Legge, James. trans. *Confucian Analects*. vol. 1, Project Gutenberg ebook, 2009. http://www.gutenberg.org/files/4094/4094-h/4094-h.htm.

Giles, Lionels. trans. *Attack by Stratagem*. Project Chinese Text. http://ctext.org/art-of-war/attack-by-stratagem.

Dictionary

Han Dian Chinese Dictionary Online, 汉典 [In Chinese.]
http://www.zdic.net/.

Websites

"Guanzhong," *Wikipedia,* last modified September 18, 2012,
http://en.wikipedia.org/wiki/Guan_Zhong.

"Han Fei," *Wikipedia,* last modified July 18, 2014,
http://en.wikipedia. org/wiki/Han_Fei.

"I Ching," trans. James Legge, *TormodKinnes,*
http://oaks.nvg.org /re5ra17.html.

"Legalism, Qin Empire and Han Dynasty," http://www.san.beck.org /EC16-Legalism.html.

"Liu Tao," *ChinaCulture.Org*, http://www1.chinaculture.org/created /2005-07/20/content_70803.htm.

"Sun Tzu The Art of War," trans. Lionel Giles, http://classics.mit.edu /Tzu/artwar.html.

"Wu Qi," *Wikipedia*, last modified June 28, 2014, http://en.wikipedia.org/wiki/Wu_Qi.

"Xiaohe," http://history.cultural-china.com/en/47History1920.html.

上海正道影视发展有限公司简介

志弘正道，修己达人。上海正道影视发展有限公司成立于2015年，致力于中华传统文化传承传播，倡导孝悌忠信、礼义廉耻、仁爱和平、以德化人、因果教育等之文化精髓，通过影视制作、音像书籍出品、多形式文化活动、新媒体技术等多种形式，创意设计、制作发布，策划执行文化传播，坚持正见、正思维、正语、正业、正命、正精进、正念、正定之正道理念，用明德引领风尚，以人化文、以文育人、以人培元。

公司出品的“正道文化”系列丛书，以儒释道文化为根基，秉承仁、义、礼、智、信、忠、孝、悌、节、恕、勇、让，修身、齐家、治国、平天下的人文精神，将思想道德、风格心志、思维方式用图文的形式呈现其内涵，教化育人，并坚定文化自信，树立民族自尊。

唐宗密《华严原人论序》云：“然孔老释迦皆是至圣、随时应物，设教殊涂。内外相资，共利群庶。策勤万行，明因果始终，推究万法，彰生起本末，……策万行，惩恶劝善，同归于治、则三教皆可遵行。”佛则云明心见性，儒则云正心诚意，道则曰澄其心而神自清，语殊而心同。跨越时空，弘扬传统文化，传承民族精神。

中华传统文化蕴含着丰富的智慧，正道文化专注研究建构、挖掘传承、诠释传播中华传统文化，使其与当代社会相适应、与现代文明相协调、与世界文化发展趋势相符合、与全人类优秀文化相汇通。

公司自媒体“正道文化交流”微信公众号，将以每日论语、小故事大智慧、群书治要、一日一课、一日一善等栏目，倡导儒释道文化教育。

正道文化

上海正道影视发展有限公司

地　址：上海虹口区东大名路558号17楼

电　话：86-21-52600038-685